COPYRIGHT © 1978, 1982, 1988, 1992, 1996 WEST PUBLISHING CO.
© West, a Thomson business, 1998, 2002, 2005, 2006
© 2009 Thomson Reuters
© 2016 LEG, Inc. d/b/a West Academic
      444 Cedar Street, Suite 700
      St. Paul, MN 55101
      1-877-888-1330

West, West Academic Publishing, and West Academic are trademarks of West Publishing Corporation, used under license.

Printed in the United States of America

ISBN: 978-1-68328-318-8

SECURITIES REGULATION

IN A NUTSHELL®

ELEVENTH EDITION

THOMAS LEE HAZEN
Cary C. Boshamer Distinguished Professor of Law
The University of North Carolina at Chapel Hill

WEST
ACADEMIC
PUBLISHING

PREFACE

This book is designed for lawyers, law students and others who are seeking an understanding of the basic content and organization of federal (and state) securities law.

The growth and elaboration of federal securities law in recent years has been phenomenal. In this "nutshell," I have tried to summarize the essential background and current status of each major area, while keeping details and citations to a minimum. I have, of course, included references to the relevant statutes, SEC rules and releases, and other governmental materials, as well as to "leading cases," where they exist, and to illustrative cases in other areas. I have not cited any secondary materials; there are simply too many of them.

This book will not answer all of your questions about securities law. It should, however, answer most of your basic ones and help you to find the answers to the others.

Readers desiring more detailed analysis and sources for research should consult Thomas Lee Hazen, Treatise on the Law of Securities Regulation (7th ed. 2016) (seven volume Practitioner's Edition), Thomas Lee Hazen, Hornbook on the Law of Securities Regulation (7th ed. 2016) (one volume edition) or Thomas Lee Hazen, Principles of Securities Regulation (4th ed. 2016).

THOMAS LEE HAZEN

July 2016

ABBREVIATIONS

The following abbreviations are used throughout this Nutshell.

1933 Act—Securities Act of 1933 (15 U.S.C. §§ 77a et seq.)

1934 Act—Securities Exchange Act of 1934 (15 U.S.C. §§ 78a et seq.)

CCH—Commerce Clearing House Federal Securities Law Reports

CEA—Commodity Exchange Act (7 U.S.C. §§ 1 et seq.)

DMM—Designated Market Maker

ECN—Electronic Communications Network

FINRA—Financial Industry Regulatory Authority

FRB—Federal Reserve Board

IAA—Investment Advisors Act of 1940 (15 U.S.C. § 80b–1 et seq.)

ICA—Investment Company Act of 1940 (15 U.S.C. §§ 80a–1 et seq.)

NASD—National Association of Securities Dealers

NYSE—New York Stock Exchange

OTC—Over-the-Counter (market)

PSLRA—Private Securities Litigation Reform Act (Pub. Law No. 104–67, 109 Stat. 737 (104th Cong. 1st Sess. December 22, 1995))

Rel.—(SEC) Release

RRI—(SEC) Rules Relating to Investigations

SEC—Securities and Exchange Commission

SIPA—Securities Investor Protection Act of 1970 (15 U.S.C.A. §§ 78aaa et seq.)

SIPC—Securities Investor Protection Corporation

SLUSA—Securities Litigation Uniform Standards Act (Pub. Law No. 105–353, 112 Stat. 3227 (105th Cong.–2d Sess. November 3, 1998))

SRO—Self-Regulatory Organization

USA—Uniform Securities Act

WKSI—Well-Known Seasoned Issuer

OUTLINE

TABLE OF CASES

References are to Pages

TABLE OF STATUTES

References are to Pages

TABLE OF RULES

References are to Pages

SECURITIES REGULATION

IN A NUTSHELL®

ELEVENTH EDITION

CHAPTER I

INTRODUCTION

Traditional securities differ from most other commodities and investments in which people deal. They have no intrinsic value in themselves—they represent rights in something else. The value of a bond, note, or other promise to pay depends on the financial condition of the promisor. The value of a share of stock depends on the profitability or future prospects of the corporation or other entity that issued it; its market price depends on how much other people are willing to pay for it, based on their evaluation of those prospects.

The distinctive features of securities give a unique coloration to regulation of transactions in securities, in contrast to the regulation of transactions in other types of goods. Most goods are produced, distributed, and used or consumed; governmental regulation focuses on protecting the ultimate consumer against dangerous articles, misleading advertising, and unfair or non-competitive pricing practices. Securities are different.

First, securities are created, rather than produced. Since they are nothing in themselves but represent only an interest in something else, they can be issued in unlimited amounts, virtually without cost. An important focus of securities laws, therefore, is assuring that, when securities are created and offered to the public, investors have an accurate idea of what that "something else" is and how much of an interest in it the particular security represents.

Second, securities are not used or consumed by their purchasers. They become a kind of currency, traded in the so-called "secondary markets" at fluctuating prices. These "secondary" transactions far outweigh, in number and volume, the offerings of newly-created securities. A second important focus of securities law, therefore, is to assure that there is a continuous flow of information about the corporation or other entity whose securities are being traded, including additional disclosure whenever security holders are being asked to vote or make a decision with respect to the securities they hold.

Third, because the trading markets for securities are uniquely susceptible to manipulative and deceptive practices, all securities laws contain general "antifraud" provisions. These have been interpreted to apply to manipulation of securities prices, trading by "insiders" on the basis of non-public information, and various kinds of misstatements by corporate management and others who have access to the company's nonpublic information.

Fourth, since a large industry has grown up to buy and sell securities for investors and traders, securities laws are concerned with the regulation of people and firms engaged in that business, such as broker-dealers, investment banks, and investment advisers. This regulation assures that they do not take advantage of their superior experience and access to overreach their non-professional customers.

Finally, securities laws provide for a variety of governmental sanctions against those who violate their prohibitions, as well as civil liability to persons injured by such violations. In addition, the courts have implied the existence of civil liabilities in situations where they are not expressly provided by statute.

§ 1.   THE SECURITIES MARKETS

The facilities through which securities are traded are known as "markets." These markets may have physical locations, but in many cases, they are simply formal or informal systems of communication through which buyers and sellers make their interests known and consummate transactions. Thanks to the Internet, there are now many virtual, rather than physical, securities markets.

In terms of dollar volume, the largest securities market is the bond market—trading in the debt instruments issued by the United States government, by state and local governments, and by corporations. However, since the bond market attracts more interest from professional and institutional investors than from the general public, and since federal, state, and local government obligations are exempt from most of the direct regulatory provisions of the federal securities laws, the bond markets have in recent years occupied only a small part of the attention of securities regulators.

The principal focus of securities regulation is on the markets for common stocks. There are two types of stock markets now operating in the United States—"exchange" markets and "over-the-counter" markets. An "exchange" market, of which the New York Stock Exchange (NYSE) is by far the largest, operates for most of its existence in a physical facility with a trading "floor" to which transactions in a particular security are directed. The orders are routed electronically through the SuperDot electronic order-routing system that links member firms to specialists' posts on the trading floor. The NYSE (and, to a lesser extent, the other exchanges) has traditionally operated in a very rigid manner, prescribing the number and qualifications of members, the functions each member may perform, and (until 1975) the commission rate to be charged on all transactions. The "over-the-counter" (OTC) market, on the other hand, has traditionally been completely unstructured and without any physical facility. Any qualified firm is free to engage in many type of activities with respect to OTC securities. Most of the securities traded through NASDAQ are now listed on NASDAQ's National Stock Market, which is now a registered securities exchange. These markets are supplemented by virtual markets known as Electronic Communications Networks (ECNs).

As far as the individual buyer or seller of stocks is concerned, the significant difference between an exchange and OTC or NASDAQ transaction is the function performed by the firm with which the investor deals. In the case of an exchange transaction, the customer's firm acts as a "broker"— that is, as an agent for the customer's account—and charges the customer a commission for its services. For many years, the only person permitted to act as a "dealer" or "make a market" in the stock on the exchange floor—that is, to buy and sell the security for the dealer's own account—is the registered "specialist" in that stock. The broker transmits the customer's order to the exchange floor where it is generally executed by buying from or selling to either the specialist or another customer whose broker has left his order on the specialist's "book." The specialist system has yielded to technological advances since so many trades are now done electronically. Firms that formerly operated as specialists are now known as designated market makers (DMMs). The NYSE's transition from a specialist system to one based on designated market makers means that operations on the NYSE more closely resemble trading in the NASDAQ markets than ever before.

In the OTC and NASDAQ stock markets, on the other hand, there is no exchange floor, only a computer and telephone communication network. The principal market for the stocks of large companies traded in the OTC market was the NASDAQ (National Association of Securities Dealers Automated Quotation) National Market System. In 2006, the NASDAQ stock market became a registered national securities exchange. In the NASDAQ markets, a number of firms may act as "dealers" or "market makers" in a particular stock and may deal directly with public customers in that stock. If the firm through which a customer orders a particular stock is not a dealer in that stock, it will normally purchase it for the customer as the customer's broker from one of the dealers making a market in that stock. In many cases, however, the firm will solicit orders from customers in stocks in which it is making a market, selling the stock to the customer as principal at a mark-up over the price it is currently quoting to brokers. Since retail firms commonly act simultaneously as brokers in exchange-listed stocks and as dealers in OTC and NASDAQ stocks, this may cause some confusion on the part of customers.

A firm selling stock to a customer as part of an underwritten offering of a new issue (whether of an exchange-listed or OTC stock) normally sells to the customer as principal at a fixed price (equal to or slightly below the current market price, in the case of a security which is already publicly traded). The dealer's compensation in that case comes out of the "spread" between the public offering price and the net proceeds paid to the issuer (or other person on whose behalf the distribution is being made). For example, if the dealer bought the stock at 15$ per share and resells it for $16.25, there is a $.25 spread.

In recent years, two factors have substantially blurred the distinctions between exchange and OTC markets. The first is modern computer and communication technology, which revolutionized the operation of the over-the-counter market, and has raised serious questions about the necessity and desirability of a physical exchange "floor." In the 1990s, the availability of online trading created a vehicle for increased individual investor access to the securities markets. The development of ECNs has opened up addition trading platforms and has enhanced competition. At the same time, trading in common stocks, particularly those listed on the New York Stock Exchange, has been increasingly dominated by "institutional investors"— predominately pension funds, mutual funds, bank trust departments, and insurance companies—with individual investors accounting for a continually decreasing percentage of trading volume.

(A) THE SECURITIES INDUSTRY

The securities industry is characterized by a wide variety of firms, both in size and function. Firms registered as broker-dealers in securities can be large firms engaged in brokerage, market-making, underwriting, investment advice, and fund management, as well as commodities, real estate dealings and a variety of other financial service activities. They also may include, at the other end of the spectrum, one-person firms engaged solely in selling mutual fund shares or dealing in a few specialized securities.

There has always been a substantial failure rate among small securities firms, which commence operations during periods of high trading volume and fold when volume declines. In 1969 and 1970, however, as a result of operational breakdowns, unsound capital structures, and rapidly declining volume and prices for securities, there was an unprecedented series of failures of large NYSE member firms, which almost caused the collapse of the industry. This near-collapse triggered a number of governmental studies, culminating in the imposition of new financial responsibility requirements on securities firms. It also led to the development of a more rational and efficient system for the clearing and settlement of securities transactions.

Since passage in 1933 of the Glass-Steagall Act, which prohibited banks from dealing in securities (except government bonds), until 1999, the securities industry consisted of a relatively separate and well-defined group of firms. However, with the increasing tendency for individuals to make their equity investments indirectly through institutions, rather than trading directly in stock for their own account, securities firms came increasingly into competition with banks, insurance companies, and other financial institutions. At the same time that securities firms began offering their customers an increasing number of financial services that traditionally had been associated with commercial banking, commercial banks entered into many areas that formerly were reserved for investment bankers and securities firms. This competition placed severe strains on the existing regulatory structure under which securities firms, banks, and insurance companies are regulated by different agencies with entirely different concerns and approaches. To deal with this strain, in 1999, Congress enacted the Gramm-Leach-Bliley Act, which repealed most provisions of Glass-Steagall and paved the way for even more competition among and between financial institutions by allowing these institutions to offer a wide variety of financial services to their customers. The Gramm-Leach-Bliley Act adopted a system of functional regulation under which the various operations of multi-service financial institutions are regulated by different government agencies depending on the nature of the activity. Thus, for example, while securities activities of banks and other institutions are regulated by the

SEC, their banking activities are governed by the applicable federal or state banking agencies, and their insurance activities are subject to state regulation. The credit crisis and financial meltdown of 2008 led many policymakers to question this deregulatory trend. Although it is unlikely to revert back to Glass-Steagall's separation of investment and commercial banking, as this book went to press there were many proposals for increased regulation. At a minimum, it appears that there will be tighter regulation of financial institutions' risk assessment and risk management.

Credit Rating Agencies

Over the past 30 years, the markets in general and many regulators, including the SEC, relied on credit ratings to help monitor the risk of debt securities; the risks related to investment banking, commercial banking, insurance companies and other regulated entities; and the risks of unregulated entities, such as hedge funds. Over that time, the SEC has come to recognize several credit rating agencies as nationally recognized statistical rating organizations (NRSROs), through the issuance of no-action letters, for regulatory and legislative purposes. For many years prior to the credit crisis and market collapse in 2008–2009, there was concern about the efficacy of these highly relied upon credit rating agencies. For example, many of the companies that failed around the turn of the twenty-first century had good credit ratings when the market was surprised by serious financial problems of these highly rated companies.

In 2006, Congress enacted the Credit Rating Agency Reform Act as an amendment to the Securities Exchange Act of 1934, granting the SEC the regulatory authority to register and oversee nationally recognized statistical rating organizations. Credit Rating Agency Reform Act of 2006, Pub. Law 109–291120 Stat. 1327 (2006). The SEC implemented rating agency regulation (see 1934 Act Rules 17g–1 through 17g–6) and has introduced proposals to refine and expand their regulation. In the aftermath of the 2008 credit crisis, there continues to be calls for increased regulation.

§ 2.   STATE AND FEDERAL SECURITIES LAWS

Securities transactions are subject to regulation under both federal and state law. Since the federal securities laws are based on Congress's power to regulate interstate commerce, they generally apply only to transactions involving "the use of any means or instruments of transportation or communication in interstate commerce or of the mails." The courts have been willing to find the requisite use of interstate commerce facilities in doubtful situations. Use of the mails to accomplish any part of the transaction, including payment or confirmation after a sale, is sufficient to support federal jurisdiction. See, e.g., Franklin v. Levy, 551 F.2d 521 (2d Cir.1977). An intrastate telephone call is sufficient to involve the use of interstate facilities. See, e.g., Dupuy v. Dupuy, 511 F.2d 641 (5th Cir.1975).

Prior to 1996, federal securities laws specifically preserved the jurisdiction of state commissions to regulate securities transactions and securities professionals, so long as their regulation did not conflict with federal law. However, in that year, the federal laws were amended to preempt many aspects of state regulation.

State securities laws, commonly known as "blue sky" laws, generally provide for registration of broker-dealers, registration of securities to be offered or traded in the state, and sanctions against fraudulent activities. The Uniform Securities Act (USA), promulgated in 1956 and revised in 1985, has been substantially or partially adopted in more than 30 states, but state securities law is still characterized by great diversity of language and interpretation. Revisions to the USA have since been adopted in many states but the diversity remains. Also, as discussed in subsection Chapter X below, in 1996 Congress enacted legislation (the National Securities Markets Improvement Act, or NSMIA) that preempted a significant amount of state regulation that previously co-existed with the federal regulatory scheme. While the state "blue sky" laws retain their vitality in broker-dealer and investment adviser regulation, their sphere of influence in regulating offerings of securities was severely curtailed by NSMIA.

Federal securities law basically consists of five statutes enacted between 1933 and 1940, which have been periodically amended in the intervening years, one statute enacted in 1970, and one statute enacted in 2002. In 2002, the Congress responded to many highly publicized corporate governance scandals and enacted numerous amendments to the existing securities laws and also some stand-alone provisions. The current statutes, which have been amended from time to time, are:

Securities Act of 1933 (1933 Act)

Securities Exchange Act of 1934 (1934 Act)

Trust Indenture Act of 1939 (TIA)

Investment Company Act of 1940 (ICA)

Investment Advisers Act of 1940 (IAA)

Securities Investor Protection Act of 1970 (SIPA)

Sarbanes-Oxley Act of 2002 (SOX)

The *Securities Act of 1933* regulates public offerings of securities. It prohibits offers and sales of securities which are not registered with the Securities and Exchange Commission (SEC), subject to exemptions for enumerated kinds of securities and transactions. It also prohibits fraudulent or deceptive practices in any offer or sale of securities.

The *Securities Exchange Act of 1934* extended federal regulation to trading in securities which are already issued and outstanding. Unlike the 1933 Act, which focuses on a single regulatory provision, the 1934 Act contains a number of distinct groups of provisions, aimed at different participants in the securities trading process. The 1934 Act established the Securities and Exchange Commission and

transferred to it the responsibility for administration
of the 1933 Act, which had originally been assigned
to the Federal Trade Commission. Other provisions
of the Act impose disclosure and other requirements
on publicly-held corporations; prohibit various
"manipulative or deceptive devices or contrivances"
in connection with the purchase or sale of securities;
restrict the amount of credit that may be extended for
the purchase of securities; require brokers and
dealers to register with the SEC and regulate their
activities; and provide for SEC registration and
supervision of national securities exchanges and
associations, clearing agencies, transfer agents, and
securities information processors.

The former *Public Utility Holding Company
Act of 1935* was enacted to correct abuses which
Congressional inquiries had disclosed in the
financing and operation of electric and gas public
utility holding company systems, and to achieve
physical integration and corporate simplification of
those systems. The SEC's functions under this Act
were substantially completed by the 1950s, and it
currently accounts for a very small part of the
Commission's work. In 1995, the SEC recommended
to Congress that PUHCA be repealed and that the
SEC's functions under the Act be transferred to the
Federal Energy Regulatory Commission. PUHCA
was eventually repealed in 2006.

The *Trust Indenture Act of 1939* applies
generally to public issues of debt securities in excess
of a specified amount, which is currently fixed by the
SEC at $10 million. See TIA § 304(a)(9), Rule 4a–3.

Even though the issue is registered under the 1933 Act, the indenture covering the securities must also be qualified under the 1939 Act, which imposes standards of independence and responsibility on the indenture trustee and requires other provisions to be included in the indenture for the protection of the security holders. In 1990, the Act was amended to simplify the process of preparing indentures and set heightened conflict-of-interest standards for indenture trustees.

The *Investment Company Act of 1940* gives the SEC regulatory authority over publicly-owned companies which are engaged primarily in the business of investing and trading in securities. The Act regulates the composition of the management of investment companies, their capital structure, and approval of their advisory contracts and changes in investment policy. Additionally, the Act requires SEC approval for any transactions by such companies with its directors, officers, or affiliates. A 1970 amendment imposed additional controls on management compensation and sales charges.

The *Investment Advisers Act of 1940,* as amended in 1960, established a scheme of registration and regulation of investment advisers comparable to, but less comprehensive than, the scheme contained in the 1934 Act with respect to broker-dealers. In 1996, the Act was amended to preempt state regulation of investment advisers with more than $25 million of assets under management, and to exempt from the Act advisers with less than

$25 million under management that are regulated by their home states.

The **Securities Investor Protection Act of 1970** established the Securities Investor Protection Corporation (SIPC), which has the power to supervise the liquidation of securities firms that get into financial difficulties and to arrange for the payment of claims asserted by their customers.

The **Sarbanes-Oxley Act of 2002** (SOX) adopted comprehensive corporate governance reforms in response to various corporate scandals, including the Enron and WorldCom scandals. Many of SOX's provisions are disclosure provisions combined with enhanced criminal penalties for violations, but the clear thrust of these amendments is to improve corporate governance. SOX goes further than any of the earlier securities laws and amendments in dealing directly with corporate governance—an area that had traditionally been reserved to the states. For example, SOX mandates accounting and auditing reforms, an increased role of public corporations' audit committees, increased accountability of executive officers, and corporate attorneys by including an obligation to internally report suspected wrongdoing. It also imposes increased criminal penalties for violations of the securities laws. SOX also created an accounting oversight board (Public Company Accounting Oversight Board, or PCAOB, sometimes pronounced "peek-a-boo") to oversee the accounting profession and to police the self-regulatory system that previously existed. Even beyond its specific provisions, SOX could be the beginning of a sea-change by focusing federal law more on corporate governance and other areas of corporate law that have traditionally been left to the states.

As a general proposition, the federal securities laws are focused on disclosure, while matters relating to corporate governance are relegated to state corporate law. SOX introduced major corporate governance reforms that now are a matter of federal law. For example, federal securities laws now require disclosures with respect to corporate codes of ethics. There are heightened independence requirements for auditors and members of the audit committee. There are also controls on executive compensation, such as a prohibition on most loans to high-ranking executives. Additionally, the listing standards of the stock exchanges and NASDAQ impose corporate governance limits on publicly-held corporations.

Other Securities Statutes. From time to time, Congress adopts amendments to the various securities laws outlined above. Although it is not uncommon for these amendments to carry their own names, since they amend existing securities statutes, they are not generally considered stand-alone laws. Thus, for example, the Williams Act amendments in 1968 to the 1934 Act introduced tender offer and other takeover regulation. The Private Securities Litigation Reform Act of 1995 (PSLRA) and the Securities Litigation Uniform Standards Act of 1998 (SLUSA) amended various provisions of the 1933 and 1934 Acts in an attempt to curtail vexatious litigation. The National Securities Markets

Improvement Act of 1996 amended the existing
federal securities laws to preempt the states from
many areas of securities regulation that had
previously been within their jurisdiction. These are
just some examples of the "named" amending
legislation.

The Proposed Federal Securities Code. During
the 1970s, the American Law Institute drafted and
promulgated a "Federal Securities Code" designed to
replace the seven laws described above. The Code
would not have made any major substantive changes
in the law. Instead, it was designed to deal with
certain "problems" under existing law, including (a)
the "complications" arising from inconsistent
definitions, as well as procedural and jurisdictional
provisions, in the different acts, (b) the overemphasis
in the disclosure provisions on "public offerings"
rather than periodic reporting requirements, and (c)
the "chaotic" development of civil liabilities resulting
from "broad judicial implication of private rights of
action" under various provisions of existing law. The
Institute gave its final approval to the proposed Code
in May 1978. However, Congress showed no interest
in even considering the Code, so it was never formally
introduced. It has nevertheless had considerable
influence on the development of the law. Many of its
approaches have been incorporated in SEC rules or
utilized by the courts to resolve ambiguous provisions
of current law, a process which the Reporter for the
Code once described as "cannibalizing it for spare
parts."

§ 3.   THE SECURITIES AND EXCHANGE COMMISSION

The Securities and Exchange Commission (SEC) is the agency charged with principal responsibility for the enforcement and administration of the federal securities laws. The 1934 Act provides that the SEC shall consist of five members appointed by the President for five-year terms (the term of one Commissioner expires each year), not more than three of whom shall be members of the same political party.

Among lawyers and among students of governmental process, the SEC generally enjoys a high reputation. It has been noteworthy for the level of intelligence and integrity of its staff, the flexibility and informality of many of its procedures, and its avoidance of the political and economic pitfalls in which many other regulatory agencies have found themselves trapped. Its disclosure and enforcement policies have also been credited with making an important contribution to the generally favorable reputation which American corporate securities and American securities markets enjoy, not only among American investors, but also in foreign countries. On the other hand, it has been subject to frequent criticism for failing to give adequate consideration to the economic costs of its rules and requirements. In 1996, the principal federal securities laws were amended to provide that the Commission, when engaged in rulemaking, shall consider, in addition to the protection of investors, whether its action will promote efficiency, competition, and capital formation. 1933 Act § 2(b); 1934 Act § 3(f); ICA § 2(c).

The SEC consists of four divisions and various offices. The division of Corporation Finance ("Corp. Fin.") has the primary responsibility for examining all registration documents and reports filed with the Commission. Corp. Fin. also has drafted most SEC rules, disclosure forms, and guides. The Division of Trading and Markets (formerly Market Regulation) oversees the operation of the markets and broker-dealer regulation. The Division of Investment Management carries out investment company and investment adviser regulation. The Division of Enforcement conducts investigations of suspected violations and can initiate court action or administrative proceedings in appropriate cases; it also can refer matters to the Department of Justice for possible criminal prosecution. Some of the more important offices include the Office of General Counsel and the Office of the Chief Accountant.

The SEC Staff. While the Commission itself is ultimately responsible for all decisions, the day-to-day administration of the Acts is largely delegated to the staff. Most of the staff are located at the Commission's head office in Washington, with the remainder in 11 regional offices in financial centers around the country. The SEC has a very small economic staff and engages in almost none of the rate-setting and franchise-granting activities that occupy a large part of the attention of most other regulatory agencies.

"Self-Regulation." Rather than relying solely on regulation by the SEC, the federal securities laws reserve a uniquely important role for "self-regulation" by industry and professional groups. Stock exchanges had been regulating the activities of their members for more than 140 years prior to the passage of the Securities Exchange Act of 1934. The 1934 Act incorporated the exchanges into the regulatory structure, subject to certain oversight powers by the SEC. When Congress decided to impose more comprehensive regulation on over-the-counter securities dealers in 1938 and on municipal securities dealers in 1975, it adopted a similar self-regulatory approach, authorizing the establishment of the National Association of Securities Dealers (NASD), which has since been replaced by the Financial Industry Regulatory Authority (FINRA), and the Municipal Securities Rulemaking Board (MSRB) as self-regulatory organizations for those respective groups.

§ 4.   SOURCES OF SECURITIES LAW

The starting point in analyzing any question of federal securities law is, of course, the statutes. The statutes are, however, quite sketchy or ambiguous in many important areas, so it is necessary to resort to supplemental sources of law. These are of two kinds: rules and other statements of general applicability issued by the SEC (or self-regulatory organizations), and reports of decided cases.

SEC Rulemaking

The SEC has broad rulemaking powers under the various statutes it administers and has exercised its authority by prescribing at least three different kinds of rules. The first category consists of procedural and technical rules (e.g., rules prescribing numbers of copies to be filed); the second category consists of definitions of terms used in the law (e.g., 1933 Act Rule 147, providing a safe harbor definition of what constitutes an intrastate offering); the third category consists of substantive rules adopted pursuant to a Congressional delegation of authority (e.g., the proxy solicitation rules under 1934 Act § 14). In 1996, Congress significantly broadened the Commission's rulemaking power by giving it general authority to exempt any classes of persons, securities, or transactions from any provisions of the 1933 or 1934 Act. See 1933 Act § 28; 1934 Act § 36.

Delegated   Rulemaking.   Administrative rulemaking by direct legislative delegation necessarily has the effect of law, so long as the rulemaking has been in compliance with the process set forth in the Administrative Procedure Act and the scope of the rule does not exceed the grant of authority in the organic statute that created this administrative rulemaking power.

Interpretive   Rulemaking.   Commission rulemaking is not limited to legislatively delegated rules. The SEC has also promulgated a number of interpretive rules which are designed to aid corporate planners and attorneys in complying with the statutes' requirements.   Unlike   the   rules promulgated pursuant to specific statutory delegation, interpretative rules do not carry with them the force of law; they simply reflect the Commission's interpretation of the law created by the statute. Nevertheless, interpretative rules are extremely important in guiding practitioners through the regulatory maze. Equally important is the fact that when interpreting the scope of a statute, federal courts traditionally give deference to administrative interpretation.

Safe Harbor Rules. A special variety of SEC interpretative rules are the so-called safe harbor rules. A safe harbor rule sets forth conditions under which the SEC will take the position that the law has been complied with. A person's compliance with a safe harbor rule will thus assure that he or she is safe from SEC prosecution with regard to the transaction in question.

SEC Forms

Supplementing the SEC's rules are its forms for the various statements and reports which issuers, broker-dealers, and others are required to file under the Acts. Since disclosure is such an important part of the regulatory pattern, these forms (which have the legal force of rules) play an important part in defining the extent of the disclosure obligation.

Informal Law-Making

Beyond the rules and forms, the SEC engages in a good deal of "informal law-making," setting forth the views of the Commission or its staff on questions of current concern, without stating them in the form of legal requirements. The principal media for these statements are SEC "Releases" which, as the name implies, are simply statements distributed to the press, to companies and firms registered with the Commission, and to other interested persons.

SEC Interpretive Releases; Staff Legal Bulletins and Interpretations. As noted above, the Securities and Exchange Commission disseminates unsolicited advisory opinions in the form of SEC Releases, which may include guidelines or suggest interpretation of statutory provisions and rules. In addition to periodic interpretative releases, each time the Commission proposes a new rule or rule amendment, the proposal is accompanied by a release. Similarly, when new rules or amendments are adopted, the SEC's formal adoption is accompanied by an interpretative release. The SEC positions announced in interpretative releases necessarily provide less precedential and predictive value than do rules that are promulgated as a result of the more formal interpretive rulemaking process.

No-Action Letters. Supplementing general public statements of policy, the staff, since the Commission's early days, has been willing to respond to individual private inquiries as to whether a certain transaction could be carried out in a specified manner. These responses are known as "no-action" letters because they customarily state that "the staff will recommend no action to the Commission" if the transaction is done in the specified manner. The staff's recommendation is conditional on the facts being as they are set forth in the no-action letter request.

Law and Lore

In addition to the aforementioned rulemaking and interpretative avenues, a body of practices has built up over time. These practices result in securities "lore" that supplements the law. Although these practices may be reflected in SEC releases and no-action responses, they are not always easily found because, unlike with formal rules, there is no convenient indexing system.

In some areas of federal securities law, notably in the registration provisions of the 1933 Act, most of the "law" is found in the rules, forms, and policy statements of the Commission, and very little in the form of decided "cases." In other areas, however, notably under the general antifraud provisions of the 1934 Act, there is very little in the way of formal rules. Instead, the law has developed in the traditional "common law" manner, with courts and other tribunals deciding each case on the basis of precedents.

SEC Enforcement

Decisions may be rendered in several different types of proceedings. The SEC itself may proceed in a number of ways if it discovers what it believes to be a violation of the law.

SEC Administrative Proceedings

If the alleged violator is a broker-dealer or investment adviser required to register with the

SEC, the Commission can bring a proceeding to revoke or suspend the firm's registration or take other disciplinary action. If the alleged violator is an issuer seeking to sell securities under a 1933 Act registration statement, the Commission can bring a proceeding to suspend the effectiveness of the statement. In either case, the Commission staff acts as "prosecutor" and the Commission itself makes the final decision (after initial findings by an administrative law judge).

In 1990, Congress significantly broadened the Commission's powers by authorizing it (a) to issue cease-and-desist orders and (b) to impose fines or order disgorgement of profits in administrative proceedings. Prior to this expansion of its powers, the Commission could only proceed against persons not registered with it by going to court to obtain relief.

One common type of court action brought by the Commission is an application to a federal district court for an injunction against future violations. In a particularly egregious case, however, the Commission may refer the matter to the Department of Justice for prosecution as a criminal violation of the securities laws.

A person who believes that he or she has been injured by a violation of the securities laws can bring a civil action in the courts for damages. The aggrieved investor may either sue under the specific civil liability provisions of those laws or assert an "implied" right of action under a provision prohibiting the activity in question. Beginning in the 1960s, there was an enormous expansion in the number of private damage actions under the federal securities laws, particularly those asserting an implied right of action under the general antifraud provisions. However, since 1975, the Supreme Court has taken a much more restrictive view of the availability of these implied rights of action.

§ 5.   WHERE TO FIND THE LAW

One comprehensive and convenient source for all of the federal securities laws; SEC rules, forms, interpretations, and decisions; and court decisions on securities matters is the loose-leaf Federal Securities Law Reporter published by Commerce Clearing House (CCH). This service is kept up to date with weekly supplements, and decisions and interpretations going back to 1941 can be found in annual or bi-annual "transfer binders." Westlaw and Lexis also contain specialized and comprehensive libraries in federal and state securities law. Pamphlet copies of the 1933 Act, the 1934 Act, and the rules and forms governing the preparation of disclosure documents under those two acts are also available from many financial printers who specialize in the preparation of such documents.

The official version of the federal securities laws is, of course, found in the United States Code (and in the United States Code Annotated) as §§ 77–80 of Title 15. Unfortunately, whoever was in charge of numbering the Code decided that the sections of the 1933 Act (15 U.S.C. § 77) should be numbered §§ 77a, 77b, 77c, etc. Thus § 5(b)(1) of the Act becomes 15 U.S.C. § 77e(b)(1), and § 12(a)(2) become § 77*l*(a)(2).

The 1934 Act is handled in similar fashion in 15
U.S.C. § 78. If you want to find a section of the 1933
or 1934 Act in the Code you can do so easily, provided
you remember the alphabet and have enough fingers
to count to 26 (sections of the 1934 Act after section
26 are rendered as §§ 78aa, 78bb, and so forth). In
addition, when Congress adds entirely new sections
to the existing securities laws, they may be
incorporated into the midst of the existing statutes
with letters. Thus, for example there is a Section 8A
of the 1933 Act (15 U.S.C. § 77h–1), which appears
between sections 8 and 9 of that Act. Since everyone
connected with securities regulation uses the section
numbers of the Acts, rather than the Code references,
the latter are omitted in the remainder of this book.

The official version of the SEC rules can be found
in volume 17 of the Code of Federal Regulations.
Here the numbering system is more rational. 1933
Act rules are found in 17 C.F.R. Pt. 230 under the
rule number, and 1934 Act rules can be found in 17
C.F.R. Pt. 240 in the same manner. Thus, for
example, 1933 Act Rule 144 is 17 C.F.R. § 230.144,
and 1934 Act Rule 10b–5 is 17 C.F.R. § 240.10b–5.

SEC releases announcing the proposal or adoption
of new rules, as well as those containing significant
interpretations of the law, can be found in the
Federal Register for the day on which the release was
issued. Other releases are not systematically or
officially published in any form other than the
releases actually distributed by the Commission and
are simply numbered serially by reference to the Act

or Acts to which they relate, such as Securities Act Release No. 33–4434.

The SEC's "no-action" letters have been made publicly available since 1970. They can be examined at the SEC office in Washington and are also available through a variety of commercial sources. A number of "no-action" letters are also available on the SEC's website.

The official texts of SEC decisions in administrative proceedings are distributed as "releases" at the time they are handed down and are eventually printed and compiled in bound volumes of "SEC Decisions and Reports" (SEC).

Although having less precedential effect than formal SEC Releases, from time to time, the SEC staff publishes bulletins or staff interpretations. These interpretations are available on the SEC website and often provide insight on selected issues.

Court decisions involving the federal securities laws are generally reported in full text in Westlaw and Lexis, as well as in the CCH Federal Securities Law Reporter. Decisions of the Courts of Appeals, of course, also appear in West's Federal Reporter (F.2d and F.3d), and the more significant District Court decisions appear in the Federal Supplement (F.Supp., F.Supp.2d, and F.Supp.3d).

Up-to-date compilations of the constitutions, rules, and interpretations of the major stock exchanges and the NASD can be found in the loose-leaf, and now online, stock exchange "Guides" and the "FINRA Manual." The FINRA, NASDAQ, and NYSE websites

are also helpful recourses (www.finra.org, www.
nasdaq.com, and www.nyse.com).

As far as state securities law is concerned, the most
current and comprehensive compilation of statutes,
rules, and administrative and court decisions is the
CCH Blue Sky Law Reporter, which contains
separate sections covering the law of each of the 50
states. The securities law of any particular state can
also be obtained through its published statutes,
published administrative regulations (if any), and
official and unofficial reports of its court decisions.

§ 6.   THE DEFINITION OF "SECURITY"

Since most of the operative provisions of the
federal securities laws apply by their terms only to
transactions involving "securities," the
determination of whether an instrument is a security
is often the threshold issue in determining whether
or not those laws apply. "Security" is defined in
§ 2(a)(1) of the Securities Act of 1933 to include "any
note, stock, treasury stock, security future, security-
based swap, bond, debenture, evidence of
indebtedness, certificate of interest or participation
in any profit-sharing agreement, collateral-trust
certificate, preorganization certificate or
subscription, transferable share, investment
contract, voting-trust certificate, certificate of deposit
for a security, fractional undivided interest in oil, gas,
or other mineral rights, . . . or, in general, any
interest or instrument commonly known as a
'security', or any certificate of interest or
participation in, temporary or interim certificate for,

receipt for, guarantee of, or warrant or right to subscribe to or purchase, any of the foregoing." Substantially identical definitions are found in the other federal securities laws, see 1934 Act § 3(a)(10), ICA § 2(a)(36), and in most state securities laws, see USA § 401(e).

Interpretive questions under these provisions have generally involved three different types of instruments: (a) instruments technically denominated "stocks" or "notes," but issued for non-investment purposes, (b) special types of investment instruments issued by financial institutions, such as insurance companies, savings, and loan associations, and (c) instruments evidencing investments in profit-seeking undertakings, which are not in the form of stock, notes, or other traditional "securities."

(A) STOCKS AND NOTES

A share of stock will almost always be deemed to be a "security." However, in United Housing Foundation v. Forman, 421 U.S. 837 (1975), the Supreme Court held that shares of stock in a cooperative housing corporation were not "securities" under federal law where "the inducement to purchase was solely to acquire subsidized low-cost living space; it was not to invest for profit." The court rejected the "suggestion that the present transaction * * * must be considered a security transaction simply because the statutory definition of a security includes the words 'any * * * stock' " and reemphasized the "basic principle that has guided all of the Court's decisions in this area" that "form should be disregarded for substance and the emphasis should be on economic reality."

Starting in 1981, several lower courts held that the sale of a business, effected by the transfer of all its outstanding stock, is not a sale of "securities" because the transfer of stock is simply the method used to vest ownership and control of the business in the purchaser. However, in Landreth Timber Co. v. Landreth, 471 U.S. 681 (1985), the Supreme Court rejected this "sale of business" doctrine. The Court held that a sale of securities which had all of the attributes commonly associated with "stock" was a sale of a "security" within the meaning of the federal securities laws, regardless of the purpose of the transaction or the percentage of the securities being sold.

In contrast to the situation regarding stock, the courts had always recognized that there are certain kinds of "notes" that should not be considered securities, such as notes secured by a mortgage on a home, notes secured by accounts receivable or other business assets, and notes evidencing loans by commercial banks for current operations. Until 1990, the different circuits applied different tests to determine what other kinds of notes fell outside the purview of the securities laws. In Reves v. Ernst & Young, 494 U.S. 56 (1990), the Supreme Court adopted the Second Circuit test—that any note which bears a "strong family resemblance" to one of the kinds of notes on the "judicially crafted list of exceptions" should be held not to be a security. The factors to be taken into account in determining whether there is a "family resemblance" are (a) the motivations of the lender and borrower in entering into the transaction, (b) whether the note is the subject of "common trading for speculation or investment," (c) how the note would be perceived by reasonable members of the public, and (d) whether the transaction is subject to another regulatory scheme which makes application of the securities laws unnecessary. The fact that a note or other debt instrument has a fixed return does not prevent it from being considered a security. SEC v. Edwards, 540 U.S. 389 (2004).

(B) FINANCIAL INSTRUMENTS

Most of the specialized types of investment instruments issued by financial institutions, such as life insurance policies and annuities, "shares" in savings and loan associations, or certificates of deposit in banks, are specifically exempted from the registration provisions (but not the antifraud provisions) of the federal securities laws. See 1933 Act § 3(a)(2), (5), (8); 1934 Act § 3(a)(12). There is some question as to whether the traditional forms of these instruments would be deemed to be "securities" even in the absence of such exemption. However, when such institutions issue instruments on which the rate of return varies with the profitability of the institution or of a portfolio of securities, they will be considered "securities." The Supreme Court has held in two decisions that "variable annuities" issued by insurance companies are "securities" required to be registered under the 1933 Act. SEC v. Variable Annuity Life, 359 U.S. 65 (1959); SEC v. United

Benefit, 387 U.S. 202 (1967). In 1987, the SEC adopted 1933 Act Rule 151, a "safe harbor" rule specifying the characteristics that would cause annuity contracts to be classified as exempt securities within the meaning of 1933 Act § 3(a)(8).

The Supreme Court has also held that withdrawable capital shares issued by a savings and loan association are "securities" for the purposes of the antifraud provisions of the 1934 Act, even though they are specifically exempted from the registration provisions of the 1933 Act. Tcherepnin v. Knight, 389 U.S. 332 (1967). However, a regular bank certificate of deposit is not a security, since the holders "are abundantly protected under the federal banking laws." Marine Bank v. Weaver, 455 U.S. 551 (1982).

Derivatives—Options, Futures, and Swaps. Puts, calls, and options are specifically included in the definition of securities under both the 1933 and 1934 Acts. Trading in options on outstanding securities, which has mushroomed over the years following the development of organized option exchanges, is fully subject to SEC regulation. Indeed, the exchanges are considered the issuers of the options and must register them under the 1933 Act. The continued proliferation of derivative investments continues to make this an increasingly important sector of the financial markets.

Contracts for future delivery of securities, however, were developed by and are traded on commodity exchanges rather than securities exchanges. Since the definition of "commodity" in the Commodity Futures Trading Commission Act includes securities, these "futures contracts" on individual securities and stock market indices are regulated by the CFTC rather than the SEC. For an opinion analyzing the often-difficult question of whether a novel financial instrument should be considered a futures contract or a security, see Chicago Mercantile Exchange v. SEC, 883 F.2d 537 (7th Cir.1989). Difficult questions can arise, for example, as to whether a stock index futures contract is sufficiently broadly-based to be subject to the exclusive jurisdiction of the CFTC or to co-regulation as a future on a security. See Board of Trade v. SEC, 187 F.3d 713 (7th Cir.1999), Commodity Exchange Act § 1a(25).

The Commodity Futures Modernization Act of 2000 (CFMA) clarified the respective roles of the SEC and CFTC in regulating certain derivatives and hybrid investments. Futures on individual stocks are now permitted and are expressly included within the definition of security; these futures contracts are regulated by both the SEC and CFTC under a "passport" system of co-regulation. The CFMA modernization legislation also excluded securities-based swap agreements from the definition of securities but, at the same time, subjected those arrangements to the securities laws' general antifraud provisions. Swap agreements that are not based on securities are similarly excluded from the securities laws but, unlike securities-based swap agreements, are not subject to the securities laws' antifraud provisions.

Swap transactions were largely unregulated until the adoption of the Dodd-Frank Act in 2010. This became a huge point of controversy following the 2008 credit crisis and financial meltdown, with many observers pointing to unregulated credit default swaps as a contributing cause. There have been a number of proposals to regulate the swap markets and derivative markets generally. It is likely that some regulatory change will be forthcoming. Under current law, swaps are excluded from the securities laws. However, although securities-based swap agreements are not "securities" under federal law, they are expressly subject to the securities laws' antifraud provisions.

(C) INVESTMENT CONTRACTS

The area of greatest difficulty has been in determining whether investments in a variety of money-raising schemes are "securities," even though there is no "note, stock, * * * or instrument commonly known as a 'security.'" The question has been whether an investment in such a scheme may nevertheless be an "investment contract" or a "certificate of interest or participation in any profit-sharing agreement." These terms have been liberally interpreted by the courts to apply to a wide range of schemes, particularly where the SEC or state regulators have sought injunctions against activities for which there was no prompt or effective relief available under other laws designed to protect the public.

Among the types of interests which have been held in certain circumstances to be "securities" are interests in oil and gas drilling programs, partnerships, real estate condominiums, cooperatives, farm lands or animals, commodity option contracts, whiskey warehouse receipts, multi-level distributorship arrangements, and merchandise marketing schemes.

The basic test laid down by the Supreme Court in SEC v. W. J. Howey Co., 328 U.S. 293 (1946), is whether "a person invests his money in a common enterprise and is led to expect profits solely from the efforts of the promoter or a third party." In that case, the sale of individual rows of orange trees, in conjunction with a service contract under which the seller cultivated, harvested, and marketed the orange crop, was held to involve a "security" within the meaning of the 1933 Act.

"Investment of Money." In Teamsters v. Daniel, 439 U.S. 551 (1979), the Supreme Court held that interests in a non-contributory pension plan were not "securities," since the contributions by employers to the plan could not really be considered an "investment of money" by their employees. The SEC subsequently took the position that only pension plans to which employees make voluntary contributions would be considered securities. Sec. Act Rel. 33–6188 (1980).

"Common Enterprise." Courts have split on the question whether investors must share in a single pool of assets ("horizontal commonality") in order to find a common enterprise, or whether a profit-

sharing arrangement between the promoter and each investor ("vertical commonality") is sufficient. See Revak v. SEC Realty, 18 F.3d 81 (2d Cir.1994). And the Supreme Court has held that a "unique [profit-sharing] agreement, negotiated one-on-one by the parties, is not a security." Marine Bank v. Weaver, *supra.*

"Expectation of Profit." As noted above, the Supreme Court held in *Forman* that shares of stock in a cooperative housing corporation would not be considered "securities" where "the inducement to purchase was solely to acquire subsidized low-cost living space; it was not to invest for profit." Similarly, the courts have held interests in pension plans not to be "securities" on the ground that the employee expects the funds for his or her pension to come primarily from contributions by the employer rather than earnings on the plan's assets. Teamsters v. Daniel, *supra*; Black v. Payne, 591 F.2d 83 (9th Cir.1979). Investments frequently offer profits based on a variable return, depending upon the profitability of the enterprise. However, a variable return is not a precondition of finding a profit, as a fixed return can satisfy the profit element so as to find a security. SEC v. Edwards, 540 U.S. 389 (2004).

"Solely from the Efforts of Others." The *Howey* requirement that profits come "solely" from the efforts of others has led to decisions holding the securities laws inapplicable to franchise arrangements where the investor takes an active part in the business. See, e.g., Wieboldt v. Metz, 355 F.Supp. 255 (S.D.N.Y.1973). However, courts have

modified the interpretation of the word "solely" to reach fraudulent pyramid sales schemes in which the investor does have to exert some "efforts" in soliciting other persons to participate in the scheme, but where "the efforts made by those other than the investor are the undeniably significant ones, those essential managerial efforts which affect the failure or success of the enterprise." SEC v. Glenn W. Turner, 474 F.2d 476 (9th Cir.1973). See SEC v. Koscot, 497 F.2d 473 (5th Cir.1974); SEC v. Aqua-Sonic, 687 F.2d 577 (2d Cir.1982).

With respect to partnerships, limited partnership interests will generally be held to be securities, since limited partners are not entitled to participate in management. See, e.g., Goodman v. Epstein, 582 F.2d 388 (7th Cir.1978). General partnership interests, on the other hand, will generally be held not to be securities, since general partners are entitled to participate in management. Most courts, however, follow the approach of Williamson v. Tucker, 645 F.2d 404 (5th Cir.1981), in holding that a general partnership interest can be a security if the investors have no effective voice in management because of (a) specific provisions in the partnership agreement, (b) their inexperience in business matters, or (c) their dependence on the unique skills of the promoter or manager. See, e.g., Koch v. Hankins, 928 F.2d 1471 (9th Cir.1991).

Limited liability company interests are treated in much the same manner as partnerships. They will be considered to be securities if the investment is a passive one to the extent that the investor is dependent upon the promoter's efforts for the business to succeed. See, e.g., SEC v. Shreveport Wireless, 1998 WL 892948 (D.D.C.1998). Limited liability company interests will not be securities when the members are active participants in the business. See, e.g., Great Lakes Chemical Corp. v. Monsanto Co., 96 F.Supp.2d 376 (D.Del.2000).

Some state courts, in construing their securities laws, have followed the lead of the California Supreme Court in Silver Hills v. Sobieski, 55 Cal.2d 811, 13 Cal.Rptr. 186, 361 P.2d 906 (1961) and found a "security" even where the investor takes an active role in the enterprise, if the funds the investor contributes are part of the "risk capital" for the initial development of the business. In United Housing Foundation v. Forman, *supra*, the U.S. Supreme Court expressly declined to decide whether the "risk capital" test should be used in interpreting federal securities law.

(D) EXEMPT SECURITIES

1933 Act § 3(a) and 1934 Act § 3(a)(12) contain lists of "exempted securities." In general, an "exempted security" is not subject to the registration and disclosure requirements of the particular statute, but may be subject to the general antifraud and civil liability provisions. While provisions of the 1933 Act do not apply to exempted securities "except as * * * expressly provided" (see, e.g., 1933 Act §§ 12(a)(1) and 17(c)), provisions of the 1934 Act do apply to exempted securities unless their operation is specifically excluded (see, e.g., 1933 Act §§ 12(a) and 15(a)(1)).

The most important class of "exempted securities" under 1933 Act § 3(a)(2) and 1934 Act § 3(a)(12) consists of obligations issued or guaranteed by the United States government or by state or local governments, including tax-exempt industrial development bonds. The 1933 Act (but not the 1934 Act) also exempts securities issued by banks, religious and other charitable organizations, savings and loan associations, bankruptcy certificates, insurance policies, and annuity contracts.

The 1933 Act § 3(a)(3) exempts notes with a maturity of nine months or less which "arise[ ] out of a current transaction," and 1934 Act § 3(a)(10) excludes from the definition of "security" all notes with a maturity of nine months or less. Many courts have construed these exclusions as applying only to high-grade "commercial paper" issued by large corporations to finance their current operations. See, e.g., Zeller v. Bogue, 476 F.2d 795 (2d Cir.1973). In Reves v. Ernst & Young, *supra*, the Supreme Court declined to adopt this limitation, but held (5–4) that a note payable on demand did not fall within the exclusion if it was not anticipated that demand would in fact be made within nine months from the date of issue.

The 1933 Act also exempts from its provisions certain "classes" of securities which are in reality transaction exemptions. Among these are securities issued in exchange for other securities (1933 Act §§ 3(a)(9) and (10)) or in intrastate offerings (1933

Act § 3(a)(11)), as well as in small offerings made in compliance with SEC rules under 1933 Act § 3(b). (See § 10 below.)

Some exemptions have been eliminated or restricted over the years. For example, the Railroad Revitalization Act of 1976 eliminated the 1933 Act exemption for securities issued by railroads (other than equipment trust certificates). 1933 Act § 3(a)(6). The Securities Exchange Act was amended in 1974 to require the banking agencies, which administer that Act's disclosure requirements with respect to bank securities, to conform their regulations to those of the SEC, unless different treatment could be justified. 1934 Act § 12(i). The Securities Acts Amendments of 1975 also required firms that deal solely in state and local government securities to register with the SEC and to comply with rules laid down by a newly-created Municipal Securities Rulemaking Board. 1934 Act § 15B.

In 1986, § 15C was added to the 1934 Act, setting up a complex regulatory scheme for brokers and dealers in U.S. Government securities. Since many banks are engaged in that activity, regulatory authority is divided between the SEC and the three federal banking agencies, with the principal rulemaking power vested in the Secretary of the Treasury.

(E) DERIVATIVE INVESTMENTS, STOCK OPTIONS, INDEX OPTIONS, FUTURES

The statutory definitions in both the 1933 and 1934 Acts make it clear that securities include not only stocks and bonds but also "any put, call, straddle, option, or privilege on any security." Thus, an investment that is derivative of a security is itself a security. Derivative investments—both those based on securities and those based on commodities or other underlying values—have become a significant segment of the investment markets. Regulation of derivative investments is more fragmented than securities regulation generally. The discussion that follows addresses the applicability of the securities laws to derivative investment.

Derivative Investments: An Overview

Over the past four decades, the securities markets have been infused with options trading in order to provide an alternative way to participate in short-term investments in securities. Put and call options on individual securities allow investors to hedge their positions and thereby limit risk. While reducing risk may be the motivation for some investors, much options trading has been on a speculative basis. Since its inception, public trading of options on securities exchanges has been an active financial market. The success of the options markets for individual securities paved the way for expansion into markets for index options, which are subject to Securities and Exchange Commission regulation, and markets for futures based on stock indexes, which are subject to the jurisdiction of the Commodity Futures Trading Commission. The index markets permit investors to diversify their holdings by not tying their investments to the stock of a particular issuer. Index options and futures are broadly-based indexes, the value of which is dependent upon the current per share price of the stocks comprising the index. By utilizing the index markets, investors can take positions in groups of stocks tied to a publicly traded index option or futures contract. The index markets also have provided additional opportunities for the breed of arbitrageurs known as risk arbitrageurs.

Options provide an important way to hedge long positions in securities. A long position exists when an investor owns securities, as opposed to a short position when an investor has sold options or securities thereby obligating him or her to purchase them at a later date. For example, an investor owning 1000 shares of ABC Co. stock which is currently trading at $12 per share may want to limit the risk of a price decline. In such a case, an appropriate hedge strategy would be to buy put options with a strike price of $10 per share. This would guarantee that at any time until the expiration date the investor could sell the stock for $10 per share. Buying the puts will cause the investor to incur the cost of the premium that the market has placed on the put, thereby increasing his or her total cost but limiting the risk of loss.

Another example of an option strategy occurs when the investor believes that the market is likely to decline and therefore he or she maintains a large cash balance. In order to hedge against the possibility that their negative market outlook is wrong, investors may want to purchase call options, in selected stocks or broader-based index options, which would allow participation in a market rise. The purchase of call options involves less cash than investing in the underlying stocks but also is much more speculative as the investor stands to lose his or her entire investment if the option expires when the stock price is below the option exercise price.

In 2000, Congress opened the door for a futures market place to parallel the securities option markets that are subject to SEC regulation. The 2000 amendments to the Commodity Exchange Act (CEA) granted for the first time to the Commodity Futures Trading Commission jurisdiction over futures contracts on individual securities. Options and futures contracts can also be based on groups of individual securities. These groups may be established according to well-established stock indexes or alternatively by a group of securities characterized by industry or other identifying factors.

Over-the-Counter Derivatives

The heart of the Commodity Exchange Act was the contract market monopoly required by section 4 of that Act. This meant that commodity-related instruments that fall within the exclusive jurisdiction of the CFTC had to be traded on a registered commodities contract market or exchange absent some exemption or exclusion from the Act. As a result, unlike the securities markets, there was no public over-the-counter market for commodity-related investments. If an instrument fell within the Act's exclusive jurisdiction but was exempt from the contract market monopoly requirement, then the instruments could be traded off-exchange. However, since such exempt commodity-related investments still fall under the Act's exclusive jurisdiction, the SEC cannot assert jurisdiction. The Commodity Futures Modernization Act of 2000 created a revolution in commodities regulation when it largely eliminated the contract market monopoly. In addition to various exemptions from CFTC regulation, there are exclusions from the Commodity Exchange Act's coverage, such as for forward contracts as opposed to futures contracts. A forward contract is a contract calling for a future delivery where the parties to the contract engage in a trade or business that utilizes the underlying commodity. As such forward contracts are not subject to the act and thus may be traded over-the-counter, other than through an organized contract market.

Swaps and Other Hybrids

During the 1980s a host of novel and exotic investment products developed. A number of commercial banks and investment banks began to develop specialized financial products geared to the investment objectives of particular clients. Among these "new exotics" were interest-rate swaps, followed by foreign-currency swaps and, eventually, by equity- or commodity-based swaps. During the 1980s, these hybrid and derivative instruments flourished, interrelating all sorts of financial variables to permit sophisticated hedging strategies. At the same time, many institutional investors got in over their heads. For example, in 1994, Orange

County, California, declared bankruptcy after losing over one billion dollars from these investments.

Even still, swap transactions have become an important part of the international economy. For example, interest-rate swaps are frequently used to manage credit risks. The prevalence of swap agreements means that there are large amounts of money tied up in these arrangements, most of which are largely unregulated. For the most part, these exotic derivatives are not subject to regulation as securities because they involve contracts between the creator and the investor where the gains of one are the losses of the other; thus, they do not involve a common enterprise. Although promoters of these derivative instruments put substantial efforts into their design and marketing, that alone is not sufficient to classify them as securities.

Even if some of the underlying instruments are regulated because they are considered securities, the regulations do not address the complex relationships that exist as a result of the swap or derivative formulas. It is these formulas that create the risks that are not easily understood even by the most sophisticated investors. In addition to the absence of meaningful securities regulation (other than the antifraud rules), these over-the-counter derivatives and swaps are generally excluded or exempt from the coverage of the commodities laws.

In 2000, Congress amended the securities and commodities laws regarding hybrid investments. Among other things, these amendments resulted in securities-based swap agreements being excluded from the definition of security but nevertheless subjected to the securities laws antifraud provisions. Also, swaps that are not security-based do not fall within either the registration or antifraud provisions of the securities laws.

Swap transactions, like any hybrid instruments containing commodities components, are likely to be categorized as subject to the exclusive jurisdiction of the Commodities Futures Trading Commission (CFTC). However, as mentioned above, the CFTC and Congress provided exemptions from the Commodity Futures Modernization Act for many swap transactions involving institutional and other sophisticated participants. This created an over-the-counter market among sophisticated participants for certain commodity-related investments that were largely unregulated until 2010.

These unregulated over-the-counter markets came under increased scrutiny as a result of the aftermath of the 2008 credit crisis and financial meltdown, and it became inevitable that they would face some form of regulation. The Dodd-Frank Wall Street Reform and Consumer Protection Act of 2010 (Dodd-Frank) responded to the crisis with a mandate for extensive regulation of swap transactions. The Dodd-Frank amendments set forth a broad definition of "swap" in the Commodity Exchange Act (CEA) § 1a(47)(A), 7 U.S.C. § 1a(47), and continues the distinction under prior law between security-based swaps, see 1934 Act, § 3(a)(68), that are subject to SEC jurisdiction and other swaps, which are not subject to SEC jurisdiction. In addition to defining swaps broadly, the Act sets forth a series of exclusions from the definition of swap. Those exclusions include futures contracts, options on futures contracts, and "any sale of a nonfinancial commodity or security for deferred shipment or delivery, so long as the transaction is intended to be physically settled." CEA, § 1a(47)(B). The legislative history makes clear that this exclusion was designed to parallel the pre-existing exclusion of forward contracts in the Commodity Exchange Act and the CFTC's policy on forward contracts.

The CEA also excludes from the definition of swap options and other contracts based on securities indexes where the option or contract is subject to SEC jurisdiction and options and derivatives of individual securities, as well as a carve-out for security-based swaps. A security-based swap is any swap where "a material term [of the swap agreement] is 'based on' the price, yield, value, or volatility of any security or any group or index of securities."

While securities regulation covers most types of investment contracts, it does not include non-securities-based derivative contracts, which include credit default swaps and interest rate swaps. 1933 Act, § 2A. The unique aspect of credit default swaps is that, unlike other risk-shifting contracts such as insurance, they were not regulated prior to Dodd-Frank. This lack of regulation was justified by many because of their usefulness in mitigating risks. However, they clearly contributed to the severity of the 2008 financial crisis and set the stage for Dodd-Frank. A credit default swap (CDS) is a derivative investment that has been the topic of much discussion over the past several months.

Additionally, Dodd-Frank created two new categories of professionals that must be registered under the Securities Exchange Act. Those two new categories are (1) security-based swap dealers and (2) major security-based swap participants. A "security-based swap dealer" is defined as a person who (i) holds itself out as a dealer in security-based swaps, or (ii) makes a market in security-based swaps, or (iii) regularly enters into swaps with counterparties as an ordinary course of business for its own account, or (iv) engages in activity commonly known in the trade as a dealer or market maker in security-based swaps. 1934 Act, § 3(a)(71). A "major security-based swap participant" is a person other than a security-based swap dealer that maintains a substantial non-hedging position in security-based swaps giving rise to substantial counterparty exposure that could impact the economy systemically. 1934 Act, § 3(a)(67). Security-based swap dealers and major swap participants that are required to register under the Exchange Act are made subject to a variety of duties, including capital and margin requirements, extensive reporting and recordkeeping, business conduct standards, disclosure duties, risk management obligations, and many other operational mandates. The specifics and implementation of the regulation will be unveiled by SEC rulemaking. Dodd-Frank's mandates for security-based swaps parallel the mandates to the CFTC for all other swaps.

CHAPTER II

REGULATION OF PUBLIC OFFERINGS

The process by which a corporation or other issuer offers and sells its securities to the public has been a principal focus of regulatory activity in the securities field. A major portion of the work of the SEC (and of lawyers engaged in securities practice) is devoted to determining if registration of these offerings is required under the Securities Act of 1933 and, if so, to registering the offering. While some people feel that there has been undue emphasis on this activity—to the detriment of other problem areas, such as—the registration practices under the 1933 Act have created a distinctive approach and tone to American securities regulation.

Unlike many state securities laws, as is the case with the other federal securities laws, the 1933 Act is essentially only a "disclosure" statute. The SEC has no authority to decide whether a particular security may be offered to the public; it can only insist that the issuer make full disclosure of all material facts.

The heart of the 1933 Act is 1933 Act § 5, which provides in general that no security may be offered or sold to the public unless it is registered with the SEC. 1933 Act §§ 6 and 8 set forth the procedure for registration, and 1933 Act §§ 7 and 10 specify the information which must be disclosed. 1933 Act §§ 3 and 4 list types of securities and types of transactions which are exempt from the registration requirement. 1933 Act §§ 3 and 4 are supplemented by 1933 Act

§ 28 which gives the SEC broad exemptive authority through its rulemaking process.

Civil liability for damages is established by 1933 Act §§ 11 and 12. 1933 Act § 11 sets forth in detail the liabilities arising from misstatements or omissions in a registration statement, 1933 Act § 12(a)(1) establishes civil liability for offers or sales in violation of 1933 Act § 5, and 1933 Act § 12(a)(2) establishes liability for misstatements or omissions in any offer or sale of securities, whether or not registered under the Act. As noted below, the Supreme Court has limited the 12(a)(2) remedy to offerings by a prospectus. Gustafson v. Alloyd, 513 U.S. 561 (1995). The only other substantive provision of the 1933 Act is 1933 Act § 17, which makes it unlawful to engage in fraudulent or deceitful practices in connection with any offer or sale of securities, whether or not registered under the Act.

§ 7. 1933 ACT DISCLOSURE REQUIREMENTS

The basic purpose of the Securities Act of 1933 is to assure the availability of adequate reliable information about securities which are offered to the public. To achieve this objective, the Act makes it illegal to offer or sell securities to the public unless they have been registered. An issuer can register an offering of securities by filing with the SEC a "registration statement" containing certain information specified in the Act and in the SEC's rules and forms. Unlike registration under the 1934 Act, which covers an entire class of securities, registration under the 1933 Act covers only the securities actually being offered, and only for the purposes of the offering described in the registration statement. Thus, it is misleading to refer to securities registered under the 1933 Act. Rather, the specific transaction or offering is registered. This means that securities which have been registered under the 1933 Act for purposes of a public offering may have to be registered again if they are being reoffered in a new transaction subject to the 1933 Act registration requirements (such as a distribution of a "controlling" block of shares).

The "registration statement" consists of two parts: Part I, the "prospectus," a copy of which must be furnished to every purchaser of the securities, and Part II, containing information and exhibits which need not be furnished to purchasers but are available for public inspection in the Commission's files.

1933 Act § 7, by reference to Schedule A of the Act (or Schedule B, in the case of securities issued by foreign governments), prescribes the information to be included in a registration statement. 1933 Act § 10(a)(1) specifies which of those items of information must be included in the prospectus furnished to purchasers.

1933 Act § 7 authorizes the Commission (a) to require any additional information to be included in a registration statement, and (b) to permit the omission of certain items of information with respect to particular classes of securities or issuers. Acting under this authority, the Commission has promulgated a number of different forms for registering different types of offerings. The basic form for registration statements is Form S–1, prescribed for use in all offerings for which no other form is authorized or prescribed. With respect to companies whose securities are already publicly traded, Form S–1 permits companies that have filed at least one annual report and who are current in their 1934 Act filings to incorporate by reference information in previously filed SEC reports, provided that the information incorporated by reference is readily available on a website maintained by the company.

In March 1982, the Commission took a major step toward integration of the 1933 and 1934 Act disclosure requirements with the adoption of an "integrated disclosure system." Sec. Act. Rel. 33–6383 (1982). The principal elements of that system are:

(a) Inclusion of all of the disclosure requirements for the basic 1933 and 1934 Act documents in Regulation S–K, with the items of the various forms simply referring to the applicable items of that Regulation.

(b) Adoption of registration former form S–2 and form S–3 for offerings by issuers already registered under the 1934 Act, which permit a large part of the information required in the registration statement to be incorporated by reference to the issuer's 1934 Act filings or reports to shareholders. (The 1934 Act disclosure requirements are described in § 13 below.)

Form S–2, which was rescinded in 2005, formerly could be used by any issuer which had filed reports under the 1934 Act for at least three years. This form permitted the issuer to supply the requisite information about itself by including in the registration statement and prospectus a copy of its latest annual report to shareholders and incorporating by reference its latest annual report to the Commission on Form 10–K.

Form S–3 can also be used by issuers that have filed reports under the 1934 Act for at least twelve months to register (a) offerings of senior securities, secondary offerings, and certain special kinds of offerings, and (b) new offerings of equity securities if the market value of the issuer's publicly-held voting stock is at least $75 million. It does not require the issuer to include in the registration statement or prospectus any information about itself but, instead, allows the issuer to simply incorporate by reference its latest annual report on Form 10–K. The rationale behind these two forms is that the information already circulating in the market with respect to such issuers obviates the need for further dissemination of that same information by means of the registration statement and prospectus.

In 1997, the Commission took a further step toward integration of the two Acts by proposing the complete elimination of the requirement of 1933 Act registration for additional issues of securities by a company registered under the 1934 Act, so long as the company provides "enhanced" disclosure on a continuing basis. Sec. Act Rel. 33–7314 (1996). This proposal has not been implemented. However, the SEC has significantly expanded the events that trigger interim reporting under 1934 Act Form 8–K, thus moving us ever closer to a continuous rather than periodic reporting system.

In response to pressure on the Commission to reduce the burden of registration on small issuers, the Commission in 1992 completely revamped its registration and disclosure forms for small issuers. Sec. Act Rel. 33–6949 (1992). The SEC adopted 1933 Act former registration Form SB–2 which was made available for offerings of any size by a "small business issuer," defined as any issuer with annual revenues of less than $25 million. Disclosures on former Form SB–2 were governed by former Regulation S–B, which superseded Regulation S–K for all forms filed by small business issuers under either the 1933 or 1934 Act. In 1993, the Commission adopted another form—former Form SB–1—which could be used by small business issuers to sell up to $10 million worth of securities in any twelve-month period. Former form SB–1 was a streamlined disclosure document in which the registrant could use either the traditional narrative disclosure approach or take advantage of the question-and-answer format now permitted in offerings under Regulation A, discussed in § 10(e) below.

In 2007, the SEC eliminated the specialized forms and Regulation S–B that formerly were available to small business issuers. At the same time, the SEC redefined the concept of small business issuers in order to enable more companies to qualify for the new "scaled disclosure requirements" available under both the 1933 and 1934 Acts for smaller reporting companies. Companies with less than $75 million in public equity float now qualify for scaled disclosure requirements under Regulation S–K as amended and under the applicable 1933 and 1934 Act forms as amended. Companies that do not have a calculable public equity float qualify for scaled disclosure if their revenues were below $50 million in the previous year. Companies that formerly were eligible for forms SB–1 or SB–2 may now take advantage of the scaled disclosures permitted under revised Form S–1.

In order to ease some of the disclosure burdens of smaller companies, in 2012 the JOBS Act introduced a new category of reporting company, the emerging growth company. Jumpstart Our Business Startups Act § 106(a), H.R. 3606, 112 Cong. 2d sess. (2012). An emerging growth company is a company with less than $1 billion in annual gross revenue during its most recent fiscal year. Emerging growth companies can take advantage of an "on-ramp" for IPOs that eases or eliminates some of the more burdensome disclosure and reporting requirements for up to five years after the company's IPO.

The on-ramp for emerging growth companies provides a significant relief from 1934 Act obligations that otherwise would apply. For example, during the years following the IPO, emerging growth companies are excused from detailed executive pay disclosures, the non-binding say on pay votes that are required for larger companies, compliance with any new accounting standards, and any future mandate that firms rotate auditors. This on-ramp also reintroduces the research analysts to the underwriting effort. In addition, emerging growth companies may "test the waters" by soliciting potential investor interest prior to the filing of a registration statement.

Other 1933 Act registration forms available for use in special situations include Form S–4, for mergers and acquisitions, Form S–8, for employee stock purchase plans, and Form S–11, for real estate companies.

Supplementing the items and instructions contained in the forms themselves is the Commission's Regulation C, consisting of 1933 Act Rules 400–499, which prescribes registration procedures and the general form of registration statements and prospectuses.

These rules and forms, however, are only the starting point in the preparation of a registration statement. The supposed objective of the 1933 Act is to produce a document which tells a prospective purchaser the things the potential investor really ought to know before buying a security. This objective, however, is not easy to attain. Among the factors which inhibit it are (1) the fact that it may be against the issuer's financial interest to tell investors the real weaknesses of the operation, and (2) the difficulty of putting complex financial arrangements or economic factors into language simple enough for the average investor to understand. The task is complicated further by uncertainty as to whether the principal purpose of disclosure under the federal securities laws is to protect investors against really bad deals by making sure that negative factors are emphasized, or to enable them to make rational choices among alternative respectable deals by requiring a balanced presentation of affirmative and negative factors.

The SEC for many years took the position that 1933 Act registration statements should contain only "hard" information, such as descriptions of current or completed activities and financial statements covering past periods. It objected to inclusion of such "soft" information as appraisals of property and estimates of future earnings. However, in the 1970s, the SEC began rethinking this position and, in 1978, issued a release encouraging issuers to include "projections, economic forecasts, and other forward-looking information" in filed documents. This policy is currently set forth in Item 10 of Regulation S–K.

In 1979, the Commission adopted "safe harbor" rules, specifying the circumstances under which "forward-looking statements" would not be deemed to be "fraudulent statements." See 1933 Act Rule 175; 1934 Act Rule 3b–6. Under these rules, an issuer will not be held liable for projections incorporated in a registration statement, which were accurate at the time they were made, even if they are no longer accurate at the time the registration statement becomes effective. Wielgos v. Commonwealth Edison, 892 F.2d 509 (7th Cir.1989). And in 1995, the securities laws were amended to provide that when forward-looking statements are accompanied by "meaningful cautionary statements," they will not give rise to liability. See 1933 Act § 27A, 1934 Act § 21E.

To provide investors with additional assistance in interpreting the "hard" information in the registration statement, Item 303 of Regulation S–K requires that it contain a "management discussion and analysis" (MD&A) providing supplementary information about liquidity, capital resources, results of operations, off-balance sheet arrangements, tabular disclosure of contractual obligations, and "such other information that the registrant believes to be necessary to an understanding of its financial condition, changes in financial condition and results of operations." For analysis of this requirement, see Sec. Act Rel. 33–6835 (1989); In re Caterpillar, Exch. Act Rel. 34–30532, 1992 WL 71907 (SEC 1992).

In 1998, the SEC adopted amendments to 1933 Act Rule 421 to require that prospectus disclosure substantially comply with principles of "plain English," including the use of (a) the active voice, (b) short sentences, (c) definite, concrete everyday words, (d) tabular presentation or bullet lists, (e) no legal or highly technical business terminology, and (f) no multiple negatives. See Sec. Act Rel. 33–7380 (1997).

§ 8.   THE REGISTRATION PROCESS

Under 1933 Act § 8(a), a registration statement automatically becomes "effective" 20 days after it is filed with the Commission, at which point the issuer is free to sell the registered securities to the public. The Commission, however, has certain powers to delay or suspend the effectiveness of the registration statement. Under 1933 Act § 8(b), it can issue an order "refusing to permit such statement to become effective" if it appears that the statement "is on its face incomplete or inaccurate in any material respect." Under 1933 Act § 8(d), it can issue a "stop order" suspending the effectiveness of a registration statement that it finds to contain a misstatement or omission of a material fact.

In practice, the SEC has not used the "refusal order" at all (because of timing and procedural problems), and has used the "stop order" only in egregious situations. Strangely enough, the "stop order" proceeding is almost never used to "stop" an ongoing sale of securities under a registration statement that has just become effective. It is normally employed either (a) to prevent a registration statement with serious deficiencies from becoming effective, or (b) to publicize the deficiencies in a registration statement under which securities have already been publicly distributed. See, e.g., Universal Camera, 19 SEC 648 (1945); Franchard, 42 SEC 163 (1964).

This is not to say, however, that the SEC has played a passive role with respect to the contents of the great majority of registration statements filed with it. On the contrary, a substantial part of the time and energy of its staff has been devoted to the review of registration statements and the communication of the staff's views in "letters of comment," also known as "deficiency letters." In these informal communications, which are not provided for in the Act, the staff may insist on or suggest changes, additions, or deletions, or may request additional information as a prelude to further comments.

The basis of this procedure, and of the willingness of issuers to go along with it, is 1933 Act § 8(a), which authorizes the Commission, subject to stated criteria, to permit a registration statement to become effective less than 20 days after filing. The issuer or underwriters making a distribution normally want to start selling the security as soon as they have set the price and other terms of the offering, which are usually omitted from the registration statement as originally filed. The inclusion of this information requires the filing of an amendment to the registration statement. Because 1933 Act § 8(a) provides that the filing of any amendment starts the 20-day period running again, the SEC's willingness to "accelerate" the effective date is crucial to every issuer wanting to proceed with its offering as soon as possible after filing the "price amendment."

In determining whether to grant "acceleration," the Commission is required to give "due regard to the adequacy of the information * * * available to the public, to the facility with which the nature of the securities * * * and the rights of holders thereof can be understood, and to the public interest and the protection of investors." In general, the Commission's decisions on acceleration rest on the issuer's willingness to make additions, deletions, or modifications in the registration statement requested by the Commission staff (or to convince the

Commission staff that they are inappropriate). However, in a "Note" to its rules, the Commission set down certain substantive conditions for acceleration, most notably a requirement that the issuer undertake not to indemnify its officers and directors against 1933 Act liability in the absence of a court determination that such indemnification would not contravene the public policy of the Act. See 1933 Act Rule 461; Item 512(h) of Regulation S–K. This condition, which the Commission justified under the "public interest and protection of investors" test, has been criticized by members of the securities bar as an unwarranted extension of the Commission's discretionary power of acceleration.

From time to time, particularly when there is a heavy volume of 1933 Act filings, the Commission has announced that it will give only "cursory" or "summary" review to registration statements which appear to present no special problems, and will automatically accelerate the effective date to the date requested by the issuer. Several commentators have consistently urged the Commission to abandon its "letter of comment" procedure altogether and "permit the Securities Act of 1933 to operate in the manner in which it was originally written."

For many years, the Commission took the position that an issuer could register only securities which it intended to offer for sale immediately, and could not register securities to have them available for quick sale at a later date. However, in 1982, it modified this position and adopted 1933 Act Rule 415, broadening the opportunities for "shelf registration." Under the

Rule, an issuer can register securities for sale from time to time over a period of up to two years, with the offering terms to be set in light of market conditions and other factors. The Rule permits an issuer to avoid the delays involved in the preparation and filing of a new registration statement at the time of each sale. It was strongly supported by large companies which make frequent offerings of debt securities and want to move quickly to take advantage of favorable interest rates. It was opposed, however, by some major underwriting firms who feared its impact on their traditional ways of doing business. As definitively approved in 1983, the Rule is available only for (a) offerings by persons other than the issuer, (b) traditional types of continuing offerings, such as employee purchase plans, and (c) any debt or equity offerings by the very large companies qualified to register their securities on Form S–3 (see § 7 above). WKSIs qualify for automatic shelf registration.

In 1987, the Commission adopted 1933 Act Rule 430A, under which information relating to the price of the securities and terms of the underwriting need not appear in the registration statement at the time it becomes effective, provided the information is contained in a final prospectus filed pursuant to 1933 Act Rule 424 within five days after the effective date. This eliminates the need for filing a special "price amendment" immediately prior to the effective date. Under Rule 430A(b), the omitted information is deemed to be part of the registration statement for purposes of liability under 1933 Act § 11. In 1995, the Commission further liberalized the rules on prospectus delivery by permitting the preliminary prospectus to be supplemented by a "term sheet," containing specified information about the offering. See 1933 Act Rule 434, adopted in Sec. Act Rel. 33–7168 (1995).

§ 9.   THE OPERATION OF 1933 ACT § 5

As noted above, the purpose of the 1933 Act is to prevent the public offering and sale of securities unless adequate information about them has been made available. The basic provisions designed to prevent such offers and sales are the prohibitions found in § 5 of the Act. In trying to understand the operation of 1933 Act § 5, you may find it helpful to keep in mind two basic patterns. The first is the sequence of participation in the movement of securities from the issuer to the public.

ISSUER→UNDERWRITERS→DEALERS→PUBLIC

This is not always the pattern, but it is the one on which the basic restrictions and liabilities in the 1933 Act are based. An "underwriter" is defined as a person "who has purchased from an issuer with a view to, or offers or sells for an issuer in connection with, the distribution of any security, or participates * * * in any such undertaking," but does not include a dealer "whose interest is limited to a commission [or discount] from an underwriter or dealer not in excess of the usual or customary distributors' or sellers' commission [or discount]." A "dealer" is a person "who engages * * * as agent, broker, or principal, in the business of offering, buying, selling, or otherwise dealing or trading in securities issued by another person."

In the normal "firm-commitment" underwriting, the underwriters purchase the securities as principal from the issuer and resell them to dealers for retail sale to the public. For example, the issuer may sell shares to the underwriters at $22, to be resold to dealers at $23, for reoffering to the public at $24. A "firm-commitment" underwriting usually involves a "fixed-price" offering in which each dealer agrees to make a bona fide public offering at the price stated in the prospectus. Contrary to a "firm-commitment" underwriting, in a "best-efforts" underwriting, the underwriters simply agree to try to sell as many securities as they can, receiving a commission from the issuer for the securities sold.

The second basic pattern to keep in mind is the time sequence established by the 1933 Act, by reference to the date on which the registration statement is filed and the date on which it becomes "effective".

FILING DATE		EFFECTIVE DATE
PRE-FILING PERIOD	WAITING PERIOD	POST-EFFECTIVE PERIOD

1933 Act § 5 has a dual thrust: (a) to prevent or restrict any public statements about the securities being offered, except those contained in the registration statement and the statutory prospectus, and (b) to assure that the statutory prospectus is made available to the investing public. Unfortunately, the structure of § 5 does not clearly reflect this division; nor does it clearly reflect the distinctions between the three different periods defined by the filing date and effective date of the registration statement. As an aid to your understanding of the structure of § 5, the following diagram indicates the respective periods in which the prohibitions contained in the five subdivisions of the section are applicable:

[B6801]

The complex structure of § 5 results from the 1954 amendments to the Securities Act. Prior to that time, the definition of "sale" in 1933 Act § 2(a)(3) included offers as well as actual sales, so that § 5(a) prohibited any sales or offers prior to the effective date of the registration statement. The purpose of the 1954 amendments was to legitimate, and indeed encourage, the use of the preliminary or "red herring" prospectus to make written offers during the waiting period. Thus, § 5(c) prohibits any offers prior to the filing of the registration statement, § 5(a) prohibits any sales prior to the effective date, § 5(b)(2) prohibits the delivery of a security after sale unless it is accompanied by the statutory prospectus, and § 5(b)(1) prohibits the use of any prospectus that does not meet the requirements of 1933 Act § 10, which was also amended in 1954 to specify what information could be omitted from the preliminary prospectus used during the waiting period.

The SEC's 2005 offering reform rules gave more certainty to the issues facing existing public companies. The rules in essence divide existing public companies into two categories—seasoned issuers and well-known seasoned issuers ("WKSIs"), which are larger and more widely held public companies. See 1933 Act Rule 405.

The following sections of the statute and SEC rules can be helpful in navigating through section 5's requirements:

		1933 Act Sections	**Rules**
A.	The Pre-Filing Period	5(c), 4(a)(1), 2(a)(3), 2(a)(4), 2(a)(11), 2(a)(12)	135, 137–139, 141, 163–163A, 168–169, 433
B.	The Waiting Period	5(a), 5(b)(1), 2(a)(10), 10(a), 10(b)	134, 137–139, 163A–164, 168–169, 430, 433, 460, 15c2–8
C.	The Post-Effective Period	5(b), 4(3), 2(a)(10), 4(a)(3),	137–139, 173, 174, 424, 427, 10b–10

1933 Act   Rules
Sections
10(a)(3),
17(a)(2), 12

The operation of § 5 is discussed below.

(A) THE PRE-FILING PERIOD

All companies, including first-time issuers, are permitted to publicly disseminate information that does not refer to a securities offering more than thirty days prior to filing the registration statement, provided the issuer takes reasonable steps to prevent further distribution of the information during the thirty days immediately preceding the public offering. See 1933 Act Rule 163A. There is an additional, more expansive safe harbor for preexisting public companies, known as seasoned issuers, that explicitly includes both "factual business information or forward-looking information." 1933 Act Rule 168(a). This exemption applies to the types of information that the company had been disseminating in the regular course of business.

1933 Act § 5(c) prohibits any offer to sell or offer to buy before a registration statement is filed. The definition of "offer" in 1933 Act § 2(a)(3), however, exempts preliminary negotiations or agreements between the issuer and the underwriters or among underwriters, so that they may commence to negotiate the terms of the offering during that period. No offer may be made to dealers during this period.

Dealers are also prohibited from offering to buy the securities, so that they cannot be pressured into trying to obtain priority for their orders before any reliable information is available.

The SEC takes a very broad view of what constitutes an "offer" for purposes of § 5(c). In addition to formal offers, any unusual publicity by the issuer or prospective underwriters about the issuer's business, or the prospects of the industry in which it is engaged, "may in fact contribute to conditioning the public mind or arousing public interest in the issuer or in the securities of an issuer in a manner which raises a serious question whether the publicity is not in fact part of the selling effort." Sec. Act Rel. 33–3844 (1957). In Loeb, Rhoades, 38 SEC 843 (1959), the Commission held that underwriters had violated 1933 Act § 5(c) by issuing a press release about a proposed offering of a Florida land development company, and that the "news" value of the offering did not justify the release.

In recognition of the fact that publicly-held companies may have an obligation to make prompt disclosure of important developments, 1933 Act Rule 135 permits an issuer to put out a press release or other written notice of an offering that sets forth no more than the name of the issuer and the purpose and basic terms of the offering (without naming the underwriters). In 1995, the SEC proposed a new rule, under which a company making an initial public offering would have been able to solicit indications of interest from prospective purchasers prior to the filing of a registration statement, by means of a written or broadcast statement. The statement must contain certain specified information and be submitted to the SEC prior to its first use. Sec. Act Rel. 33–7188 (1995). Although adopted for the Regulation A exemption (see § 10(e) below), this "testing the waters" process was not adopted for public offerings. The 1933 Act Rules 137–139, adopted in 1970, and amended in 2005, also permit broker-dealers to publish certain types of recommendations of securities, even when securities of the same issuer are currently being publicly distributed. However, in certain complex situations, such as an exchange offer by one company of its securities to shareholders of another company, an issuer may be found to have violated § 5(c) by making statements about its securities that it is required to make under the disclosure provisions of the 1934 Act. See Chris-Craft v. Bangor Punta, 426 F.2d 569 (2d Cir.1970); Sec. Act Rel. 33–5927 (1978).

The 1933 Act Rule 169 provides a safe harbor for "factual business information" that is not directed to investors but is issued as part of the company's ordinary business. Thus, for example, product advertisements are protected by the safe harbor. Rule 169's safe harbor applies to non-reporting companies (a company not subject to 1934 Act § 13 or § 15(d)), as well as to reporting companies (a company subject to § 13 or § 15(d)). The safe harbor does not apply to communications made as part of the offering and also is limited to the types of information the company had made in the past. The 1934 Act reporting companies are given a broader safe harbor in Rule 168 which permits not only the dissemination of factual information but also forward-looking information. As is the case with Rule 169, Rule 168's safe harbor for reporting companies applies only if "[t]he timing, manner, and form in which the information is released or disseminated is consistent in material respects with similar past releases or disseminations" and also excludes from the safe harbor "communication[s] containing information about the registered offering or released or disseminated as part of the offering activities in the registered offering." The safe harbors in Rules 168 and 169 apply both to § 5(c) gun jumping and to information during the waiting and post effective periods, as the rules refer to section 2(a)(10)'s definition of prospectus as well.

In 2012, a limited testing the waters provision for registered offerings by emerging growth companies was added by the JOBS Act. Jumpstart Our Business Startups Act § 106(a), H.R. 3606, 112 Cong. 2d sess. (2012). An emerging growth company is an issuer with less than $1 billion in annual gross revenue during its most recent fiscal year. 1933 Act § 2(a)(19), 15 U.S.C. § 77b(a)(19); 1934 Act § 3(a)(80), 15 U.S.C. § 78c(a)(80). These emerging growth companies and their underwriters are now permitted by § 5(d) of the 1933 Act to test the waters by contacting qualified institutional buyers and institutional accredited investors to determine if there is sufficient investor interest before filing a registration statement. The JOBS Act also added a provision permitting pre-filing research reports for emerging growth companies. The pre-filing reports are limited to those provided to accredited institutional investors and qualified institutional buyers. Emerging growth companies may submit a draft registration to the SEC on a confidential basis. Twenty-one days after the public filing of the registration statement, emerging growth companies may conduct road shows.

(B) THE WAITING PERIOD

As amended in 1954, 1933 Act § 5 permits offers, but not sales, during the waiting period between filing and effectiveness. There is no restriction on oral offers during this period. However, 1933 Act § 2(a)(10) makes any offer in writing a "prospectus," and § 5(b)(1) makes it unlawful to transmit any prospectus after the filing of the registration statement, unless the prospectus contains the information called for by 1933 Act § 10. Some of the information required by § 10 is generally unavailable until the underwriting agreements have been signed and the offering price has been set. To meet this problem, the 1933 Act and rules provide avenues for the use of two kinds of written offering material during the waiting period—the preliminary prospectus and the "tombstone ad."

1933 Act § 10(b) provides that the Commission may permit for the purposes of § 5(b)(1) the use of a preliminary prospectus which omits or summarizes some of the information required by § 10(a). Pursuant to that authority, the Commission has adopted Rule 430, which provides that the offering price and related information may be omitted from a prospectus used prior to the effective date. A special

legend must be printed on every such preliminary
prospectus. Reg. S–K, Item 501(c)(8). The
preliminary prospectus is also known as a "red
herring" prospectus.

Acting under its general definitional power in 1933
Act § 19, the Commission also adopted 1933 Act Rule
134, providing that the term "prospectus," as defined
in 1933 Act § 2(a)(10), will not include a notice that
contains only certain specified information about the
proposed issue, such as factual information about the
issuer and the title of the security. The notice also
must set forth certain legends prescribed by the rule.
Because of the black borders customarily placed
around these notices, they are known as "tombstone
ads."

Rules 163 and 164 permit a free writing
prospectus, which is a written communication
(including graphic and electronic communications)
that constitutes an offer to sell. See 1933 Act Rule
405. A free writing prospectus may not, however,
contain information that contradicts information in
current SEC filings, including the 1933 Act
registration statement. In addition, as a general
proposition, a precondition to a company's use of a
free writing prospectus is that it contain a statement
to the effect that the offering is being made pursuant
to a registration statement. The free writing
prospectus should also indicate how the registration
statement or statutory prospectus can be obtained or
accessed.

A company's classification based on the public
trading of its securities affects the availability of the

use of a free writing prospectus. See 1933 Act Rules 163 and 164. WKSIs are generally free to use free writing prospectuses regardless of whether a registration statement has been filed. WKSIs and seasoned issuers need not make physical delivery of a statutory prospectus. Instead, it is sufficient if the person disseminating the free writing prospectus relating to a WKSI or seasoned issuer includes a legend notifying the recipient that a registration statement has been filed, the web address or hyperlink to the SEC website, and a toll-free number for requesting a statutory prospectus. For issuers other than WKSIs, the use of a free writing prospectus is generally limited to after filing of the registration statement. With respect to non-reporting and unseasoned reporting companies, in most instances, a free writing prospectus prepared by or on behalf of the issuer must be accompanied or preceded by a hard copy of the most recent statutory prospectus. In many instances, before it is used, a free writing prospectus must be filed with the SEC. An immaterial inadvertent failure to file the free writing prospectus with the SEC does not automatically render the communication in violation of § 5(b) of the Act.

As is the case during the pre-filing period, Rules 168 and 169 provide safe harbors for dissemination of factual information by 1933 Act registrants and of forward-looking information by 1934 Act reporting companies.

The language of the 1933 Act contemplates physical delivery of a prospectus in order to satisfy

§ 5(b)'s prospectus delivery requirements. However, 1933 Act Rule 173 implements an *access equals delivery* approach to the statutory prospectus in providing that notice of the availability of a statutory prospectus will satisfy § 5(b)'s prospectus delivery requirement.

While above-mentioned provisions permit the dissemination of written information to potential investors during the waiting period, they do not require it. In the 1960s, the SEC became concerned about the fact that an offeree might never see a preliminary prospectus and not receive the final prospectus until after the investor had purchased the securities. In Sec. Act Rel. 33–4968 (1969), therefore, the SEC announced that, before taking action to accelerate the effective date of a registration statement, it would require a written statement from the managing underwriter that copies of a preliminary prospectus had been mailed to all prospective purchasers at least 48 hours before the confirmations of sale were to be sent to them. This requirement is now incorporated in 1934 Act Rule 15c2–8, adopted under the antifraud provisions of the 1934 Act, which also requires dealers to take reasonable steps to see that copies of the preliminary prospectus are made available to each sales representative engaged in offering the securities and to any customer who makes a written request for one.

In 1999, the SEC liberalized its rules concerning communications relating to a tender offer or business combination requiring the registration of shares under the 1933 Act. Under 1933 Act Rule 165, communications after the effective date of a registration statement that are made prior to the public announcement of a business combination will not be deemed a prospectus for the purposes of § 5(b)(1).

(C) THE POST-EFFECTIVE PERIOD

After the registration statement becomes effective, underwriters and dealers are free to make offers and sales to anyone; the question is under what circumstances a copy of the final prospectus must be delivered to the purchaser. In general, a prospectus must be delivered or made available through an online link (a) on any sale of securities which are part of the underwriters' original allotment which have not yet been publicly sold, and (b) on any resales by dealers, for a specified period after the commencement of the offering, of securities sold to the public and repurchased by the dealer. This results from the following complex of provisions.

1933 Act § 5(b)(2), by its terms, requires that a prospectus be delivered on every sale of a security in interstate commerce. The 1933 Act § 4(a)(1), however, exempts sales by anyone who is not an "issuer, underwriter, or dealer." 1933 Act § 4(a)(3) exempts all sales by a "dealer" (a term defined in 1933 Act § 2(a)(12)), except for two classes of sales:

(1) the original sale by the dealer of the securities which are being distributed by the issuer or by or through an underwriter, no matter how long the dealer has held them (1933 Act § 4(a)(3)(C)); and

(2) resales by the dealer of securities which were sold to the public in such a distribution and reacquired by the dealer, but only if they take place within a specified period after the original public offering (1933 Act § 4(a)(3)(A) and (B)).

The period specified in § 4(a)(3) for the latter class of sales is forty days, in the case of securities of an issuer which has made a prior registered offering under the 1933 Act, and 90 days in the case of securities of an issuer which has not previously made a registered offering (1933 Act § 4(a)(3), last sentence). However, the SEC, utilizing the exemptive power contained in that section, adopted another exemption in Rule 174, under which a dealer need not deliver a prospectus on any resale of a security of an issuer which, prior to filing, was already subject to the reporting requirements of the 1934 Act, no matter how soon after the public offering the resale takes place. In 1987, Rule 174 was amended to reduce the prospectus delivery period to 25 days for any securities which are listed on a stock exchange or traded in the NASDAQ system. For any issue in which dealers are required to deliver prospectuses on resale, Reg. S–K, Item 502(e) requires that the prospectus set forth the date on which the requirement terminates.

The purpose of paragraph (A) of § 4(a)(3) is to permit dealers to trade in a security which was illegally offered to the public without registration, after a lapse of 40 days from the time the offering was made. In Kubik v. Goldfield, 479 F.2d 472 (3d Cir.1973), the court held that "for the purposes of determining a dealer exemption under [§ 4(a)(3)], a 'bona fide' offer to the public may occur when a stock first appears in the 'pink sheets,' even though the stock may be 'illegally' unregistered." (The "pink sheets" are a daily publication of prices of OTC stocks.)

If a dealer is required to deliver a prospectus a substantial time after the effective date, two problems may arise. First, 1933 Act § 10(a)(3) requires that any prospectus used more than nine months after the effective date be updated so that the information contained in it is not more than 16 months old. Second, whether or not nine months have elapsed, the dealer must be sure that the prospectus still contains an accurate and up-to-date description of the company. Delivery of a prospectus which is misleading at the time it is used may constitute a violation of 1933 Act § 17(a)(2) and subject the dealer to liability under 1933 Act § 12(a)(2), even if the prospectus was completely accurate on the effective date. It may also be held to constitute a violation of 1933 Act § 5(b)(2), subjecting the dealer to liability under 1933 Act § 12(a)(1). Compare SEC v. Manor, 458 F.2d 1082 (2d Cir.1972) with SEC v. Southwest, 624 F.2d 1312 (5th Cir.1980). A prospectus can be modified or supplemented to reflect events occurring after the effective date; however, if the changes are "substantive," five copies of the modified prospectus must be filed with the SEC under 1933 Act Rule 424 before it is used. In the case of securities which are registered for a delayed offering pursuant to 1933 Act Rule 415 (see § 8 above), certain kinds of changes must be made by means of a post-effective amendment to the registration statement, in accordance with undertakings required by Item 512(a) of Regulation S–K.

§ 10. EXEMPTIONS FROM REGISTRATION UNDER THE 1933 ACT

1933 Act § 5, by its terms, requires registration for *any* sale by *any* person of *any* security, unless it is specifically exempted from the registration provisions by 1933 Act § 3 or § 4. 1933 Act §§ 3(a)(2)– (8) and 3(c) exempt certain kinds of securities from the registration requirements. 1933 Act §§ 3(a)(1), (9)–(11), § 3(b), and § 4 exempt securities which are sold in certain kinds of transactions. The most important exemption in this latter category is 1933 Act § 4(a)(1), which exempts "transactions by any person other than an issuer, underwriter, or dealer." This provision, together with 1933 Act § 4(a)(3), which exempts most transactions by dealers, effectively remove almost all secondary trading (i.e., trading in already outstanding securities) from the registration requirements of the Act. However, as set forth in the remainder of this section, there are some important exemptions for transactions which do involve the issuer, and there are some situations in which securities must be registered for sale even though they are being sold by someone other than the issuer.

It should also be noted that, while all of the exemptions described below are found in, or based on, specific provisions of the 1933 Act, that Act was amended in 1996 to give the SEC power to exempt any transactions or classes of transactions from the registration requirements. Thus, future exemptions will not necessarily be confined to these statutory categories. See 1933 Act § 28. To date the SEC has invoked § 28 very sparingly.

(A) PRIVATE PLACEMENTS

The most important exemption for an ordinary corporate issuer wishing to raise money without registration is the exemption in 1933 Act § 4(a)(2) for "transactions by an issuer not involving any public offering." Very large amounts of securities have been sold pursuant to this exemption.

The vast bulk of these offerings consists of "private placements" of large blocks of securities with institutional investors—typically the sale of notes or debentures to one or more insurance companies or pension funds. The SEC has generally raised no objections to the consummation of these transactions in reliance on the § 4(a)(2) exemption, since the purchasers are customarily in a position to insist upon the issuer providing them with information more extensive than that contained in a registration statement and to give them other protections not available to purchasers in a registered public offering.

The private offering exemption is of course available for any other kind of offering which meets its basic criteria. Two areas where it has been effectively utilized are in offerings to key employees of the issuing company and in exchange offers to acquire the stock of closely-held companies.

The area of greatest difficulty has been the use of the § 4(a)(2) exemption for promotional offerings to limited numbers of people. Restrictive interpretations by the SEC and the courts as to the manner in which, and the persons to whom, a "non-public" offering could be made, coupled with strict liability under 1933 Act § 12(a)(1) if the terms of the exemption were not strictly complied with, made many lawyers dubious as to whether the § 4(a)(2) exemption could ever be safely used in this situation.

In SEC v. Ralston Purina, 346 U.S. 119 (1953), the Supreme Court rejected the suggestion that the applicability of § 4(a)(2) should depend on the number of persons to whom the offer was made or the limitation of the offer to a defined class of persons (in that case, "key" employees of the issuer). Instead, the Court held that the exemption should depend on whether the class of persons to whom the securities are being offered "need the protection of the Act." In the situation before it, the Court found that the employees involved "were not shown to have access to the kind of information which registration would disclose" and were therefore "entitled to compliance with § 5."

The SEC subsequently amplified the test enunciated by the Supreme Court, indicating that it would consider, among other things, the identity of the offerees and their relationship to the issuer, the size of the offering and of the units in which it was made, the use of investment bankers or stock exchange facilities, and the length of time for which the original purchasers held the securities. Sec. Act

Rel. 33–4552 (1962). However, two restrictive decisions by the Fifth Circuit in 1971 and 1972 (including one in which the SEC took an extremely narrow view of the exemption) led to doubts as to whether the exemption would ever be available for offerings to small numbers of people to raise the initial capital for new ventures, unless the offerees had access to all material information about the issuer by virtue of their status as "insiders." Hill York v. American Int'l, 448 F.2d 680 (5th Cir.1971); SEC v. Continental Tobacco, 463 F.2d 137 (5th Cir.1972). These decisions intensified pressure for development of a more "objective" test of what constitutes a "private" offering exempt from 1933 Act registration requirements.

In April 1974, the SEC adopted 1933 Act Rule 146 (since repealed and superseded by Rule 506) to provide more "objective" standards. However, Rule 146 was extremely complex and technical, and there were many complaints that it was too burdensome on small and growing businesses seeking to raise capital in non-public offerings. As part of Regulation D (see § 10(b) below), the SEC replaced former Rule 146 with a somewhat simplified 1933 Act Rule 506 and also turned to another section of the 1933 Act (1933 Act § 3(b)) to provide relief in these cases.

(B) SMALL OFFERINGS

1933 Act § 3(b) authorizes the SEC, "by its rules and regulations," to exempt offerings, not exceeding a specified dollar amount, when it finds that registration is not necessary "by reason of the small amount involved or the limited character of the public offering[.]" The dollar limit has been periodically raised by Congress from its initial level of $100,000, with the most recent increase coming in 1980 and raising the limit from $2 million to the present level of $5 million. Under this authority, the Commission has adopted a number of rules providing exemptions for certain specialized kinds of offerings, as well as the general exemption in Regulation A (described in § 10(e) below). The $5 million dollar ceiling lost much significance as a cap on SEC rulemaking in 1996 when Congress added 1933 Act § 28 giving the SEC more generalized exemptive authority. As seen below, the $5 million dollar ceiling has not been lifted with respect to most of the SEC rule-based exemptions.

To provide simplified exemptions for small offerings by issuers, the Commission in 1975 adopted former 1933 Act Rule 240, followed in 1980 by former 1933 Act Rule 242. Also in 1980, Congress added § 4(a)(5) to the 1933 Act, exempting any offering of not more than $5 million made solely to "accredited investors" (defined to include specified types of institutions and other classes of investors that the SEC might specify by rule).

These developments set the stage for the coordination of the private offering and small offering exemptions that are now contained in Regulation D.

(C) REGULATION D

In 1982, the Commission took a major step in simplifying and coordinating the exemptions for limited offerings by repealing former Rules 146, 240, and 242, and adopting in their place Regulation D, composed of 1933 Act Rules 501 through 508.

Definitions. 1933 Act Rule 501 defines the terms used in Regulation D. The most important of these is the term "accredited investor," which is defined to include (1) any bank, insurance company, investment company, or employee benefit plan, (2) any business development company, (3) any charitable or educational institution with assets of more than $5 million, (4) any director, executive officer, or general partner of the issuer, (5) any person with a net worth of more than $1 million, (6) any person with an annual income of more than $200,000 (or, together with his or her spouse, more than $300,000), and (7) any trust with more than $5 million in assets which is managed by a "sophisticated person."

1933 Act Rule 502 sets forth certain conditions applicable to all offerings under Regulation D:

Integration. Offerings that are separated in time by more than six months are not deemed to be parts of a single offering. Whether offerings within six months of each other will be considered part of a single offering depends on application of the five factors traditionally employed by the SEC: whether the offerings (1) are part of a single plan of financing, (2) involve the same class of security, (3) are made at or about the same time, (4) involve the same type of consideration, and (5) are made for the same general purpose.

Information. If an issuer sells securities under
1933 Act Rule 504 or to accredited investors only,
there are no specific requirements for furnishing
information to offerees or purchasers. If securities
are sold to non-accredited purchasers under 1933 Act
Rule 505 or 506, the following information must be
furnished to all non-accredited purchasers:

> If the issuer is not registered under the 1934
> Act, the information that would be contained in
> (a) if the offering does not exceed $2 million, an
> offering circular under Regulation A (see § 10(e)
> below), (b) if the offering is between $2 million
> and $7.5 million, a scaled disclosure permitted
> on Form S–1, and (c) if the offering exceeds $7.5
> million, a registration statement on the form the
> issuer would be entitled to use.

> If the issuer is registered under the 1934 Act,
> its most recent annual report to shareholders
> and proxy statement, or the information
> contained in its most recent annual report to the
> Commission, plus specified updating and
> supplemental information.

Manner of Offering and Limitations on Resale. No
general solicitation or general offering is permitted.
Securities sold pursuant to Regulation D are
considered to have been purchased in a non-public
offering and cannot be resold without registration
unless an exemption is available under 1933 Act
§ 4(a)(1) or 1933 Act Rule 144 (see § 10(i) below). The
issuer must take certain specified precautions to
insure that the purchasers do not make resales.

Notice. Under 1933 Act Rule 503, notices of any sales pursuant to Regulation D must be filed with the Commission. Failure to file this report does not destroy the exemption, but, under 1933 Act Rule 507, an issuer which has been sanctioned for failure to file such a report is disqualified from making any further offerings under Regulation D.

Rule 504. Under 1933 Act Rule 504, an issuer can sell an aggregate of $1 million of securities in any twelve-month period to any number of purchasers, accredited or non-accredited, with no requirements for furnishing of any information to the purchasers. The 1933 Act Rule 502 restrictions on the manner of offering and 1933 Act Rule 144 restrictions on resales by purchasers do not apply if the offering is subject to state disclosure requirements similar to the 1933 Act prospectus requirements. The exemption is available to all issuers except investment companies, companies registered under the 1934 Act, and "blank check" companies (companies which issue stock without any stated business plans for using the proceeds).

Rule 505. Under 1933 Act Rule 505, an issuer can sell up to $5 million of securities in any twelve-month period to any number of accredited investors and up to 35 unaccredited other purchasers without being required to file a registration statement. If there are any non-accredited purchasers, the information prescribed by Rule 502 must be furnished to them. The exemption is available to any issuer other than an investment company or an issuer that would be disqualified by Rule 252 from using Regulation A (see § 10(e) below).

Rule 506. Under 1933 Act Rule 506, an issuer can sell an unlimited amount of securities to any number of accredited investors and up to 35 unaccredited purchasers without it being considered a "public offering." Prior to the sale, the issuer must reasonably believe that each non-accredited purchaser, or his or her "purchaser representative" (a term defined in Rule 501), has such knowledge or experience in financial and business matters that the purchaser representative is capable of evaluating the merits and risks of the prospective investment. If there are any non-accredited purchasers, the information prescribed by Rule 502 must be furnished to them. The exemption is available to all issuers. Rule 506 does not permit general solicitation of investors generally. However, in 2013, the SEC eliminated the general solicitation prohibition for Rule 506 offerings provided the general solicitation is made only to accredited investors. Any other general solicitation of investors is not permitted under Rule 506.

Offerings complying with the terms of Rule 504 or 505 are deemed to be exempt under 1933 Act § 3(b); offerings pursuant to Rule 506, since they may exceed $5 million, cannot be exempt under § 3(b) and are considered to be non-public offerings under 1933 Act § 4(a)(2). Rule 506 is not the exclusive means of making a non-public offering; the Preliminary Note to Regulation D states specifically that failure to satisfy all the terms and conditions of Rule 506 shall not raise any presumption that the exemption provided by § 4(a)(2) is not available. Because Rule 506 was promulgated under § 4(a)(2), an offering which qualifies under 1933 Act Rule 506 is exempt from all state registration and disclosure requirements. See 1933 Act § 18(a), (b)(4)(D).

Rule 508. 1933 Act Rule 508 provides that "insignificant deviations" from Regulation D's requirements will not destroy the exemption so long as the issuer made a reasonable and good faith effort to comply with Regulation D and the deviation did not pertain to a term or condition designed to protect the complaining party.

Section 4(a)(5). Recall that 1933 Act § 4(a)(5) exempts offerings solely to accredited investors that are not made as part of a general solicitation. The Commission in 1982 also adopted 1933 Act Rule 215, defining the term "accredited investor" for purposes of 1933 Act § 4(a)(5) to include the various categories of purchasers listed in 1933 Act Rule 501. 1933 Act § 4(a)(5) is thus an alternative exemption for an offering of up to $5 million made solely to accredited investors.

(D) INTRASTATE OFFERINGS

1933 Act § 3(a)(11) exempts from the registration requirements of the 1933 Act "[a]ny security which is part of an issue offered and sold only to persons resident within a single State * * * where the issuer of such security is * * * a corporation, incorporated by and doing business within, such State." Note that this exemption is distinct from the jurisdictional provisions of the 1933 Act relating to use of facilities of interstate commerce; an offering may qualify for the intrastate exemption even if the mails or other interstate communication facilities are used, as long as the issuer and all the offerees and purchasers have the requisite connection with the state.

Because of the strict requirements of the exemption with respect to offerees, it is virtually useless for making public offerings except in isolated areas far from any state border. Not only each purchaser, but each offeree, must be a "resident" (usually defined as comparable to "domiciliary" in that a person can have only one residence for § 3(a)(11) purposes). This means that an offer to one non-resident can destroy the entire exemption. In addition, resales by the original purchasers to non-residents before the securities have "come to rest" may retroactively destroy the exemption. However, in one case where the first sales to non-residents occurred seven months after the offering, the court held that the seller had established its prima facie right to the exemption, and that the purchaser had the burden of proving that the original purchasers had taken with an intent to resell. Busch v. Carpenter, 827 F.2d 653 (10th Cir.1987). As far as the issuer is concerned, the SEC and the courts have construed the "doing business" requirement to mean not only that the issuer is doing some business in the state, but that it is doing "substantial" business in the state. See SEC v. Truckee Showboat, 157 F.Supp. 824 (S.D.Cal.1957); Chapman v. Dunn, 414 F.2d 153 (6th Cir.1969). The SEC's basic position has been that the exemption was designed for "local financing for local industries, carried out through local investment." Sec. Act Rel. 33–4434 (1961).

To provide greater certainty for issuers in determining when the requirements of 1933 Act § 3(a)(11) are met, the Commission in 1974 adopted 1933 Act Rule 147 as a safe harbor for defining certain of the terms in that section. Under Rule 147, an issuer is deemed to be "doing business" in a state only if (a) it is deriving at least 80% of its gross revenues from the state, (b) has at least 80% of its assets in the state, (c) intends to use at least 80% of the proceeds of the offering in the state, and (d) has its principal office in the state. Also, in connection with the question whether the offering has "come to rest" within the state, or is merely the first step in an interstate distribution, Rule 147 provides that the offering will be considered "intrastate" if no resales are made to non-residents of the state for a period of at least nine months after the initial distribution of the securities is completed.

(E) REGULATION A

The oldest, and at one time most widely used of the section 3(b) exemptions for small issues, is the qualified exemption from registration established pursuant to Regulation A.[1]

As it has developed over the years, Regulation A has become not so much an exemption as a simplified form of registration for small issues. Unlike the

---

[1]   Often referred to as "Reg. A," which is pronounced like but should not be confused with reggae.

exemptions described above, it is not satisfied by a finding that specified conditions exist, but only upon compliance with procedures similar in many ways to the 1933 Act registration process.

The exemption provided in Regulation A is dependent upon the securities being offered through the use of an offering circular, in a manner similar to the use of a prospectus in a registered offering. In order to use the Regulation A exemption, an issuer may not offer securities that exceed an aggregate amount of $50 million in any one year. As has been the case with section 3(b), the dollar ceiling for a Regulation A offering has increased over time. Because of the disclosure burdens imposed and the former $5 million ceiling on offerings, Regulation A had been used relatively infrequently when compared to the exemptions from registration available under Regulation D. However, Regulation A is likely to get renewed vitality since, as noted above, the JOBS Act raised the ceiling to $50 million. In March 2015, the SEC amended its Regulation A by dividing the exemption into two tiers—Tier One provides an exemption for offerings up to $20 million per year and Tier Two exempts offerings up to $50 million per year.

In order to qualify for the Regulation A exemption, the issuer (and selling shareholders, in the case of a secondary distribution) must comply with the Regulation's notification and disclosure requirements, including the offering circular delivery requirements that, in essence, have the same effect as a "mini registration." The Regulation A disclosure statements contain much of the information that would be included in a full-blown registration statement, and Rule 253's provisions for an offering circular are analogous to the § 5(b) prospectus delivery requirements. Similarly, Rule 255 provides for the use of a preliminary offering circular prior to the date on which the offering becomes qualified for Regulation A sales. As compared with a registered offering, Regulation A has broader provisions for pre-filing gun jumping sales solicitations. In particular, Rule 254 permits a solicitation of investor interest prior to the use of an offering statement. This procedure is colloquially referred to as "testing the waters."

Regulation A thus bears many similarities to a registered offering. However, it must be remembered that Regulation A provides an *exemption* from registration and is not a different form of registration. As a result of not qualifying as a registration of securities, any misstatements in the Regulation A notification form and offering circular violate the 1933 Act's antifraud provisions, but there is no liability under § 11, which concerns only material misstatements and omissions in a *bona fide* registration statement.

(F) CROWDFUNDING

Crowdfunding is a relatively new method for fundraising. Social networks have been used as a medium for financing films and other forms of art, as well as for charitable solicitations. These and similar fundraising endeavors are known as crowdfunding.

Crowdfunding is the fundraising analog to crowdsourcing, which refers to mass collaboration efforts through large numbers of people, generally using social media or the Internet. Crowdfunding has been used to finance business ventures in other countries but would have required 1933 Act registration in the United States until 2012 when Congress enacted the JOBS Act, adding 1933 Act § 4(a)(6). Supplementing the federal crowdfunding exemption, a growing number of states have created an exemption from their registration requirements for crowdfunding offerings that qualify for § 3(a)(11)'s exemption from federal registration for intrastate offerings. Crowdfunding, Sec. Act Rel. No. 33–9974, Sec. Exch. Act Rel. No. 24–76324, 2015 WL 7273273 (SEC Oct. 30, 2015) ("[I]ssuers can rely on other exemptions to offer and sell securities to accredited investors and institutional investors. As discussed above, concurrent offerings to these types of investors are possible if the conditions of each applicable exemption are met.").

Section 4(a)(6) provides an exemption for crowdfunding offerings up to $1 million per year and is conditioned on disclosure to investors. The new exemption also requires registration of crowdfunding portals and preempts much of the states' ability to regulate crowdfunding. The crowdfunding exemption limits the amount of money that a company may raise from any investor. With respect to investors having an annual income or net worth below $100,000, a company may not sell securities to any investor exceeding the greater of either $2,000 or 5% of the investor's annual income or net worth within a twelve-month period. For investors over the $100,000 annual income or net worth threshold, the twelve-month investment is capped at 10% of the investor's annual income or net worth but may not exceed $100,000 over the twelve-month period. In addition, the maximum amount a company can raise under the crowdfunding exemption is $1 million every twelve months.

The crowdfunding exemption is conditioned on providing investors with certain disclosures that must also be filed with the SEC. The required disclosures include the offering's purpose, the targeted amount to be raised, the deadline for reaching such amount, and the offering price. Significantly, risks to investors also must be disclosed as well as any additional information as the SEC may prescribe. The Act also expressly requires information about the company, its officers, directors and major shareholders in addition to a description of the company's business, business plan, capital structure and financial condition. Audited financial statements are required for offerings over $500,000 and for any other thresholds that may be imposed by SEC rulemaking. The only advertising permitted is advertising that directs interested investors to the funding portal or broker handling the offering. The company may not compensate promoters of the offering unless the compensation is disclosed. The Act also imposes reporting obligations beyond the offering. For companies not subject to the Securities Exchange Act's periodic reporting requirements, crowdfunded companies must file annual reports and provide investors with reports detailing results of operations and financial statements annually. The JOBS Act further directs the SEC to exempt, conditionally or unconditionally, companies relying on the crowdfunding exemption from the 1934 Act's registration and periodic reporting obligations.

The intermediary for a crowdfunding offering must be registered with the SEC either as a broker-dealer or under the new registration category as a crowdfunding portal. In addition to SEC registration, the SEC is directed to adopt rules requiring the broker or funding portal to provide disclosures to investors relating to risks and investor education materials. These rules will also require the broker or funding portal to take steps to ensure that investors review the disclosures, answer various questions and affirm that they understand the risk of loss. The broker or registered funding portal will also be required to investigate the background of regulatory compliance by the company's officers, directors and major shareholders. The broker or funding portal must make certain information available to investors and the SEC at least twenty-one days in advance of the offering. The broker or funding portal must also follow SEC rules designed to assure that purchasers have not exceeded the investment cap for all crowdfunding offerings by any issuer during a twelve-month period. The Act further requires the broker or funding portal to be sure that the offering proceeds are turned over to the issuer only when the target offering amount is reached.

In late October 2013, the SEC proposed its crowdfunding rules. The SEC adopted its crowdfunding rules in October 2015 with an effective date of May 16, 2016. The rules are found Regulation CF and are codified in 17 C.F.R. §§ 227.100 et seq.

(G) EMPLOYEE COMPENSATION PLANS

In 1988, the SEC adopted an exemption under 1933 Act § 3(b) for certain employee compensation plans. Under 1933 Act Rule 701, a company whose shares are not publicly traded can offer shares to employees pursuant to such a plan, without providing any specified information to the offerees. When adopted, the maximum amount that could be offered under Rule 701 varied from $500,000 to $5 million, depending on the size of the company and the number of shares it has outstanding. However, in 1999, utilizing its new general exemptive authority under 1933 Act § 28, the SEC eliminated Rule 701's $5 million ceiling but the company's size and number of shares are still limiting factors. Securities sold pursuant to Rule 701 are "restricted securities" for purposes of 1933 Act Rule 144 (see § 10(i) below).

(H) MERGERS AND REORGANIZATIONS

When an issuer offers securities, not for cash, but in exchange for other securities (issued either by itself or by another issuer), the offer and subsequent exchange are considered an "offer" and "sale" for purposes of the 1933 Act. The transaction may, of course, be exempt as a non-public or intrastate offering, or may be exempt under 1933 Act § 3(a)(9) (exchange by the issuer with its own security holders where no commission is paid to anyone for soliciting the exchange) or § 3(a)(10) (exchange approved after a hearing by a state bank or insurance commissioner or other governmental authority).

The Act does not make clear, however, whether there is an "offer" and "sale" when the exchange takes place pursuant to a merger, sale of assets, or recapitalization, under state corporation law, in which the favorable vote of a specified majority of the shareholders operates to authorize the transaction and obligate all shareholders to accept the exchange. For almost 40 years, the SEC took the position that no "sale" was involved in such a transaction, at least insofar as the registration requirements of 1933 Act § 5 were concerned. Accordingly, no registration statement had to be filed, and no prospectus had to be delivered to shareholders whose votes were solicited for approval of the merger or other transaction. The SEC's proxy rules under the 1934 Act did require that the shareholders be furnished with detailed information about the proposed transaction if their securities were of a class registered under that Act.

In 1972, the SEC reversed its long-standing position and adopted 1933 Act Rule 145, under which the solicitation of shareholders' votes for approval of a reclassification, merger, or sale of assets is considered an "offer" for 1933 Act purposes, requiring the filing of a registration statement and delivery of a prospectus to each shareholder. To coordinate this requirement with existing 1934 Act disclosure requirements, the Commission adopted a new Form S–14, in which the information called for is basically that which the issuer is or would be required to provide under the 1934 Act proxy regulations to the shareholders whose votes are being solicited. Form S–14 was replaced in 1986 by Form S–4.

"Spin-Offs" and "Shell Corporations"

Spin-Offs. The SEC has taken special steps to deal with two kinds of "reorganizations" which promoters have used to distribute shares to the public without registration under the 1933 Act. See Sec. Act Rel. 33–4982 (1969). The "spin-off" involves the issuance by a company, with little or no business activity, of some of its shares to a publicly-owned company for a nominal consideration. The publicly-owned company then "spins off" the shares as a distribution to its shareholders, creating a public trading market into which the insiders can sell the remaining shares. The courts have held that the total transaction requires registration under the 1933 Act, even though the distribution to the shareholders of the public-owned company is not technically a "sale." SEC v. Datronics, 490 F.2d 250 (4th Cir.1973); SEC v. Harwyn, 326 F.Supp. 943 (S.D.N.Y.1971). In 1997, the SEC clarified its position on the applicability of the registration requirements to certain spin-off transactions. The SEC staff takes the position that 1933 Act registration will not be required for spin-off transactions that meet the following five conditions: (1) the stockholders of the parent corporation do not provide consideration for the shares being spun off, (2) the shares are spun off on a pro rata basis to the parent corporation's shareholders, (3) the parent corporation provides adequate information both to its shareholders and to the trading markets, (4) the parent has a valid business purpose for the spin-off transaction, and (5) in the event that the parent corporation is spinning off securities that are restricted within the context of 1933 Act Rule 144, it must have held those securities for at least one year.

Shell Corporations. The "shell corporation" is one which has ceased active operations and has little or no assets, but has substantial amounts of stock held by members of the public. Promoters obtain control of the company, engage in a series of "acquisitions" or other transactions which cause the market price of the stock to rise dramatically, then take advantage of the inflated market to sell the shares that they have acquired. The courts have accepted the SEC's position that transactions of this type violate both the registration and antifraud provisions. See SEC v. North American, 424 F.2d 63 (2d Cir.1970); SEC v. A. G. Bellin, 171 F.Supp. 233 (S.D.N.Y.1959).

(I)   SALES BY PERSONS OTHER THAN THE ISSUER

As noted above, 1933 Act § 4(a)(1) exempts from the registration requirements "transactions by any person other than an issuer, underwriter, or dealer" and 1933 Act § 4(a)(3) exempts most transactions by dealers. Therefore, the only transactions not involving the issuer which require registration are those which involve an "underwriter."

The term "underwriter" is defined in 1933 Act § 2(a)(11) as "any person who has purchased from an issuer with a view to, or offers or sells for an issuer in

connection with, the distribution of any security[.]"
Solely for the purpose of this definition, the term
"issuer" is defined to include any person who
"controls" the issuer. "Control" is defined in 1933 Act
Rule 405 as "the power to direct or cause the direction
of the management and policies of a person, whether
through the ownership of voting securities, by
contract, or otherwise." Control is basically a
question of fact; a particular corporation may be
found to be controlled by one or a number of
shareholders, by its chief executive officer, by some
or all of its directors, or by some other person or
combination.

Under these definitions, there are two types of
transactions which may be found to involve an
"underwriter," even though there is no investment
banker performing the traditional functions of the
"underwriter" in a formal public offering:

(1) when a person who "controls" an issuer
sells securities of that issuer through a broker or
dealer, the broker or dealer is deemed to be
"selling for an *issuer*" and may therefore be an
"underwriter";

(2) when a person has purchased securities
directly from an issuer, and subsequently resells
them, he may be deemed to have "purchased
from an issuer with a view to distribution" and
thus himself be an "underwriter."

The first situation was involved in Ira Haupt, 23
SEC 589 (1946). Schulte, who controlled Park &
Tilford, sold a total of 93,000 shares of Park & Tilford

through Haupt, his broker, in transactions on the New York Stock Exchange. The SEC asserted that the transactions should have been registered because Haupt was an "underwriter." Haupt argued that there was no "distribution"; Schulte had simply given a series of orders to sell 200 or 300 shares at a time. The SEC rejected this defense; the circumstances clearly put Haupt on notice that a "distribution" was intended. Haupt then argued that, even if it was an "underwriter," the transaction was exempt under 1933 Act § 4(a)(4), which exempts "brokers' transactions executed upon customers' orders on any exchange * * * ." The SEC held that this exemption did not apply to situations where the broker-dealer was an "underwriter," but was designed only to permit dealers to execute brokerage transactions for ordinary retail customers at a time when, as dealers, they might be prohibited from engaging in transactions for their own account. Broker-dealers effecting transactions are under a reasonable duty of inquiry to determine if the transaction is by a control person or whether it qualifies for the § 4(a)(4) exemption. World Trade Financial Corp. v. SEC, 739 F.3d 1243 (9th Cir. 2014). Under such circumstances, a broker is "not merely an 'order taker' " and must make reasonable inquiry into the facts underlying the transaction.

The second type of situation arose in innumerable instances where people bought securities from an issuer in a private transaction and wished to resell them. Since the determination whether the person was an underwriter depended on whether he had "purchased * * * with a view to distribution," there had to be an examination of his subjective intent at the time of purchase, and a search for a "change in circumstances" that would justify selling now even though the investor had originally taken the securities "for investment." The SEC took the position that holding the securities for a specified period of time did not satisfy the requirement of "investment intent." The Commission accordingly was deluged with requests for "no-action" letters permitting sales under specified factual conditions.

Finally, in 1972, the Commission adopted 1933 Act Rule 144, applying a relatively objective (if rather complex) set of rules to both types of "underwriter" transactions. Sec. Act Rel. 33–5223 (1972). The Rule has been heavily utilized, and substantially liberalized, over the years. As amended, under Rule 144, any sale of securities by an "affiliate" of the issuer (i.e., a controlling person) must comply with the following requirements:

(1) A person's sales under Rule 144 during any three-month period may not exceed the greater of (a) 1% of the total number of units of the security outstanding and (b) the average weekly trading volume for the preceding four weeks.

(2) If the person acquired the securities from the issuer in a non-public transaction, he must have held them for at least one year before reselling them, or six months with respect to securities of 1934 Act reporting company. Securities are not considered fungible for this purpose; securities held for more than one year may be sold, even if the seller has recently

acquired additional securities of the same class from the issuer. The one-year (or six-month) holding period runs from the time the securities were purchased from the issuer or an affiliate of the issuer. Accordingly, a non-affiliate who purchased restricted securities from another non-affiliate can tack his or her holding period on to that of the previous holder. Rule 144's definition of restricted securities include securities issued in a non-public offering under 1933 Act § 4(a)(2) or Rules 505 (offerings of up to $5 million) or 506 (safe harbor for non-public offerings) (see § 10(c) above). In 1999, the SEC expanded Rule 144 to cover securities issued under Rule 504 (unless the offering was subject to state disclosure requirements analogous to the 1933 Act's prospectus requirements). The 1999 amendments also extended Rule 144's definition of restricted securities to securities issued offshore under Regulation S (see § 43 below).

(3) The issuer must be subject to, and in current compliance with, the periodic reporting requirements of the 1934 Act, or there must otherwise be publicly available information comparable to that which would be found in such reports.

(4) The securities must be sold in ordinary brokerage transactions, or transactions directly with a "market maker," not involving any special remuneration or solicitation.

(5) A notice of each sale must be filed with the SEC at the time the order is placed with the broker.

The resale limitations of Rule 144 also apply to certain persons who receive securities in mergers or asset acquisitions, by virtue of 1933 Act Rule 145. Under Rule 145(c), controlling persons of an acquired company in a merger or sale of assets transaction are considered "underwriters" of the securities of the acquiring company which they acquire and subsequently resell in public transactions. Rule 145(d) permits such persons to resell without registration provided they comply with the quantity limitations and other restrictions of Rule 144 (except that they are not subject to the two-year holding period requirement).

One question not addressed by Rule 144 is whether a person who has purchased securities from the issuer in a non-public transaction can resell those securities in another *private* transaction, and, if so, what limitations apply to such resales. Since this situation is not technically covered by either 1933 Act § 4(a)(1) or § 4(a)(2), it is sometimes said to be covered by the "§ 4(1½) exemption." See Ackerberg v. Johnson, 892 F.2d 1328 (8th Cir.1989).

In a partial response to requests for codification of the "§ 4(1½)" exemption, the SEC in 1990 adopted 1933 Act Rule 144A. Rule 144A, however, does not deal with the question of the resale by an individual purchaser to another individual who might have qualified as a purchaser in the original offering. What the rule does is permits unlimited resales of securities that have never been registered under the 1933 Act, as long as all such sales are made to a specified class of "qualified institutional buyers," defined generally as including any institution with more than $100 million of investments. The exemption is available only for securities of a class that is *not* traded on any U.S. securities exchange or in the NASDAQ system. It does not require the institutions to deal directly with one another; it permits securities firms to participate in the transactions, either as agent or principal, and in fact permits an active trading market in these securities, a substantial proportion of which are securities of foreign issuers who are unwilling to subject themselves to U.S. disclosure requirements.

(J) INTEGRATION OF OFFERINGS

In determining whether an offering qualifies for a particular exemption, it is necessary to determine whether it is in fact a separate offering, or whether it is part of a larger offering. This question often arises where an issuer, or a group of related issuers, engage in a series of "non-public" or "intrastate" offerings, or some combination thereof.

The SEC has stated that the factors to be considered in determining whether offerings should be "integrated" are whether the offerings (1) are part of a single plan of financing, (2) involve the same class of security, (3) are made at or about the same time, (4) involve the same type of consideration, and (5) are made for the same general purpose. Sec. Act Rel. 33–4552 (1962). In SEC v. Murphy, 626 F.2d 633

(9th Cir.1980), the court applied these criteria in finding that the sale of limited partnership interests in 30 separate partnerships constituted a single offering. In the case of limited offerings under Regulation D and intrastate offerings under 1933 Act Rule 147, the rules provide that offerings separated by a period of at least six months during which no offers or sales of that class of securities are made will not be integrated; if that test is not met, they are judged by the above criteria.

Under Regulation A, an issuer may sell up to the $5,000,000 limit each year, even if the successive financings are part of a prearranged plan. However, a closely related offering purportedly made pursuant to another exemption may reduce the maximum available under Regulation A if it would be considered part of the same offering under the SEC's enunciated criteria.

The limitations on sales by or through "underwriters" in 1933 Act Rule 144 also permit a prearranged program of sales, as long as the rolling six-month ceiling is not exceeded. However, the rule contains complicated provisions for "aggregating" sales by persons who have agreed to act in concert, or who have certain specified relationships to each other, in computing the maximum amount that may be sold.

The integration doctrine is not limited to successive exempt transactions. It also can be applied to a non-public offering followed by a public offering. *See* 1933 Act Rule 152. In 2001, the SEC adopted 1933 Act Rule 155 to provide a safe harbor from integration for a discontinued or abandoned private offering followed by a registered public offering and also for an abandoned public offering followed by a private offering.

(K) INTERRELATIONSHIP OF EXEMPTIONS

An offering must fall completely within a single exemption to escape registration. For example, an issuer cannot make a public offering in its home state simultaneously with "private" sales of the same security to selected residents of other states; if the offering is a single offering, it will be neither "intrastate" nor "private." On the other hand, an offering may qualify for more than one exemption. An issuer which is attempting to comply with the private offering exemption, but is not sure all the offerees meet the applicable standard, can protect itself by offering only to residents of its home state; the offering may be "intrastate" even if it is not "private."

(L) CONSEQUENCES OF A FAILED EXEMPTION

The SEC and the courts have consistently held that the exemptions from the 1933 Act registration requirements are to be strictly construed, and that the person claiming the exemption has the burden of establishing all the facts necessary to support it. This burden is especially onerous because the exemption generally relates to the offering as a whole, rather than the transaction with each investor. Thus, if an offer is made to a single ineligible person in a "private" placement, or if one of the directors of the issuer was the subject of an SEC proceeding that disqualified the issuer from using Regulation A, the basis for the exemption is destroyed, meaning every offer or sale made by the issuer has violated § 5. Under 1933 Act § 12(a)(1), any person who sells a security in violation of 1933 Act § 5 is liable to the purchaser to refund the full purchase price. A purchaser whose investment has gone down in value may therefore be able to recover his or her entire purchase price, without evidence of fraud or misstatement, if the seller is unable to establish the necessary conditions for the exemption on which it relied. See Henderson v. Hayden, Stone, 461 F.2d 1069 (5th Cir.1972). The SEC's adoption of 1933 Act Rule 508 (see § 10(c) above), providing that an "insignificant" failure to comply with the Regulation D exemption in the sale to a particular purchaser does not necessarily destroy the exemption with respect to other purchasers, represents the first effort at amelioration of this harsh rule.

§ 11. CIVIL LIABILITY FOR MISSTATEMENTS

While the prohibitions found in 1933 Act § 5 are designed to assure that securities will not be offered to the public without registration, sanctions are necessary to assure that the information contained in the registration statement is complete and accurate.

The most powerful incentive to careful preparation of the registration statement is found in 1933 Act § 11, which sets forth the civil liabilities to purchasers with respect to any material misstatements or omissions. In contrast to the vague outlines of common law fraud liability, § 11 sets forth in great detail who may sue, what they must show, who can be held liable for how much, and the defenses and cross-claims available to various classes of defendants.

The 1933 Act § 11 was considered such a draconian measure at the time of its enactment that some observers thought that it would dry up the nation's underwriting business and that "grass would grow in Wall Street." It is somewhat ironic, therefore, (or perhaps simply a testimonial to the care with which people approached the task of preparing registration statements) that the first fully litigated decision interpreting the civil liability provisions of § 11 did not come until 35 years later, after more than 27,000 registration statements had become effective, covering offerings to the public of more than $384 billion of securities. When that decision did come down, however, in Escott v. BarChris Construction Corp., 283 F.Supp. 643 (S.D.N.Y.1968), it spread new waves of concern among issuers, directors, underwriters, and their counsel and accountants, as they realized that the practices that had been followed during the new-issue boom of the early 1960s simply did not measure up to the standard of "due diligence" laid down in § 11(b).

Because 1933 Act § 11 liability is a matter of such overriding concern, it is a major influence in deciding what provisions and conditions will be included in the agreement between the issuer and underwriters, and in assigning responsibilities to the various parties involved in the registration statement. Any lawyer involved in underwriting work, therefore, should have a precise knowledge of the provisions of the section, how they have been interpreted, and how they relate to the other civil liability provisions of the federal securities laws.

The provisions of § 11, which apply only to offerings registered under the 1933 Act, are supplemented by the civil liability provisions of 1933 Act § 12, which have broader applicability. The differences and interrelationships between § 11 and § 12 liabilities are also considered in this section.

(A)   ELEMENTS OF A 1933 ACT § 11 CLAIM

In basic outline, § 11 provides that if a registration statement, at the time it became effective, "contained an untrue statement of a material fact or omitted to state a material fact required to be stated therein or necessary to make the statements therein not misleading," any person who acquired any security covered by the registration statement can sue certain specified persons to recover the difference between the price the purchaser paid for the security (but not more than the public offering price) and either the price at which he or she disposed of it or, if the purchaser still owns it, its value at the time of suit.

Who Can Sue? Section 11 of the 1933 Act gives a right of action to "any person acquiring such security." While there is no direct antecedent for the "such," the courts have construed it as meaning any security registered by that registration statement. Prior to 1995, courts had consistently held that the purchaser need not have purchased the security in the course of the original distribution; she would still have a right of action if she purchased it in a secondary transaction after it had been resold by the original purchaser, as long as the shares were "traceable" to the shares sold in the original distribution. See Barnes v. Osofsky, 373 F.2d 269 (2d Cir.1967). Some lower courts have interpreted the Supreme Court's 1995 decision in Gustafson v. Alloyd (see § 11(c) below) as holding that liability under § 11 extends only to people who purchase in the initial public offering and not to those who purchase in the secondary market. See Gould v. Harris, 929 F.Supp. 353, 358 (C.D.Cal.1996); Van de Walle v. Salomon, 1997 WL 633288 (Del.Ch.). These decisions seem clearly inconsistent with provisions of § 11 which contemplate purchases in the aftermarket. For example, § 11(a) requires the plaintiff to show reliance if the purchase is made after the issuer has made available an earning statement covering a period of 12 months beginning after the effective date, and § 11(e) measures a plaintiff's damages by the "amount paid for the security (not exceeding the price at which the security was offered to the public)." If these decisions are followed, defendants may be able to avoid all liability under 1933 Act § 11 in the common situation in which all the original purchasers resell their shares at a profit, and the people who suffer losses when the misstatements become known all purchased in the secondary market. Happily, the more recent cases have rejected such a limitation. See Joseph v. Wiles, 223 F.3d 1155

(10th Cir.2000); Hertzberg v. Dignity Partners, Inc., 191 F.3d 1076 (9th Cir.1999).

If the registration statement covers additional securities of a class which is already publicly traded, the plaintiff must show that the securities he or she bought in a secondary transaction were part of the block sold in the new offering, and not part of those previously outstanding. Barnes v. Osofsky, 373 F.2d 269 (2d Cir.1967). This can pose an insuperable obstacle to plaintiffs in the case of securities listed on a stock exchange, where there is usually no way for a buyer to ascertain the identity of the person who sold the securities to him or her.

Materiality and Reliance. All that the purchaser must show to recover is (a) that there was a material misstatement or omission in the registration statement and (b) that the investor lost money. Normally the plaintiff need not show that he or she relied on the misstatement or omission, or even that the purchaser received a copy of the prospectus. However, if the plaintiff purchased the security *after* the issuer had made generally available an earning statement covering a period of at least 12 months *beginning after* the effective date of the registration statement, the plaintiff must show reliance on the misstatement or omission, but this reliance can be established without showing that the purchaser actually read the registration statement. 1933 Act § 11(a).

The term "material" is defined in 1933 Act Rule 405 as meaning "those matters to which there is a substantial likelihood that a reasonable investor would attach importance in determining whether to purchase the security registered." This has been construed for § 11 purposes as meaning "a fact which if it had been correctly stated or disclosed would have deterred or tended to deter the average prudent investor from purchasing the securities in question." Escott v. BarChris Construction Corp., *supra.*

Affirmative Defenses. Under § 11(a), a claim made by any purchaser can be defeated if the defendant can show that the purchaser knew of the untruth or omission at the time he or she acquired the security.

Under § 11(e), a claim may be defeated or reduced to the extent that the defendant can show that the decline in value of the security resulted from causes other than the misstatement or omission in the registration statement. Thus, if a defendant can show that a decline in the value of the issuer's securities was comparable to that suffered by other companies in the same industry (particularly if it occurred before the misstatement or omission in the registration statement was revealed), it may escape liability for that decline. See Beecher v. Able, 435 F.Supp. 397 (S.D.N.Y.1975). The negative causation defense can also be established by showing that "the misstatement was barely material and that the public failed to react adversely to its disclosure." Akerman v. Oryx, 810 F.2d 336 (2d Cir.1987). On the other hand, where the issuer has gone bankrupt for reasons unrelated to the misstatements or omissions in the registration statement, that fact alone should not completely defeat a purchaser's right of action; a plaintiff should still be able to recover the difference between what the purchaser paid and what the securities would have been worth at the time of purchase if adequate disclosure had been made.

(B) PERSONS LIABLE

The 1933 Act § 11(a) entitles the purchaser to sue (a) every person who signed the registration statement (1933 Act § 6 requires that it be signed by the issuer itself, by the principal executive, financial and accounting officers, and by a majority of the board of directors), (b) every director, (c) every person who consented to being named as a director or prospective director, (d) every accountant, engineer, appraiser, or other expert who has consented to being named as having prepared or certified a part of the registration statement, and (e) every underwriter.

All of these persons are made jointly and severally liable (i.e., a purchaser can sue any one of them to recover his entire damages) with two exceptions. First, an expert is only liable with respect to misstatements or omissions in the portion of the registration statement that the expert prepared or certified. And second, the aggregate liability of an underwriter who purchased only a portion of the issue (and who did not receive any special compensation from the issuer) is limited to the aggregate public offering price of the securities which it underwrote. For example, in a public offering of 1,000,000 shares at $10 a share, if each of 10 underwriters agrees, *severally and not jointly,* to purchase 100,000 of the shares, § 11(e) limits the liability of each underwriter to $1,000,000.

The "Due Diligence" Defense. Except as to the issuer, which has absolute liability for any material misstatements or omissions in the registration statement, § 11(b) provides an affirmative defense for any other defendant who can demonstrate that he or she met a prescribed standard of diligence with respect to the information contained in the registration statement. For this purpose, the registration statement is divided into two portions: the "expertised" and the "unexpertised" portions. The "expertised" portions are those "purporting to be made on the authority of an expert," i.e., those specifically referred to in the expert's certificate or opinion included in the registration statement. The court in the *BarChris* case rejected the suggestion that the lawyers who prepared the main body of the registration statement were "experts" for purposes of § 11, or that the accountants had "expertised" any parts of the registration statement other than their audited financial statements. The standards enunciated many years ago in *Escott v. BarChris* remain applicable today. See, e.g., In re WorldCom, Inc. Securities Litigation, 2005 WL 638268 (S.D.N.Y. 2005).

With respect to the "expertised" portions of the registration statement, the "due diligence" obligation of any defendant (other than the "expert" who prepared that portion) is worded negatively: that "he had no reasonable ground to believe and did not believe" that there was any material misstatement or omission. With respect to the "unexpertised" portions (and with respect to the liability of the "expert" for the portion he or she has "expertised") the obligation is worded affirmatively: that "he had, after reasonable investigation, reasonable ground to believe and did believe" that there was no material misstatement or omission.

Section 11(c) provides that "[i]n determining * * * what constitutes reasonable investigation and reasonable ground for belief, the standard of reasonableness shall be that required of a prudent man in the management of his own property." The *BarChris* decision made clear that a defendant could not establish that he had made a "reasonable investigation" by showing that the defendant had relied on others to do the investigating on the defendant's behalf. However, it also indicated that the type and extent of investigation required to establish the "due diligence" defense of any particular defendant would depend on his area of expertise and his relationship to the issuer. For example, a lawyer-director engaged in the preparation of the registration statement would be expected to examine all corporate minutes, contracts, and other legal documents, while a non-lawyer "outside" director would not normally be expected to do so. Subsequent commentary and decisions indicated that "inside" directors—those having intimate knowledge of corporate affairs and transactions—may find it virtually impossible to establish their "due diligence" and that "[t]heir liability approaches that of the issuer as guarantor of the accuracy of the prospectus." Feit v. Leasco, 332 F.Supp. 544 (E.D.N.Y.1971). Some later decisions, however, have indicated that outside directors can place substantial reliance on management and are not required to conduct their own independent investigation to establish their due diligence. See Weinberger v. Jackson, 1990 WL 260676, CCH ¶ 95,693 (N.D.Cal.1990); Laven v. Flanagan, 695 F.Supp. 800 (D.N.J.1988).

In 1995, Congress added 1933 Act § 11(f)(2), which provides that the liability of outside directors is to be determined in accordance with the provisions of 1934 Act § 21D(g) (see § 20(b) below). Under those provisions, an outside director can be held jointly and severally liable for the full amount of the damages only if the trier of fact specifically determines that the defendant knowingly committed a violation of the securities laws. In all other cases, defendant can be held liable "solely for the portion of the judgment that corresponds to [his] percentage of responsibility," as determined by the trier of fact.

The adoption in 1982 of the Commission's "integrated disclosure system" for 1933 and 1934 Act filings (see § 7 above) raised new questions about the due diligence obligations of underwriters and others, particularly with respect to information incorporated in 1933 Act registration statements by reference to reports previously filed under the 1934 Act. The SEC therefore adopted 1933 Act Rule 176, specifying certain "relevant circumstances" to be taken into account in determining whether a particular person had made a reasonable investigation and had reasonable grounds for belief. The circumstances so specified are (a) the type of issuer, (b) the type of security, (c) the type of person, (d) the office held (if an officer), (e) other relationships to the issuer (if a director), (f) reasonable reliance on appropriate persons, (g) the underwriting arrangements (if an underwriter), and (h) whether, with respect to another document incorporated by reference, the person had any responsibility for that document at the time it was filed.

Indemnification and Contribution. Many state corporation laws, as well as corporate charters or by-laws, permit or require corporations to indemnify their officers and directors against liabilities they may incur in the conduct of their corporate functions. Underwriting agreements customarily contain provisions under which the issuer and the underwriters agree to indemnify each other with respect to liability for misstatements in the portions of the registration statement for which each was primarily responsible.

For a long time, the SEC has taken the position that it would be against public policy for an issuer to indemnify any officer, director, or controlling person (or any underwriter with which any such person was affiliated) against 1933 Act liabilities. It has made a practice of refusing to accelerate the effective date of registration statements unless the issuer undertakes to submit the question of "whether such indemnification * * * is against public policy" to a court before making any indemnification payment in these circumstances. See Item 512(h) of Regulation S–K. While the precise question of the enforceability of provisions indemnifying officers and directors has yet to be judicially determined, the courts have indicated support for the SEC position in cases involving indemnification of underwriters.

In Globus v. Law Research Service, 418 F.2d 1276 (2d Cir.1969), an underwriter sought contractual indemnification from the issuer for liability it had incurred under 1933 Act § 12(a)(2) as a result of misstatements in an offering circular used in an offering that was exempt from the 1933 Act registration requirements. The court held that the public policy enunciated by the SEC barred the underwriter from recovering indemnification under its contract, where it was found to have had "actual knowledge" of the misstatements. The court's holding was thus broader than the SEC's position in denying indemnification to an underwriter which had no other affiliation with the issuer; on the other hand, it purported only to deal with the situation where the person seeking indemnification had "committed a sin graver than ordinary negligence."

In Eichenholtz v. Brennan, 52 F.3d 478 (3d Cir.1995), the court went even further than the *Globus* court and held that the public policy underlying the securities acts bars any indemnification of underwriters against § 11 liability, reasoning that "[i]f the court enforced an underwriter indemnification provision, it would effectively eliminate the underwriter's incentive to fulfill its investigative obligation."

With respect to contribution, 1933 Act § 11(f) provides that any person held liable may recover contribution from others who could have been held similarly liable, unless the person seeking adequate basis for that evaluation. *Franklin v. Levy,* above.

Causation and Reliance. Under § 12(a)(2), the sale must be made "by means of" the misleading prospectus or oral communication. The purchaser need not show that the communication had a "decisive effect" on his or her decision, but the purchaser must show at least some causal relationship to his or her decision. *Jackson v. Oppenheim,* 533 F.2d 826 (2d Cir.1976). There is no requirement that the purchaser establish reliance on the misstatement, *Johns Hopkins v. Hutton,* 422 F.2d 1124 (4th Cir.1970), or even that the investor actually saw it, *Sanders v. John Nuveen,* 619 F.2d 1222 (7th Cir.1980).

Prior to 1995, most courts took the position that, i[n] an action under § 12(a)(2), it was not necessary fo[r] the plaintiff to prove that his or her loss resulted fro[m] the facts misstated or omitted. See *Caviness* [v.] *Derand Resources Corp.,* 983 F.2d 1295 (4th Cir.1993). Congress changed this rule in 1995 [by] adding 1933 Act § 12(b), which provides [an] affirmative defense to a defendant who proves tha[t] portion or all of the decline in the value of the secur[ity] was caused by factors unrelated to the misstatem[ent] or omission.

Good Faith Defense. The seller has an affirma[tive] defense if the defendant can establish that he or [she] did not know, and in the exercise of reasonable [care] could not have known, of the untruth or omiss[ion.] One court of appeals has held that a securities de[aler] can only assert that defense if it has made the

contribution was, and the other was not, guilty of fraudulent misrepresentation. In subsequent proceedings in the *Globus* case, the court followed that approach under 1933 Act § 12(a)(2). *Globus v. Law Research Service,* 318 F.Supp. 955 (S.D.N.Y.1970).

(C) LIABILITY UNDER 1933 ACT § 12

Section 12 of the 1933 Act imposes civil liability on sellers of securities in two situations: where a security is sold in violation of 1933 Act § 5 (i.e., in an unregistered, non-exempt transaction) and where a security is sold by means of a prospectus or oral communication which contains a material misstatement or omission. In contrast to the complex provisions in 1933 Act § 11 relating to plaintiffs and defendants, 1933 Act § 12 simply provides that the person who "offers or sells" the security is "liable * * * to the person purchasing such security from him." The purchaser (provided the purchaser did not know of the untruth or omission) may sue to recover the consideration paid, upon tender of the securities, or for damages if the plaintiff no longer owns them.

While the standard of liability for misstatements in § 12(a)(2) is similar to that set forth in § 11, its scope is different. Prior to 1987, it was generally assumed to apply to misstatements or omissions in any form, in any transaction, whether or not subject to the registration provisions of the 1933 Act, provided there was some use of the mails or facilities of interstate commerce in the course of the transaction. See *Franklin v. Levy,* 551 F.2d 521 (2d

Cir.1977). However, beginning in 1987, a number of courts held that § 12 applies only to initial distributions, and cannot be used to impose liability on brokers for recommendations of stocks traded in the secondary market. See Ballay v. Legg Mason, 925 F.2d 682 (3d Cir.1991).

When the issue reached the Supreme Court in 1995, the Court, in a 5–4 decision which surprised almost everyone, held not only that 1933 Act § 12(a)(2) does not reach secondary trading, but that it does not even apply to initial offerings unless they are made public by means of a statutory prospectus. Gustafson v. Alloyd, 513 U.S. 561 (1995). Unless this holding is limited by subsequent decisions, it appears that there will be no liability under any provision of the 1933 Act for written or oral misstatements in offerings which are exempt from that Act's registration requirements, and that persons making such misstatements can only be sued under 1934 Act Rule 10b–5 (See § 18 below). In the wake of the *Gustafson* decision, some lower courts have held that there is no liability under 1933 Act § 12(a)(2) for misstatements in an offering memorandum used in a non-public offering exempted under 1933 Act § 4(a)(2). See Glamorgan v. Ratner's, 1995 WL 406167 (S.D.N.Y.). The JOBS Act expanded exemptions for small business offerings and also expressly extended to § 12(a)(2) two exemptions that are conditioned on disclosure to investors. In creating the new exemption for crowdfunding offerings, Congress authorized a private remedy tracking § 12(a)(2) for material misstatements and omissions in crowdfunding offerings. 1933 Act § 4A(c). Section

3(b) was expanded to mandate that the SEC adopt an exemption for offerings up to $50 million per year with requirements similar to existing Regulation A. The § 12(a)(2) remedy now expressly applies to offerings using this expanded section 3(b)(2) exemption. 1933 Act § 3(b)(2)(D). The remedy should also apply to smaller Regulation A offerings.

Persons Liable. Under 1933 Act § 12, a purchaser can only sue the person from whom he or she bought the security. An issuer which sells securities to underwriters for resale to the public therefore has no direct liability to the purchasers. See Collins v. Signetics, 605 F.2d 110 (3d Cir.1979). The Supreme Court has held, however, that liability under § 12 extends not only to the actual seller, but also to any person "who successfully solicits the purchase, motivated at least in part by a desire to serve his own financial interests or those of the securities owner." Pinter v. Dahl, 486 U.S. 622 (1988).

Recovery Under § 12(a)(1). To recover under § 12(a)(1), the plaintiff need only establish that (1) the defendant sold the security to him or her, and (2) it was not registered. The burden then shifts to the defendant to establish the availability of a exemption.

Recovery Under § 12(a)(2). To recover un § 12(a)(2), the plaintiff must establish that there a material misstatement or omission in prospectus or oral communication. However court has held that a dealer's implied represen as to the quality of certain securities w actionable misstatement if the dealer did not h of investigation that would enable it to assert a "due diligence" defense under 1933 Act § 11, but two Justices of the Supreme Court expressed strong disagreement with this position. Sanders v. John Nuveen, 619 F.2d 1222 (7th Cir.1980), cert. denied 450 U.S. 1005 (1981) (Powell and Rehnquist, JJ., dissenting).

CHAPTER III

INTRODUCTION TO THE REGULATION OF PUBLICLY-HELD COMPANIES

§ 12.   OVERVIEW OF THE 1934 ACT

Unlike the Securities Act of 1933, which focuses largely on a single provision and has been amended only slightly since its enactment, the Securities Exchange Act of 1934 contains provisions dealing with a number of different areas and has been subject to very substantial amendments and additions, most notably in 1964, 1968, 1975, and 1995. The scope and organization of the Act can best be understood by reference to the following table of many of the Act's key sections:

I.   SECURITIES AND EXCHANGE COMMISSION

		Section
A.	Establishment and Constitution	4
B.	Delegation of Functions	4A
C.	Transfer of Functions	4B
D.	Investigations and Injunctions	21
E.	Civil Remedies in Administrative Proceedings	21B

VI.   LIABILITIES AND PENALTIES

VII.   SCOPE AND JURISDICTION

Sections 12, 13, 14, and 16 of the Securities Exchange Act impose disclosure and other requirements on publicly-traded companies.

1934 Act § 12(a) requires any issuer that has a class of securities traded on a national securities exchange to register with the SEC. This registration of a class of securities under the 1934 Act must be distinguished from registration of an offering of securities under the 1933 Act; a company which has registered a class of securities under the 1934 Act will still have to register a particular offering of securities of that class under the 1933 Act if the provisions of that Act so require.

In addition to the above-mentioned registration, reporting, and other disclosure requirements for exchange-listed securities, the Securities Exchange Act of 1934 also imposes registration requirements on certain over-the-counter securities. Until April 2012, by virtue of § 12(g)(1) of the Exchange Act and former Rule 12g–1, 1934 Act registration was required for issuers having both a class of equity securities with 500 or more shareholders of record and having more than ten million dollars in total assets. In 2012, the JOBS Act amended § 12(g) to increase the threshold from 500 to 2,000 shareholders of record, but it retains the lower 500 record holder threshold with respect to investors who are not accredited investors. The record holder calculation excludes shareholders who receive shares as part of an employee compensation plan that is exempt from 1933 Act registration. Section 12(g) was also amended to exclude from the shareholder calculation holders of shares issued pursuant to an exempt crowdfunding offering. As noted earlier, § 12 registration in turn subjects the company to the 1934 Act's periodic reporting and, among other requirements, proxy regulation, tender offer and other takeover regulation, and reporting of insider transactions in the company shares.

1934 Act § 12(j) empowers the SEC to revoke or suspend the registration of a security, after notice and opportunity for hearing, if it finds that the issuer has violated any provision of the 1934 Act or the rules and regulations under it. Under 1934 Act § 12(k), the SEC can (a) summarily suspend trading in any security for a period of not more than 10 days, (b) with the approval of the President, suspend all trading in all securities for a period of not more than 90 days, or (c), in the event of a "major market disturbance," take whatever action respecting the markets as it determines to be in the public interest and for the protection of investors. Prior to 1975, the SEC often imposed successive 10-day suspensions that prohibited trading in a particular security for months or even years at a time, when the Commission felt there was inadequate public information to enable investors to make an intelligent judgment as to the value of the stock. However, in SEC v. Sloan, 436 U.S. 103 (1978), the Supreme Court held that the statute did not authorize this practice, and that 10 days is the maximum time period for which trading can be suspended for any single set of circumstances.

1934 Act § 13 requires every issuer which has securities registered under 1934 Act § 12 to file periodic and other reports with the SEC, and 1934 Act § 14 regulates the solicitation of proxies from holders of such securities, in each case subject to rules prescribed by the SEC. Sections 13(d) and (e) and 14(d), (e), and (f), added by the "Williams Act" in 1968, regulate take-over bids, tender offers, and purchases by companies of their own shares.

Section 16 requires every officer, director, and 10% shareholder of an issuer that has securities registered under 1934 Act § 12 to report his or her purchases and sales of any equity securities of the issuer. This section also requires the officer, director, or shareholder to turn over to the company any profit derived from a purchase and sale of such securities within a six-month period.

There are some publicly held companies that, even though they are not required to register under § 12 of the 1934 Act, nevertheless are subject to the periodic reporting requirements mentioned above. Section 15(d) of the 1934 Act provides that issuers having issued securities under a 1933 Act registration statement with more than 300 record holders of such securities are subject to 1934 Act requirements. Section 15(d) reporting companies are subject to a lower level of regulation than companies registered under the 1934 Act. For example, unlike companies registered under § 12 of the 1934 Act, § 15(d) reporting companies are not subject to the proxy regulations under 1934 Act § 14, the takeover and tender offer provisions of the Williams Act, nor the insider trading and reporting provisions found in 1934 Act § 16.

§ 13. PERIODIC DISCLOSURE REQUIREMENTS

One principal thrust of the Securities Exchange Act of 1934 was to assure the public availability of adequate information about companies with publicly-traded stocks. As amended in 1964, the Act's disclosure requirements apply not only to companies with securities listed on national securities exchanges, but also to all companies with more than 500 shareholders and more than $1,000,000 of assets (raised to $10 million by Rule 12g–1). 1934 Act § 12(a), (g). Certain special types of issuers are exempted, including investment companies, 1934 Act § 12(g)(2)(B), and insurance companies if they are subject to comparable state requirements, 1934 Act § 12(g)(2)(G). Banks are subject to the requirements, but administration and enforcement with respect to them are vested in the federal banking agencies rather than the SEC. 1934 Act § 12(i). As part of its effort to reduce administrative burdens on small companies, the SEC in April 1982 adopted 1934 Act Rule 12g–1, which currently exempts any issuer with less than $5 million of assets from the Act's disclosure requirements. In May 1996, the SEC amended the rule to raise the threshold to $10 million in assets.

The specific requirements for disclosure of information about the issuing company are found in 1934 Act §§ 12, 13, and 14. Section 12 requires the filing of a detailed statement about the company when it first registers under the 1934 Act, and § 13 requires a registered company to file with the SEC "such annual reports * * * and such quarterly reports * * * as the Commission may prescribe." The Sarbanes-Oxley Act (SOX) enhanced many of the existing reporting requirements with enhanced auditor and audit committee independence requirements.

The basic reports required to be filed with the SEC under 1934 Act § 13 are (a) an annual report on Form 10–K, (b) a quarterly report on Form 10–Q, and (c) a current report on Form 8–K for any month in which certain specified events occur. As part of SOX, Congress mandated increased real-time disclosure by expanding the items requiring prompt disclosure under Form 8–K.

Over the years, the Commission has taken steps to integrate the disclosure requirements for these 1934 Act reports with those applicable to registration statements under the 1933 Act. The principal step has been the adoption of Regulation S–K, which specifies the information to be included in statements and reports filed under both Acts. In 1992, the Commission adopted Regulation S–B, which sets forth the disclosure requirements under both Acts for "small business issuers," defined as entities with annual revenues of less than $25 million. See Sec. Act Rel. 33–6949 (1992).

In an effort to improve the readability of reports on Forms 10–K and 10–Q, the Commission in 1980–81 amended those forms to permit much of the required information to be incorporated by reference to the company's annual and quarterly reports to shareholders. At the same time, the Commission stiffened its requirements with respect to the annual report to shareholders (see § 14 below). It also adopted a controversial requirement that the Form 10–K annual report be signed not only by the issuer but also by its principal executive, financial and accounting officers, and at least a majority of its board of directors (the same as the signature requirements applicable to a 1933 Act registration statement). The Commission stated that the expanded signature requirement was not intended to affect legal liabilities on the report but to "refocus" the attention of management toward 1934 Act filings. See Exch. Act Rels. 34–17114 (1980), 34–17524 (1981). SOX introduced an even more controversial requirement—namely that the Chief Executive Officer (CEO) and Chief Financial Officer (CFO) personally certify the accuracy of the disclosures contained in 10–K and 10–Q filings. Although as signers, these officers already had some accountability for the accuracy of the periodic reports, the CEO and CFO certification requirements enhance their exposure.

Under 1934 Act § 18, any person who makes, or causes to be made, a false or misleading statement in any report or other document filed under the 1934 Act can be held liable in damages to any person who buys or sells securities in reliance on such statement and at a price affected by such statement. See Heit v. Weitzen, 402 F.2d 909 (2d Cir. 1968). The plaintiff in such a case must allege and prove "eyeball" reliance on the filed document; reliance on similar statements in other documents is insufficient. See, e.g.,

Wachovia Bank v. National Student Marketing
Corp., 650 F.2d 342 (D.C.Cir.1980).

§ 14. PROXY SOLICITATION

1934 Act § 14 makes it unlawful for a company
registered under 1934 Act § 12 to solicit proxies from
its shareholders "in contravention of such rules and
regulations as the Commission may prescribe as
necessary or appropriate in the public interest or for
the protection of investors." In 1964, the reach of § 14
was broadened by the addition of § 14(c), under which
a company, even if it does not solicit proxies from its
shareholders in connection with a meeting, must
furnish them with information "substantially
equivalent" to that which would be required if it did
solicit proxies. Under 1934 Act § 14(f), added in 1968,
a corporation must also make disclosures to
shareholders when a majority of its board of directors
is replaced by action of the directors, without a
shareholders' meeting, in connection with the
transfer of a controlling stock interest.

Disclosure. Under this authority, the Commission
has promulgated detailed regulations prescribing the
form of proxy and the information to be furnished to
shareholders. Prior to every meeting of its security
holders, a registered company must furnish each of
them with a "proxy statement" containing the
information specified in 1934 Act Schedule 14A,
together with a form of proxy on which the security
holder can indicate his approval or disapproval of
each proposal expected to be presented at the
meeting. 1934 Act Rules 14a–3, 14a–4. Where

securities are registered in the names of brokers, banks, or nominees, the company must inquire as to the beneficial ownership of the securities, furnish sufficient copies of the proxy statement for distribution to all of the beneficial owners, and pay the reasonable expenses of such distribution. 1934 Act Rule 14a–3(d).

Definitive copies of the proxy statement and form of proxy must be filed with the SEC at the time they are first mailed to security holders. In addition, if the proxy solicitation relates to any matters other than election of directors, approval of accountants, or shareholder proposals, preliminary copies of both documents must be filed with the SEC ten days before they are to be mailed. 1934 Act Rule 14a–6. Although the proxy statement does not have to become "effective" in the same manner as a 1933 Act registration statement (see § 8 above), the SEC will often comment on, and insist on changes in, the proxy statement before it is mailed.

When the proxies are being solicited for use at an annual meeting for election of directors, the proxy statement must be accompanied by an annual report containing comparative financial statements for the last two fiscal years and other specified information. 1934 Act Rules 14a–3, 14c–3. The requirements of these rules have been progressively expanded by the SEC to increase the categories of information required to be included and to subject more of these categories of information to the specific disclosure requirements of Regulation S–K (see § 13 above). The annual report to shareholders, while still not required to be filed with the SEC, is thus becoming to a large extent an SEC-regulated document.

Proxy Contests. The SEC proxy rules apply to all solicitations of proxies, consents, or authorizations from security holders by the management or anyone else, subject to exceptions specified in 1934 Act Rule 14a–2.

Shareholder Proposals. Under 1934 Act Rule 14a–8, if any security holder of a registered company gives timely notice to the management of his intention to present a proposal for action at a forthcoming meeting, the management must include the proposal, with a supporting statement of not more than 500 words, in its proxy statement and afford security holders an opportunity to vote for or against it in the management's proxy. To be eligible to have such a proposal included, the security holder must own at least $1,000 worth, or 1%, of the securities entitled to be voted at the meeting.

This rule has been extensively utilized by proponents of "shareholder democracy," to require inclusion of proposals relating to management compensation, conduct of annual meetings, shareholder voting rights, and similar matters. It has also been utilized by persons opposed to discrimination, pollution, and other evils in an attempt to force changes in company policies that affect those matters.

Since management generally resists the inclusion of shareholder proposals, the provisions of the rule specifying the kinds of proposals that can be omitted have been the subject of constant controversy and frequent change. As presently in effect, Rule 14a–8(i) permits management to exclude a proposal if, among other things, it

(1) is, under governing state law, not a proper subject for action by security holders;

(2) would require the company to violate any law;

(3) is contrary to the SEC proxy rules;

(4) relates to redress of a personal claim or grievance;

(5) relates to operations which account for less than 5% of the company's business;

(6) is beyond the company's power to effectuate;

(7) deals with the company's ordinary business operations;

(8) relates to an election to office;[2]

---

[2] In 2009, the SEC proposed amending Rule 14a–8 to allow limited shareholder access to management's proxy statement with respect to director nominations. In addition, the Delaware legislature supplemented the Delaware Supreme Court's approach. As part of various amendments to the Delaware corporate law, companies may but are not required to adopt bylaws that would give shareholders access to a company's proxy statement for the purpose of nominating directors, subject to certain conditions. In addition, the amendments also permit a Delaware corporation's bylaws to provide for reimbursement of expenses incurred by shareholders when soliciting proxies to in an election of directors.

(9) is counter to a management proposal;

(10) has been rendered moot;

(11) is duplicative of another proposal included in the proxy statement; or

(12) is substantially similar to a proposal previously submitted during the past five years, which received affirmative votes from less than a specified percentage of the shares voted.

In case of a dispute between management and a shareholder as to whether a particular proposal may be excluded from the proxy statement, the decision in the first instance is for the SEC. The Commission initially took the position that its refusal to direct a company to include a proposal is not an "order" subject to judicial review under 1934 Act § 25, but one court disagreed with this position. Medical Committee v. SEC, 432 F.2d 659 (D.C.Cir.1970), vacated as moot, 404 U.S. 403 (1972). However, the Commission subsequently discovered that it could avoid judicial review by delegating to its staff the power to decide individual cases and declining to review the staff decision. Kixmiller v. SEC, 492 F.2d 641 (D.C.Cir.1974).

Civil Liability

A company that distributes a misleading proxy statement to its shareholders may incur liability under 1934 Act § 18 to any person who purchases or sells its securities in reliance on the misleading statement. (See § 13 above.) In addition, 1934 Act Rule 14a–9 makes it unlawful to solicit proxies by

means of any proxy statement or other
communication "containing any statement which
* * * is false or misleading with respect to any
material fact, or which omits to state any material
fact necessary in order to make the statement therein
not false or misleading * * * ." While the 1934 Act
does not explicitly create any civil liability for a
violation of § 14 or the SEC's rules under it, the
question arose whether a shareholder, who alleged
that the votes to approve a merger or other
transaction were obtained by means of a misleading
proxy statement, had a right of action for damages or
other relief. In J.I. Case v. Borak, 377 U.S. 426
(1964), the Supreme Court held that a shareholder
had such an implied right of action under 1934 Act
§ 14, by virtue of the "broad remedial purposes" of
§ 14(a) and of the language of 1934 Act § 27, which
grants federal district courts jurisdiction of all
actions "to enforce any liability or duty created by"
the Act. Subsequent Supreme Court decisions have
seriously questioned both of these bases for implying
a private right of action (see § 36 below). However,
they have not overruled the *Borak* decision itself, and
the recognition of a private right of action under
§ 14(a) continues to create a number of difficult
questions of interpretation and implementation.

Causation. One question is what showing the
plaintiff must make that shareholder approval of the
transaction was a result of the misstatement,
particularly where a substantial portion of the shares
were held by "insiders" who had full knowledge of the
true facts. In Mills v. Electric Auto-Lite, 396 U.S. 375
(1970), the Supreme Court held that, where some

votes of "outside" shareholders were necessary for approval, plaintiff was only required to show that the misstatement or omission was "material," not that it actually had a decisive effect on the voting.

A more difficult question arises if the "insiders" have enough shares to approve the transaction without the votes of any of the "outside" shareholders. Even in that situation, one court of appeals had held that, in view of the alternatives available to shareholders if the true facts had been revealed, the proxy solicitation was "an essential part of the merger." Cole v. Schenley, 563 F.2d 35 (2d Cir.1977). However, in Virginia Bankshares v. Sandberg, 501 U.S. 1083 (1991), the Supreme Court, in a 5–4 decision, rejected that approach and held that causation was not established where the votes of the outside shareholders were not necessary to approve the transaction.

Materiality. In *Mills,* Justice Harlan stated the test for materiality of a misstatement or omission in a proxy statement as whether "it *might* have been considered important by a reasonable shareholder" (emphasis added). However, in TSC v. Northway, 426 U.S. 438 (1976), the Supreme Court adopted a stricter standard, holding that "an omitted fact is material if there is *a substantial likelihood* that a reasonable shareholder would consider it important in deciding how to vote. * * * Put another way, there must be a substantial likelihood that the disclosure of the omitted fact would have been viewed by the reasonable investor as having significantly altered the 'total mix' of information made available" (emphasis added). In *Sandberg, supra,* the Court held that even a statement couched in conclusory or qualitative terms could be a material misstatement if it "expressly or impliedly asserted something false or misleading about its subject matter."

Culpability. In Gerstle v. Gamble-Skogmo, 478 F.2d 1281 (2d Cir.1973), the court held that in an action under 1934 Act Rule 14a–9, unlike an action under 1934 Act Rule 10b–5 (see § 20(b) below), negligence in the preparation of the proxy statement would be sufficient to warrant recovery. No evil motive or reckless disregard of the facts need be shown.

Relief. Where there appears to be material misstatements or omissions in proxy soliciting material, a preliminary injunction requiring circulation of corrected materials is a particularly appropriate remedy, especially where it would not be feasible to undo the transaction after the shareholder votes. Berkman v. Rust Craft, 454 F.Supp. 787 (S.D.N.Y.1978).

In appropriate cases, a court may grant equitable relief after the vote, such as ordering a new election of directors when proxies for the election of the incumbents were procured by a misleading proxy statement. Gladwin v. Medfield, 540 F.2d 1266 (5th Cir.1976). However, a plaintiff's showing of a violation does not automatically entitle the plaintiff to equitable relief. In *Mills,* the court said that a merger should not be set aside unless such action would be in the best interest of all the shareholders, and the plaintiff in that case was remitted to the plaintiff's damage remedy.

Computation of damages in a merger situation can involve difficult questions, such as the appropriate value of the acquired company or the acquiring company's liability for all profits resulting from the merger. In *Mills* itself, the courts ultimately held that, since the terms of the merger were not unfair, plaintiff was not entitled to any damages, even though there had been a material omission from the proxy statement. Mills v. Electric Auto-Lite, 552 F.2d 1239 (7th Cir.1977).

Remedies Under 1933 Act. As a result of the adoption of 1933 Act Rule 145 (see § 10(d) above), most proxy statements used in connection with mergers, reclassifications, and sales of assets are now also 1933 Act registration statements. Thus, the civil liability provisions of § 11 of that Act provide an alternative avenue of relief for aggrieved shareholders of acquired companies who can establish material misstatements or omissions in the proxy statement.

§ 15.   TAKEOVER BIDS AND TENDER OFFERS

Since the 1960s, aggressive corporate and individual investors, in increasing numbers, have embarked on campaigns to acquire controlling stock interests in publicly-held corporations. They may acquire the stock by paying cash, issuing their own securities in exchange, or some combination of the two. They may acquire stock in private transactions, by purchases through brokers in the open market, or by making a public offer to the shareholders of the target company to tender their shares, either for a fixed cash price or for a package of securities of the offering corporation. These "takeover bids" or "tender offers" are often bitterly opposed by the management of the target corporation, and the contests feature flamboyant public claims and charges on both sides, efforts to manipulate the market, and confusing and coercive approaches to the shareholders of the target corporation.

Where the takeover bid involves a public offer of securities of the aggressor corporation in exchange for shares of the target corporation, the securities must of course be registered under the Securities Act of 1933 and a prospectus delivered to the shareholders being solicited. In the case of a cash tender offer, however, there was, prior to 1968, no requirement for any filing with the SEC.

(A) FEDERAL REGULATION OF TAKEOVERS

The "Williams Act," passed in 1968, was designed to give the SEC and the courts power to deal with problems arising in the course of takeovers or tender offers. While the original impetus for the legislation came from the managements of companies that were or might be takeover targets, the SEC and Congress took the position that the purpose of the legislation was to prevent overreaching of public shareholders, rather than to tip the scales between the incumbent management and the takeover bidder. Consequently, although most of the litigation under the Williams Act is between the contending parties, the courts tend to look primarily to whether the relief sought will help protect public shareholders.

The Williams Act added several provisions to the 1934 Act. The Williams Act amendments directly applicable to takeover bids are 1934 Act § 13(d) and §§ 14(d) and (e). 1934 Act § 13(e) applies to a company's acquisitions of its own shares. 1934 Act § 14(f) introduced a requirement that agreements relating to a turn-over in management and control be disclosed.

Filing of Statement. Under 1934 Act § 13(d), any person (or "group") that becomes the owner of more than 5% of any class of securities registered under 1934 Act § 12 must file a statement with both the issuer of the securities and the Commission, within 10 days, that sets forth the following: (a) the background of such person, (b) the source of the funds used for the acquisition, (c) the purpose of the acquisition, (d) the number of shares owned, and (e) any relevant contracts, arrangements, or understandings. Some courts have recognized an implied right of action by the issuer to seek appropriate injunctive relief against violations of § 13(d), see, e.g., Dan River v. Unitex, 624 F.2d 1216 (4th Cir.1980), but others have questioned whether any such right exists under the more restrictive approach now being followed by the Supreme Court, see, e.g., Liberty National v. Charter, 734 F.2d 545 (11th Cir.1984). Even where the right of action is recognized, the issuer is not entitled to an injunction restraining the voting of the securities or acquisition of additional securities without showing "irreparable harm and other usual prerequisites for injunctive relief." Rondeau v. Mosinee, 422 U.S. 49 (1975).

One difficult question under 1934 Act § 13(d) arises where a number of shareholders of a company, owning in the aggregate more than 5% of its shares, agree to act together for the purpose of affecting the control of the company, but do not acquire any additional shares. The courts have split as to whether the agreement to act together constitutes an "acquisition" by the "group," triggering the filing requirement. Compare GAF v. Milstein, 453 F.2d 709 (2d Cir.1971), with Bath v. Blot, 427 F.2d 97 (7th Cir.1970).

Tender Offer Procedures. Under 1934 Act § 14(d), no person may make a tender offer that would result in his owning more than 5% of a class of securities registered under 1934 Act § 12 unless the person making the tender offer has filed with the Commission, and furnishes to each offeree, a statement containing certain of the information required under 1934 Act § 13(d). Sections 14(d) and (e), and the rules adopted by the SEC under them, also impose significant substantive restrictions on the terms of tender offers. A tender offer must remain open for at least 20 days, and for at least 10 days after any change in its terms. 1934 Act Rule 14e–1. The offer must be open to all holders of the class of securities sought, and the same price must be paid to all tendering shareholders. 1934 Act Rule 14d–10. Where the offer is for less than all of the outstanding shares, and is oversubscribed, shares must be taken up on a pro rata basis. 1934 Act § 14(d)(6). And tendered shares may be withdrawn at any time while the tender offer remains open. 1934 Act Rule 14d–7.

What Is a "Tender Offer"? The term "tender offer" is not defined in the Act. It has been held not to encompass purchases in the open market, whether or not made for purposes of obtaining control. Kennecott v. Curtiss-Wright, 584 F.2d 1195 (2d Cir.1978). However, it has been held to include "any public invitation to a corporation's shareholders to purchase their stock," even though it is not a "hostile bid opposed by incumbent management." Smallwood v. Pearl, 489 F.2d 579 (5th Cir.1974).

It has also been interpreted to apply to a coordinated plan by which 35% of a company's stock was purchased from 24 large stockholders in simultaneous, unpublicized take-it-or-leave-it transactions. The court held that the transaction had all the characteristics of a tender offer, other than a widespread solicitation of public shareholders, since it was an offer for a substantial portion of the company's shares at a firm price substantially above the current market, was contingent on the tender of a fixed number of shares within a limited period of time, and subjected the offerees to pressure to make a quick decision. Wellman v. Dickinson, 475 F.Supp. 783 (S.D.N.Y.1979).

In the *Wellman* case, the court identified eight factors, the presence of which would influence the court in determining whether or not there was a tender offer: (1) active and widespread solicitation of public shareholders; (2) solicitation of a substantial percentage of the issuer's stock; (3) offer made at a premium over the prevailing market price; (4) terms of the offer firm rather than negotiable; (5) offer contingent on tender of a fixed number of shares; (6) offer open only for a limited period of time; (7) offeree subjected to pressure to sell his stock; and (8) public announcement of purchasing program accompanying rapid accumulation of shares. These factors were subsequently applied by the Ninth Circuit in finding a repurchase program not to be a tender offer. SEC v. Carter, 760 F.2d 945 (9th Cir.1985). The Second Circuit, however, has rejected these criteria. In deciding that the acquisition of 25% of a company's stock in five private purchases and one open market purchase was not a "tender offer," the court held that, since the purpose of 1934 Act § 14(d) was to protect *public* shareholders from being forced to make uninformed decisions, it should only apply where there is "a substantial risk that solicitees will lack information needed to make a carefully considered appraisal of the proposal put before them." Hanson v. SCM, 774 F.2d 47 (2d Cir.1985).

Misstatements in Tender Offers. 1934 Act § 14(e) makes it unlawful for any person in connection with a tender offer to (1) misstate or omit a material fact, or (2) engage in any fraudulent, deceptive, or manipulative acts or practices. There is no express private right of action for a violation of this prohibition. However, in Electronic v. International, 409 F.2d 937 (2d Cir.1969), the court held that the target corporation had standing to seek an injunction against an aggressor which had made misleading statements in the course of a tender offer.

On the other hand, the Supreme Court held in Piper v. Chris-Craft, 430 U.S. 1 (1977), that a defeated tender offeror had no standing to sue for damages allegedly resulting from misleading statements made by its opponents in the struggle for control. While the Court did not pass on the standing of a tender offeror to seek equitable relief, or the standing of the target corporation, it indicated that it would imply a private right of action under 1934 Act § 14(e) only where it would benefit the shareholders of the target corporation, the group which Congress intended to protect. Applying this reasoning, some courts have held that a competing party in a contested tender offer does have standing to seek an injunction against misleading solicitations by its opponent, on the ground that requiring the dissemination of corrected materials will benefit the shareholders of the target company. See Florida Commercial Banks v. Culverhouse, 772 F.2d 1513 (11th Cir.1985).

Under the reasoning of *Piper,* shareholders of the target company might have an implied right to sue under 1934 Act § 14(e) if they tendered their shares on the basis of misleading statements by the offeror. See Plaine v. McCabe, 797 F.2d 713 (9th Cir.1986). However, courts have held that shareholders cannot sue the management of the target company for making misleading statements that cause a tender offer to be abandoned. Their reasoning is that since the shareholders never had an opportunity to tender their shares, they could not have relied on the misleading statements. Lewis v. McGraw, 619 F.2d

192 (2d Cir.1980); Panter v. Marshall Field, 646 F.2d 271 (7th Cir.1981).

(B) STATE REGULATION OF TAKEOVERS

In addition to the federal legislation, more than 30 states enacted laws during the 1960s and 1970s regulating takeovers of companies incorporated or doing business in those states. These statutes tended to be strongly tilted toward the interests of incumbent management. They generally required disclosures more extensive than those required by federal law, imposed a waiting period of from 10 to 60 days between the announcement and commencement of the tender offer, and provided for a hearing before a state administrative official.

The constitutionality of these statutes was extensively litigated, with lower federal and state courts reaching a variety of results. The first of these cases to reach the Supreme Court was Edgar v. MITE, 457 U.S. 624 (1982), in which the Court held that the Illinois statute containing provisions of this nature was unconstitutional because the indirect burdens which it placed on interstate commerce outweighed any legitimate state interests. Some members of the Court also felt that it was unconstitutional as a direct burden on interstate commerce and that it was preempted by the Williams Act because it conflicted with the balance drawn by Congress in that Act.

In the wake of the *Edgar* decision, a number of states passed "second-generation" takeover laws, focused on companies incorporated in the state and regulating the voting rights of persons who acquired more than a specified percentage of the outstanding stock, rather than imposing administrative obstacles. In the first of these cases to reach the Supreme Court, CTS v. Dynamics, 481 U.S. 69 (1987), the Court upheld the validity of an Indiana statute of this type, on the ground that it fell squarely within the traditional power of the states to regulate the internal affairs of corporations organized under their laws.

Despite this victory, the major commercial states have not followed the Indiana approach. Delaware and New York, the two states in which the largest number of NYSE-listed companies are incorporated or headquartered, have opted for statutes which do not restrict a bidder from acquiring or voting shares of the target company, but do prohibit it from merging with the acquired company for a specified period of years after the acquisition. This in effect makes it impossible for the bidder to use the target company's assets to secure the debt incurred by the bidder to finance the takeover. See Del.Gen.Corp.L. § 203; N.Y.Bus.Corp.L. § 912. A Wisconsin "third generation" statute similar to the Delaware law was upheld against constitutional attacks in Amanda v. Universal, 877 F.2d 496 (7th Cir.1989).

In addition to these special state takeover laws, corporations have taken a variety of defensive measures under traditional provisions of state corporation law. Litigation over these measures has generally focused on whether management was entitled to the protection of the "business judgment rule" in taking action to fend off a tender offer, or whether its action was primarily motivated by its self-interest in maintaining itself in office, in which case it would be judged by the "intrinsic fairness" test. The courts of Delaware, in which many of the actions were brought, developed a "proportionality test," under which the directors would be required to show (a) "that they had reasonable grounds for believing that a danger to corporate policy and effectiveness existed because of another person's stock ownership" and (b) the "defensive measure [was] reasonable in relation to the threat posed." Unocal v. Mesa, 493 A.2d 946 (Del.1985); see also Revlon v. MacAndrews, 506 A.2d 173 (Del.1985) Paramount v. Time, 571 A.2d 1140 (Del.1989).

Some of the defensive measures raised questions about the appropriate boundary line between state corporation law and federal securities law. For example, in the *Unocal* case, the Delaware Supreme Court upheld the validity under Delaware corporation law of a counter tender offer by the target company to purchase shares from all shareholders other than the bidder. The SEC, construing its mandate under 1934 Act §§ 14(d) and 13(e) as including an obligation to assure "fair and equal treatment of all holders of the class of securities that is the subject of a tender offer," subsequently adopted rules under which a tender offer must be open to all holders of such class. In Polaroid v. Disney, 862 F.2d 987 (3d Cir.1988), this "all holders" rule was attacked as not being within the Commission's rule-making authority, by virtue of the Supreme Court's decision

in Schreiber v. Burlington (§ 17(c) below). The Third
Circuit upheld the validity of the rule.

Another area of conflict between state and federal
law arose with respect to voting rights. A large
number of companies attempted to protect
themselves against takeovers by creating classes of
non-voting shares or super-voting shares, limiting
the number of votes any one shareholder could cast,
or barring shareholders from voting until they had
held their shares for a specified period of time. These
restrictions ran afoul of the New York Stock
Exchange rules, which bar the listing of the common
stock of any company that has non-voting common
shares or departs in any other way from the rule of
"one share, one vote." Companies listed on the NYSE
put pressure on the Exchange to change its rule, and
the Exchange submitted to the SEC a plan to permit
listed companies to adopt "disparate voting rights" as
long as they were approved by their independent
directors and "public" shareholders. The SEC
declined to approve the NYSE proposal, opting
instead to adopt its own rule, requiring all exchanges
and NASDAQ to delist the shares of any company
which took any action to "nullify, restrict, or
disparately reduce the per share voting rights of
holders of outstanding common stock." The validity
of the rule was challenged as being outside the
Commission's rule-making authority. In Business
Roundtable v. SEC, 905 F.2d 406 (D.C.Cir.1990), the
rule was struck down as an attempt by the SEC to
regulate corporate internal affairs, a power which the
court found Congress had not delegated to the
Commission. However, the major stock exchanges

and NASDAQ subsequently adopted uniform rules strictly limiting the situations in which disparate voting rights would be permitted.

§ 16. LIABILITY FOR "SHORT-SWING" PROFITS

The last of the provisions applicable to companies which have securities registered under 1934 Act § 12 is 1934 Act § 16, which is designed to discourage corporate "insiders" from taking advantage of their access to information by engaging in short-term trading in the corporation's securities. 1934 Act § 16(a) requires every person who beneficially owns, directly or indirectly, more than 10% of a class of equity securities registered under 1934 Act § 12, and every officer and director of every company that has a class of equity securities registered under that section, to file a report with the SEC. A report must be filed (a) at the time the beneficial owner, officer, or director acquires such status and (b) by the end of the second business day after he or she acquires or disposes of any equity securities of that company. "For the purpose of preventing the unfair use of information which may have been obtained by" any such officer, director, or 10% shareholder, 1934 Act § 16(b) permits the company, or any security holder suing on its behalf, to recover any "profit" realized by any person from any purchase and sale, or sale and purchase, of any equity security of the company within a period of less than six months.

There are several important things to note about 1934 Act § 16. First, although its purpose is to prevent unfair use of inside information, it does not reach all instances of such use; it only reaches specified combinations of transactions by specified classes of people. When the statute does apply, it is not necessary to show that the defendant actually took advantage of, or had access to, inside information. Smolowe v. Delendo, 136 F.2d 231 (2d Cir.1943). In interpreting the specific words such as "purchase," "sale," and "beneficial owner," however, most courts have followed the "pragmatic" approach of attempting to determine whether the particular transaction presented the possibilities for the type of abuse with which Congress was concerned. See Kern County v. Occidental, 411 U.S. 582, 594 n.26 (1973).

Second, the SEC has only limited powers under 1934 Act § 16. It has power to enforce the filing requirements under § 16(a), and it has statutory power under § 16(b) to exempt by rule transactions which it finds to be "not comprehended within the purpose of [that] subsection." See Greene v. Dietz, 247 F.2d 689 (2d Cir.1957). In 1991, the Commission replaced all of its rules under 1934 Act § 16 with a completely new set of rules, incorporating many substantive changes. Exch. Act Rel. 34–28869 (1991). However, the SEC has no power to enforce the liability imposed by § 16(b). Liability can be asserted only in a suit brought by the issuer or a security holder suing on its behalf. Since corporate management will seldom be inclined to sue its own members, and since the financial benefit to any individual security holder bringing suit on the issuer's behalf will ordinarily be infinitesimal, the principal incentive to enforcement of the section is the fee which the court awards to the attorney for the plaintiff out of the profits recovered by the company. While the principal financial interest in a § 16(b) suit is that of the attorney, rather than the "client," the courts have refused to bar such actions on the basis of improper motivation or unprofessional conduct, reasoning that Congress must have intended to accept such conduct as the price of effective enforcement of that particular type of provision. See Magida v. Continental, 176 F.Supp. 781 (S.D.N.Y.1956).

"Profit Realized." There is a "profit" for 1934 Act § 16(b) purposes whenever there is a purchase that can be matched against a sale at a higher price that is made less than six months after, or before, the purchase. Securities are fungible for § 16(b) purposes; there is no need to trace certificates. Smolowe v. Delendo Corp., above. Indeed, sales of common stock can be matched against purchases of debentures convertible into common stock to produce a "profit." Chemical Fund v. Xerox, 377 F.2d 107 (2d Cir.1967); see 1934 Act Rule 16b–6. Also, there is no provision for offsetting "losses" against "profits." Where a defendant has engaged in a series of transactions at varying prices, the "profit" recoverable by the company is determined by matching the highest-price sales against the lowest-price purchases, so that the defendant may be held liable for "profits" even where the defendant has suffered an overall trading loss during the six-month period involved. Chemical Fund v. Xerox, above.

"Officer" or "Director." The term "officer" is defined to mean the president, the principal financial and accounting officers, any vice president in charge of a principal business unit, division, or function, and any other officer or person who performs similar policy-making functions for the issuer. 1934 Act Rule 16a–1(f); see C.R.A. v. Crotty, 878 F.2d 562 (2d Cir.1989).

A purchase or sale made by a person after he or she has ceased to be a director or officer can be matched against a sale or purchase made within six months previously while the officer or director still held that position. See 1934 Act Rule 16a–2(b); Feder v. Martin, 406 F.2d 260 (2d Cir.1969). However, a purchase and sale both made within the six-month period following resignation as a director are not covered. See 1934 Act Rule 16a–2(b); Levy v. Seaton, 358 F.Supp. 1 (S.D.N.Y.1973).

A partnership or corporation that is found to have "deputized" one of its members or officers to serve as a director of another company will itself be liable as a "director" under § 16(b) for profits made on its own trades. Blau v. Lehman, 368 U.S. 403 (1962); Feder v. Martin, above. However, "deputization" is a question of fact, and where a partner is found not to have been representing the partnership on the board of the company, § 16(b) liability will attach only to his pro rata share of profits on the partnership's trading activities. Blau v. Lehman, above.

Transactions by directors or officers may or may not be matched against transactions by their spouses or other family members, depending on whether the director or officer is found to have a "direct or indirect pecuniary interest" in the securities. See Rule 16a–1(a)(2). Compare Whiting v. Dow, 523 F.2d 680 (2d Cir.1975) with CBI v. Horton, 682 F.2d 643 (7th Cir.1982).

"10% Shareholder." To be liable as a beneficial owner, a person must own more than 10% of a class of *registered equity securities.* Ownership of more than 10% of the common stock, or of a registered preferred stock (i.e., a class traded on a national securities exchange or held by more than 2000 persons, see 1934 Act § 12(g)), will of course suffice. However, ownership of more than 10% of a class of convertible debentures (which are considered "equity securities" under 1934 Act § 3(a)(11) only because they are convertible into common stock) does not make the holder liable under 1934 Act § 16(b) unless the common stock into which his debentures are convertible, plus any other common stock the insider owns, would amount to more than 10% of the common stock outstanding. Chemical Fund v. Xerox, *supra*; see 1934 Act Rule 16a–1(a)(2)(ii)(F). For the purpose of determining whether a person is a 10% beneficial owner, the term "beneficial owner" is defined by reference to the rules under 1934 Act § 13(d). See 1934 Act Rule 16a–1(a)(1).

In contrast to the situation with respect to directors and officers, § 16(b) specifically provides that a beneficial owner can be held liable only if he or she was a 10% shareholder at the time of both the purchase and the sale. The Supreme Court has held that the purchase which makes a person a 10% shareholder cannot be matched against a subsequent sale to create liability. Foremost-McKesson v. Provident, 423 U.S. 232 (1976). It has also held that a holder of more than 10% who first sells enough to bring its holdings down to 9.9%, and then sells the remainder, cannot be held liable for the profit on the second transaction, even if the two sales were parts of a single prearranged plan. Reliance v. Emerson, 404 U.S. 418 (1972).

"Purchase" and "Sale." Under 1934 Act Rule 16b–6, as amended in 1991, the receipt or disposition of a put or call option on common stock, or of securities convertible into common stock, is treated as a purchase or sale of the underlying common stock. The exercise of an option or the conversion of a convertible security is not treated as a purchase or a sale for purposes of § 16(b). (This reverses the position previously taken by the SEC that the exercise of an option constitutes a purchase or sale of the underlying common stock.)

Surrender of securities of one company for securities of another company in a statutory merger may constitute a "sale" and "purchase" if the defendant had power to put through the merger and there was a possibility for use of inside information. Newmark v. RKO, 425 F.2d 348 (2d Cir.1970). However, where the defendant is a "forced seller" (e.g., a defeated tender offeror which is forced to exchange its shares because it has insufficient votes to prevent the merger from going through), its disposition is not considered a "sale" for § 16(b) purposes. Kern County v. Occidental, above.

Transactions by officers and directors pursuant to employee stock option plans and other employee benefit plans are exempt from § 16(b) if the plan is approved by the shareholders of the company and the transactions comply with the requirements set forth in 1934 Act Rule 16b–3.

"Within Any Period of Less than Six Months." If a person purchases stock on March 15, what is the earliest date on which she can sell without incurring liability? In Stella v. Graham-Paige, 132 F.Supp. 100 (S.D.N.Y.1955), the court defined the six-month period by taking the date on which the stock was purchased, finding the corresponding date six months later, and then subtracting one day to determine the date on which the six-month period terminates. In the above example, therefore, the six-month period would end on September 14, and the purchaser could sell on that date without incurring liability because that period would constitute exactly six months, not less than six months. See also Jammies v. Nowinski, 700 F.Supp. 189 (S.D.N.Y.1988).

CHAPTER IV
ANTIFRAUD PROVISIONS

Most of the preceding sections of this book have dealt with specific, and often very elaborate, provisions of law or regulations designed to deal with particular kinds of transactions or practices. However, some of the most important developments in federal securities law have grown out of the "antifraud" provisions found in those laws, which are generalized prohibitions against "fraud or deceit" or "manipulative or deceptive devices or contrivances."

Provisions of this type are found in 1933 Act § 17(a), 1934 Act §§ 10(b), 14(e), and 15(c)(1), and IAA § 206. Because 1934 Act § 10(b) has the broadest jurisdictional reach, it is the provision most frequently invoked, but many of the doctrines developed under it are also applicable to the other sections.

§ 17. MARKET MANIPULATION

In the hearings which led to enactment of the 1934 Act, one of the most serious abuses in the securities markets on which Senate investigators focused was the operation of "pools." These "pools" ran up the prices of securities on an exchange by a series of well-timed transactions, effected solely for the purpose of "manipulating" the market price of the security, then unloaded their holdings on the public just before the price dropped. Accordingly, 1934 Act §§ 9 and 10(a) prohibit a variety of manipulative activities with respect to exchange-listed securities, and 1934 Act

§ 10(b) contains a catch-all provision permitting the SEC to prohibit by rule any "manipulative or deceptive device or contrivance" with respect to any security.

By and large, these provisions have been effective in preventing a recurrence of the widespread manipulation on exchanges which flourished in the 1920s. There continue, however, to be isolated instances of manipulation which give rise to enforcement actions. See, e.g., SEC v. Lorin, 877 F.Supp. 192 (S.D.N.Y.1995); United States v. Mulheren, 938 F.2d 364 (2d Cir.1991). At the beginning of the twenty-first century, a number of new manipulations came to light. The most notable manipulations were those involving IPO (Initial Public Offering) practices and mutual fund sales practices.

There are several areas in which there have been continuing problems in drawing the line between manipulative activity and legitimate transactions. One is the extent to which securities dealers and others participating in a public offering or "distribution" of securities may simultaneously bid for or purchase the same security. Another is the extent to which corporations may influence the price of their own shares by purchasing them in the open market. A third is the activities of the participants in contested takeover bids.

(A) DISTRIBUTIONS

The success of a public offering of securities may depend in large measure on whether the market price of the security goes up or down during the period of the distribution. Accordingly, there is a strong incentive for those participating in the distribution to maintain the market price at a high level during that period. On the other hand, the injection of a large new block of securities into the trading market may exert a temporary depressing influence on the market price and make it impossible for the underwriters to market the new shares at a price near the previously prevailing market price. The SEC therefore faced the question whether to permit the underwriters to "stabilize" the price—i.e., to place a bid for the securities in the market at or near the public offering price, and to purchase (for resale) shares coming into the market that might otherwise cause the market price to drop.

As early as 1936, the Commission decided that "certain stabilizing operations" were not within the Act's prohibitions against manipulation, and permitted underwriters to support, within limits, the price of the security being distributed. Since 1939, the SEC has required that the prospectus set forth the possibility of underwriters' stabilizing purchases and that the underwriters file detailed reports with the SEC when they do in fact stabilize. See Reg. S–K, Item 502(d); 1934 Act Rule 17a–2.

Precise guidelines as to when, and at what price, underwriters may enter stabilizing bids were finally laid down in 1955 with the adoption of 1934 Act Rules 10b–6, b–7, and b–8. In 1997, those rules were replaced by Regulation M, with its Rules 100–105. Regulation M makes it unlawful for the issuer, any selling stockholder, or any underwriter or other person participating in a "distribution" to bid for or purchase any units of the security being distributed, with certain specified exceptions. The term "distribution" is defined in Rule 100 as "an offering of securities, whether or not subject to registration under the Securities Act, that is distinguished from ordinary trading transactions by the magnitude of the offering and the presence of special selling efforts and selling methods."

Rule 101 of Regulation M prohibits an underwriter or other "distribution participant" from bidding for or purchasing any units of the security being distributed during the "restricted period," which begins one day (or five days in the case of thinly-traded securities) before the beginning of such person's participation and ends on completion of such participation. These restrictions do not apply to distributions of high-grade debt securities or equity securities that have an average trading volume of at least $1 million and a public float of at least $150 million. Rule 102 imposes comparable restrictions on issuers and selling security holders.

Rule 103 of Regulation M permits a NASDAQ market maker participating in a distribution to continue "passive" market making during the distribution, with limitations on the volume of its purchases and the prices at which it may bid for the security. Rule 104 of Regulation M prescribes the conditions under which underwriters may enter bids or make purchases for the purpose of "stabilizing" the price of the security being distributed, and Rule 105 prohibits any person from purchasing securities from any underwriter or distribution participant to cover a "short sale" made less than five days before the commencement of the distribution.

"Hot Issues." The opposite side of the "stabilizing" problem is presented by the "hot issue"—a new issue which jumps to a substantial premium over the offering price as soon as secondary trading commences. This phenomenon typically occurs during periods of speculative frenzy, when almost any issue of a small, unknown company will jump to an immediate premium because of large demand and a small supply of stock. The efforts of the SEC and the NASD (now FINRA) have been concentrated on assuring that the underwriters do not artificially stimulate demand or restrict the supply of stock, and that they do not profit by "free riding," i.e., withholding some of the stock from the public during the initial offering in expectation of selling it at a higher price in the secondary market.

IPO Practices. From time to time, initial public offerings have been plagued by fraudulent and manipulative practices. Problems arise both in the context of "hot issues" that generate a good deal of buying interest and soft issues where there is a temptation to stimulate buying interest to get the offering off started with a positive reception from investors. During the IPO boom of the 1990s, companies and their underwriters engaged in a number of questionable practices. These practices were contrary to existing law but apparently were widespread in many sectors of the securities industry. When the stock markets turned sour in the late 1990s and early twenty-first century, the IPO bubble burst. Investors and regulators began looking into the practices that may have contributed to huge losses to market participants who had invested in hot IPO stocks.

For example, the states, under the leadership of former New York Attorney General Elliot Spitzer, investigated investment banking practices, including analysts' conflict of interest and improper IPO activities. The SEC and the NASD also became involved in the investigation and ensuing regulation. The investigation culminated in a $1.4 billion "global settlement" with ten of the largest investment banks in the U.S.

The problematic IPO practices included activity that, although not explicitly prohibited by rules particularizing the conduct in question, violate the fraud and manipulation prohibitions of the securities laws. Those practices included, but were not limited to various types of conduct including "laddering" and "spinning." Laddering, or pre-selling the aftermarket, is a practice under which IPO purchasers are asked to commit to purchase additional shares in the aftermarket. Laddering not only provides improper consideration for the allocation of IPO shares but also creates additional demand in the aftermarket. This increase in demand ensures rising prices once the shares are publicly traded. "Spinning" involves allocating IPO shares to favored customers in exchange for a quid pro quo or to IPO purchasers who plan to "flip" the shares by reselling immediately. These are just some of the practices that are addressed in the sections that follow.

The SEC commissioned an advisory committee whose study led to rule revisions designed to eliminate these and other improper IPO practices. In 2003, the SEC approved the NASD's revamped approach to regulating certain public offering practices. See Sec. Exch. Act Rel. No. 34–48701 (2003). The former NASD rules related to "hot issues." In contrast, the amended version of the NASD rules make it clear that they address the offering process with respect to all IPOs. NASD Rule 2790 (now a FINRA rule) expands and clarifies many of the NASD's policies that were already in place. Subject to some enumerated exceptions, IPO shares may not be allocated to "restricted persons," who are individuals or entities having an interest in the issuer or in the offering.

(B) CORPORATE REPURCHASES

Corporations may purchase their own shares in the open market (or cause such shares to be purchased for employee pension or profit-sharing plans). Such purchases may have the effect (and sometimes the purpose) of raising the market price of the company's stock above the level that would otherwise prevail. They may raise problems even when the company is not technically engaged in a distribution and therefore not subject to the prohibitions of Regulation M.

Between 1961 and 1966, Georgia-Pacific acquired a number of other companies in exchange for its own stock, with the total number of shares to be delivered depending on whether G-P stock reached a specified price level within a certain period. The SEC brought an injunction action against G-P, charging that, during that period, G-P had purchased 23,000 shares of its own stock for its employee bonus plan, and that "such purchases were intentionally effected in a manner which would and did, directly and indirectly cause the last sale price of G-P common stock on the NYSE to rise in order that G-P's obligation to issue additional shares * * * would be avoided or reduced[.]" At the SEC's request, the court issued an injunction restraining G-P from repurchasing any shares while the terms of an acquisition or exchange offer were being determined, or from repurchasing shares at any time (a) through orders placed with more than one broker, (b) at the opening or close of the market, (c) at a price above the last sale or current bid price, or (d) in excess of 10% of the current weekly trading volume or 15% of the current daily trading volume. SEC v. Georgia-Pacific, CCH ¶ ¶ 91,680, 91,692 (S.D.N.Y.1966).

In 1968, as part of the "Williams Act" to regulate take-over bids and tender offers, Congress enacted 1934 Act § 13(e), specifically authorizing the SEC to regulate repurchases by corporations of their own securities, for the purpose of preventing "fraudulent, deceptive or manipulative acts or practices." However, in November 1982, the Commission abandoned its effort to write a rule under 1934 Act § 13(e), and instead adopted a "safe harbor" rule under 1934 Act § 10(b). Under 1934 Act Rule 10b–18, repurchases by an issuer and its affiliates during any trading day are deemed not to violate the anti-manipulative provisions of 1934 Act § 9(a)(2) and 1934 Act Rule 10b–5 if (a) they are made through only one broker or dealer, (b) none of them are made as the opening transaction or during the last half hour of trading on that day, (c) none of them are made at a price exceeding the highest current independent bid price or the last independent sale price, whichever is higher, and (d) the total of such purchases does not exceed 25% of the average daily trading volume for the preceding four weeks. Sec. Exch. Act Rel. 34–19244 (1982).

(C) CONTESTED TAKEOVER BIDS

In the course of a contest for control of a target company (see § 15 above), one contestant may make purchases of stock of the target company for the purpose of affecting its market price or in a way which violates the specific prohibitions of former 1934 Act Rules 10b–6 and 10b–13, now found in Regulation M and 1934 Act Rule 14e–5. The courts have held, however, that the opposing contestant, against whom such practices are directed, has no standing to sue for damages resulting from the violation. Piper v. Chris-Craft, 430 U.S. 1 (1977) (technical violation of Rule 10b–6); Crane v. American Standard, 603 F.2d 244 (2d Cir.1979) (deliberate manipulation in violation of 1934 Act § 9).

The Supreme Court has also held that an agreement between a tender offeror and the management of the target company, under which shareholders of the target received less than they would have under the original offer, was not a "manipulative" device within the meaning of 1934 Act § 14(e). Schreiber v. Burlington, 472 U.S. 1 (1985).

§ 18.   THE JURISPRUDENCE OF 1934 ACT RULE 10b–5

1934 Act § 10(b) is a catch-all provision, designed to deal with abuses that escaped the specific prohibitions of 1934 Act §§ 9 and 10(a). Section 10(b) makes it unlawful for any person to use the mails or facilities of interstate commerce:

> "To use or employ, in connection with the purchase or sale of any security * * * any manipulative or deceptive device or contrivance in contravention of such rules and regulations as the Commission may prescribe as necessary or appropriate in the public interest or for the protection of investors."

Note that § 10(b) by its terms does not make anything unlawful unless the Commission has adopted a rule prohibiting it.

In 1942, the Commission was presented with a situation in which the president of a company was buying shares from the existing shareholders at a low price by misrepresenting the company's financial condition. While 1933 Act § 17(a) prohibited fraud and misstatements in the *sale* of securities, there was no comparable provision prohibiting such practices in connection with the *purchase* of securities. The SEC's Assistant Solicitor accordingly lifted the operative language out of 1933 Act § 17(a), made the necessary modifications, added the words "in connection with the purchase or sale of any security," and presented the product to the Commission as 1934 Act Rule 10b–5. It was unanimously approved without discussion. Remarks of Milton Freeman, 22 Bus. Lawyer 922 (1967).

As adopted (and it has not been amended), Rule 10b–5 states:

> "It shall be unlawful for any person, directly or indirectly, by the use of any means or instrumentality of interstate commerce, or of the mails or of any facility of any national securities exchange,
>
> "(a) To employ any device, scheme, or artifice to defraud,
>
> "(b) To make any untrue statement of a material fact or to omit to state a material fact necessary in order to make the statements made, in the light of circumstances under which they were made, not misleading, or
>
> "(c) To engage in any act, practice, or course of business which operates or would operate as a fraud or deceit upon any person,
>
> "in connection with the purchase or sale of any security."

In the 67 years since its adoption, this deceptively simple rule has been invoked in countless SEC and private proceedings, and applied to almost every conceivable kind of situation.

In the 1960s and early 1970s, many federal appellate courts and district courts developed expansive interpretations of Rule 10b–5 (and other antifraud provisions of the securities laws). They applied it to impose liability for negligent as well as deliberate misrepresentations, for breaches of fiduciary duty by corporate management, and for failure by directors, underwriters, accountants, and lawyers to prevent wrongdoing by others. In private actions for damages, the courts were willing to imply a private right of action in anyone whose losses were even remotely connected with the alleged wrongdoing, or even in someone who had suffered no loss if his or her suit would help to encourage compliance with the law. The Supreme Court aided and abetted this development, giving an expansive reading to the terms "fraud" and "purchase or sale" and to the "connection" that had to be found between them.

Starting in 1975, a new conservative majority on the Supreme Court sharply reversed this trend, in a series of decisions giving a narrow reading to the terms of Rule 10b–5 and other antifraud provisions, and limiting the situations in which a private right of action will be implied. The tone of these subsequent Supreme Court decisions is even more important than their actual holdings. They cast doubt on the continued vitality of many of the expansive decisions of the preceding years, even those decisions that have not been specifically overruled. This fact should be kept in mind in evaluating the discussion in the following sections, which summarize the current law governing the application of the Rule.

(A)   ELEMENTS OF 1934 ACT RULE 10b–5

There are three separate clauses in Rule 10b–5, not arranged in a very logical order. Clauses (a) and (c) speak in terms of "fraud" or "deceit" while clause (b) speaks in terms of misstatements or omissions. It is generally assumed, however, that clause (c), which prohibits "any act, practice, or course of business which operates or would operate as [1] a fraud or deceit [2] upon any person [3] in connection with [4] the purchase or sale [5] of any security," has the broadest scope. Each of the five elements of this formulation has given rise to interpretive questions.

"Fraud or Deceit." Rule 10b–5 is an "antifraud" provision. It was adopted by the SEC under authority of a section designed to prohibit "any manipulative or deceptive device or contrivance," and two of its three operative clauses are based on the concept of "fraud" or "deceit". The Supreme Court has held that no person can be found to have violated Rule 10b–5, in either an SEC or a private action, unless the defendant is shown to have acted with "scienter." Aaron v. SEC, 446 U.S. 680 (1980); Ernst and Ernst v. Hochfelder, 425 U.S. 185 (1976). The scienter requirement, in the view of some courts, does not require that the person acted willfully, but may be met by showing that the defendant acted recklessly. See, e.g., Sanders v. John Nuveen, 554 F.2d 790 (7th Cir.1977). Interestingly, the Supreme Court has held

that a violation of clause (2) or (3) of 1933 Act § 17(a) (from which the language of the corresponding clauses of 1934 Act Rule 10b–5 was adapted) can be established without showing scienter. Aaron v. SEC, above. Thus, the language of clauses (b) and (c) of 1934 Act Rule 10b–5, because it is based on 1934 Act § 10(b), has a different meaning than the corresponding language in 1933 Act § 17(a).

A recurrent problem in litigation under 1934 Act Rule 10b–5 has been whether the complaint meets the requirements of Rule 9(b) of the Federal Rules of Civil Procedure that, in cases alleging fraud, the circumstances constituting fraud must be "stated with particularity." See, e.g., O'Brien v. National, 936 F.2d 674 (2d Cir.1991). In the Private Securities Litigation Reform Act of 1995 (discussed in § 20(b) below), Congress provided that, where liability requires "proof that the defendant acted with a particular state of mind, the complaint shall * * * state with particularity facts giving rise to a strong inference that the defendant acted with the required state of mind." 1934 Act § 21D(b). See, e.g., Tellabs, Inc. v. Makor Issues & Rights Ltd., 551 U.S. 308 (2007) (setting forth the applicable pleading standards); In re Silicon Graphics, Inc. Securities Litigation, 183 F.3d 970, 988 (9th Cir.1999) (requiring "deliberate recklessness"). The Act also provides that, where liability of any defendant for money damages depends on his state of mind, the court, on defendant's request, must "submit to the jury a written interrogatory on the issue of each such defendant's state of mind at the time the alleged violation occurred." 1934 Act § 21D(d).

"Upon Any Person." Since the SEC's rule-making power under 1934 Act § 10(b) is to be exercised "for the protection of investors," it can be argued that the only persons entitled to the protection of 1934 Act Rule 10b–5 are those who can be classified as "investors." However, the definition has been stretched in a number of ways. One of the most important came in Hooper v. Mountain States, 282 F.2d 195 (5th Cir.1960), involving a suit by a corporation which had been defrauded into issuing shares for an inadequate consideration. The defendant argued that the issuance of stock was not a "sale" and that the corporation was not an "investor." The court rejected both arguments, holding that the issuance was a "sale" and that the corporation, having parted with shares which had economic value, was in the same position as an investor. This decision is important as the basis for a large number of derivative actions (discussed in § 21(c) below), in which shareholders have alleged that management or controlling shareholders defrauded the corporation by causing it to issue shares to them or their affiliates for an inadequate consideration.

"In Connection with." While the fraud must be "in connection with the purchase or sale," it need not relate to the *terms* of the transaction. In Superintendent v. Bankers Life, 404 U.S. 6 (1971), a group that obtained control of an insurance company caused it to sell certain securities which it owned, then misappropriated the proceeds for their own benefit. The Supreme Court, reversing the court of appeals, held unanimously that "[s]ince there was a

'sale' of a security and since fraud was used 'in connection with' it, there is redress under § 10(b), whatever might be available as a remedy under state law." Subsequent lower court decisions have read this decision narrowly, holding that the fraud must have infected the securities transaction itself, rather than merely involving a misappropriation of the proceeds, see In re Investors Funding, 523 F.Supp. 563 (S.D.N.Y.1980), and that there is no liability when there is a substantial time gap or no direct causal link between the sale and the alleged fraud. See Ketchum v. Green, 557 F.2d 1022 (3d Cir.1977); Rochelle v. Marine Midland, 535 F.2d 523 (9th Cir.1976).

The most important extension of the "in connection with" language came in SEC v. Texas Gulf Sulphur, 401 F.2d 833 (2d Cir.1968). In that case, the court held that misstatements in a press release issued by a publicly-held corporation, which was not at the time engaged in buying or selling any of its own shares, violated 1934 Act Rule 10b–5 because they were made "in connection with" the purchases and sales being made by shareholders in the open market. This holding has formed the basis for a large number of shareholder class actions (discussed in § 20(b) below), alleging damages suffered because of misstatements in a company's reports or press releases. The Second Circuit has continued to give an expansive reading, for example by holding that an advertisement for a drug that appeared in a medical journal could be found to have been made "in connection with the purchase or sale" of a security. In re Carter-Wallace, Inc. Securities Litigation, 150

F.3d 153 (2d Cir.1998). It is not necessary that the
fraud relate directly to the value of the security. See
Comerchero v. Emtek Health Care Systems, Inc., 189
F.3d 472 (9th Cir.1999). And the fraud need not be in
connection with a particular securities transaction.
See SEC v. Zandford, 535 U.S. 813 (2002); United
States v. O'Hagan, 521 U.S. 642 (1997). Thus, for
example, misappropriation of funds from a securities
account implicates Rule 10b–5 event though the
wrongdoing was not traceable to a securities
transaction. SEC v. Zandford, 535 U.S. 813 (2002).

"Purchase or Sale." In the *Hooper* case, *supra,* the
court held that the issuance by a corporation of its
own shares was a "sale" under Rule 10b–5. In its first
decision interpreting 1934 Act Rule 10b–5, the
Supreme Court held that a merger involved a "sale"
of the stock of the disappearing company and a
"purchase" of the stock of the surviving company for
the purposes of the rule. SEC v. National Securities,
393 U.S. 453 (1969). Other types of reorganizations
may or may not be considered a "sale." Compare
International Controls v. Vesco, 490 F.2d 1334 (2d
Cir.1974) (holding a spin-off of a subsidiary to be a
sale), with In re Penn Central, 494 F.2d 528 (3d
Cir.1974) (holding an exchange of shares of an
operating company for those of a newly-formed
holding company not to be a sale).

An oral option to purchase a security satisfies Rule
10b–5's purchase or sale requirement. Wharf
Holdings Limited v. United International, 532 U.S.
588 (2001). This is true even when the alleged fraud

is a secret intention not to honor the rights of the option holder. Id.

The Supreme Court has held that a pledge of securities is a "sale" for purposes of the 1933 Act, since 1933 Act § 2(a)(3) defines "sale" to include "every contract of sale or disposition of a security or interest in a security, for value." Rubin v. United States, 449 U.S. 424 (1981). It is unclear whether a similar result would be reached under the 1934 Act, since 1934 Act § 3(a)(14) defines "sale" only to include "any contract to sell or otherwise dispose of." See Mallis v. FDIC, 568 F.2d 824 (2d Cir.1977), cert. dismissed, 435 U.S. 381 (1978).

"Of Any Security." Rule 10b–5 applies to any purchase or sale by any person of any security. There are no exemptions. It applies to securities which are registered under the 1934 Act, or which are not so registered. It applies to publicly-held companies, to closely-held companies, and to any kind of entity which issues something that can be called a "security." It even applies to "exempted securities," as defined in 1934 Act § 3(a)(12) (including federal, state, and local government securities), which are specifically exempted from certain other provisions of the Act. The Supreme Court's rejection of the "sale of business" doctrine (see § 6(a) above) means that this will probably continue to be the case, despite occasional complaints from judges that Congress could not have intended these local and private disputes to be decided in the federal courts. See Trecker v. Scag, 679 F.2d 703 (7th Cir.1982) (Posner, J., concurring).

(B) CIVIL LIABILITY FOR VIOLATIONS

Rule 10b–5 is worded as a prohibition; there are no express provisions anywhere in the securities laws prescribing any civil liability for its violation. However, starting in 1946, courts have been applying to it the common law tort rule that a person who violates a legislative enactment is liable in damages if the defendant invades an interest of another person that the legislation was intended to protect. Kardon v. National Gypsum, 69 F.Supp. 512 (E.D.Pa.1946). This question of the existence of an "implied private right of action" for violations of the Rule did not reach the Supreme Court until 1971, at which time the Court simply stated in a footnote, without discussion, that "a private right of action is implied under 1934 Act § 10(b)." While the Court, in subsequent decisions, has questioned the rationale for implying private rights of actions under the federal securities laws (see § 37 below), it has not thus far indicated any intention to reexamine the availability of such a right under Rule 10b–5. In fact, the Court has reaffirmed Rule 10b–5's implied remedy.

Overlap with Other Provisions. Recognition of a private right of action for fraudulent misstatements under Rule 10b–5 raises the possibility that such an action may be brought where the misstatement is covered by another, more specific, provision of federal securities law. In SEC v. National Securities, 393 U.S. 453 (1969), the Supreme Court held that Rule 10b–5 could be applied to misstatements in proxy statements, even though proxy solicitation was governed by specific SEC rules under 1934 Act § 14.

Subsequently, the Court has held that suit can be brought under Rule 10b–5 to recover damages resulting from misstatements in a 1933 Act registration statement, even though such misstatements give rise to a specific right of action under 1933 Act § 11. Herman & MacLean v. Huddleston, 459 U.S. 375 (1983). Lower courts have also held that such suits can be brought with respect to misstatements in documents filed under the 1934 Act, as to which there is specific civil liability under 1934 Act § 18. See Ross v. A.H. Robins, 607 F.2d 545 (2d Cir.1979).

The "Purchaser-Seller" Requirement. The most significant court-imposed limitation on private litigation under Rule 10b–5 is the requirement that the plaintiff be either a "purchaser" or "seller" of securities in the transaction being attacked. The problem can arise where a minority shareholder attacks the sale of a controlling block of stock, at a premium over the current market price, as a "fraud" on the minority shareholders. In Birnbaum v. Newport, 193 F.2d 461 (2d Cir.1952), one of the earliest cases under Rule 10b–5, the court held that the purpose of the rule was to protect purchasers and sellers of securities from being defrauded, and that since neither the minority shareholders nor the corporation had purchased or sold any securities, they had no cause of action. (The Second Circuit subsequently held, in a landmark decision, that the transaction attacked in *Birnbaum* involved a breach of the controlling shareholder's fiduciary duty under state law. Perlman v. Feldmann, 219 F.2d 173 (2d Cir.1955).)

The "purchaser-seller" requirement of *Birnbaum* was reaffirmed by the Supreme Court in Blue Chip v. Manor, 421 U.S. 723 (1975). In *Blue Chip,* defendants were obliged under an antitrust decree to offer plaintiffs certain shares in a new company. Plaintiffs alleged that defendants had violated 1934 Act Rule 10b–5 by giving a deceptively pessimistic portrayal of the new company in the prospectus, for the purpose of inducing the plaintiff *not* to buy the shares. While the facts were highly unusual, the court rested its decision denying standing to any person other than a purchaser or seller on the broad policy ground that it would deter "vexatious litigation" which "has a settlement value to the plaintiff out of any proportion to its prospect of success at trial" and which may raise "many rather hazy issues of historical fact the proof of which depend[s] almost entirely on oral testimony." Justice Rehnquist's majority opinion is replete with expressions of hostility to private actions against corporate management, leading dissenting Justice Blackmun to remark that "the Court exhibits a preternatural solicitousness for corporate well-being and a seeming callousness toward the investing public quite out of keeping * * * with our own traditions and the intent of the securities laws."

One important exception to the purchaser-seller requirement is that a person whose shares are automatically converted into shares of another company in a merger put through by means of misleading statements is entitled to sue under Rule 10b–5 as a "forced seller." Vine v. Beneficial Finance, 374 F.2d 627 (2d Cir.1967). Courts have continued to apply the "forced seller" exception after the Supreme

Court decision in *Blue Chip*. See Alley v. Miramon, 614 F.2d 1372, 1387 (5th Cir.1980). However, the forced seller doctrine is narrowly interpreted. Jacobson v. AEG Capital Corp., 50 F.3d 1493, 1499 (9th Cir.1995) (asserting that the "forced sale doctrine does not cut a wide swath"). A would-be-seller—someone who held the securities rather than sell—does not have standing under Rule 10b–5. In Merrill Lynch, Pierce, Fenner & Smith v. Dabit, 547 U.S. 71 (2006), the Supreme Court held that the Securities Litigation Uniform Standards Act (SLUSA) preempts state law claims that could be brought by someone who held, rather than sold, securities. The Court noted that the absence of a Rule 10b–5 remedy reinforced the application of SLUSA's preemptive effect.

Causation. In actions under Rule 10b–5, courts have generally held that the plaintiff must show both "transaction causation," i.e., that the fraud caused the plaintiff to enter into the transaction, and "loss causation," i.e., that the transaction caused the loss to the plaintiff. See, e.g., Schlick v. Penn-Dixie, 507 F.2d 374 (2d Cir.1974). More recently, some courts have gone further and required that the plaintiff demonstrate that the loss was a result of the facts which were misrepresented by the defendant. See, e.g., Bastian v. Petren, 892 F.2d 680 (7th Cir.1990). Congress in 1995 codified this approach by providing that in any private action under the 1934 Act, "the plaintiff shall have the burden of proving that the act or omission of the defendant alleged to violate [the Act] caused the loss for which the plaintiff seeks to recover damages." 1934 Act § 21D(b)(4). See also

Dura Pharmaceuticals, Inc. v. Broudo, 544 U.S. 336 (2005) (discussing loss causation under Rule 10b–5).

§ 19.   INSIDER TRADING

One of the most important applications of 1934 Act Rule 10b–5 is its use as a sanction against "insider trading"—purchases or sales by persons who have access to information that is not available to those with whom they deal or to traders generally.

Early applications of the rule focused on the situation with which it was specifically designed to deal—purchases in direct transactions by the corporation or its officers without disclosure of material favorable information about the company's affairs. Ward la France, 13 SEC 373 (1943); Speed v. Transamerica, 99 F.Supp. 808 (D.Del.1951). In this context, it was available to supplement state common law, which in most states did not afford a remedy to the aggrieved seller in this situation in the absence of affirmative misstatements or "special circumstances."

In a series of administrative decisions and injunctive proceedings, commencing in 1961, the SEC greatly broadened the applicability of Rule 10b–5 as a general prohibition against any trading on "inside information" in anonymous stock exchange transactions as well as in face-to-face dealings. The three most significant decisions were Cady Roberts, 40 SEC 907 (1961), SEC v. Texas Gulf Sulphur, 401 F.2d 833 (2d Cir.1968), and Investors Management, 44 SEC 633 (1971). However, the subsequent decisions of the Supreme Court in Chiarella v. United

States, 445 U.S. 222 (1980), and Dirks v. SEC, 463 U.S. 646 (1983), have cast doubt on some of the doctrines developed in those decisions.

(A) ELEMENTS OF THE VIOLATION

In *Cady Roberts,* a partner in a brokerage firm received a message from a director of Curtiss-Wright that the board of directors had just voted to cut the dividend. He immediately placed orders to sell Curtiss-Wright stock for some of his customers, and the sales were made before the news of the dividend cut was generally disseminated. In *Texas Gulf Sulphur,* officers and employees of the company made substantial purchases of the company's stock after learning that exploratory drilling on one of the company's properties showed promise of an extraordinary ore discovery (although the drilling had not gone far enough to establish whether there was a commercially exploitable body of ore). In *Investors Management,* an aircraft manufacturer disclosed to a broker-dealer, which was acting as principal underwriter for a proposed debenture issue, that its earnings for the current year would be substantially less than it had previously forecast publicly. The broker-dealer's underwriting department passed the information to members of its sales department, who in turn passed it to representatives of major institutional clients. The institutions sold large amounts of stock before the revised earnings estimate became public.

In all three cases, the persons who effected the transactions (or who passed information to those persons) were held to have violated Rule 10b–5.

In *Chiarella,* an employee of a financial printing firm, who was working on documents relating to contemplated tender offers, ascertained the identities of the companies which were the targets of those offers, purchased stock in those companies, and sold the stock at a profit after the tender offers were announced. The Supreme Court reversed his conviction of a criminal violation of Rule 10b–5.

In *Dirks,* a security analyst received confidential information from a former employee of Equity Funding Corporation (EFC) to the effect that a large percentage of EFC's policies were fake. The employee's motivation in giving Dirks the information was to obtain his aid in exposing the fraud. While attempting to ascertain the truth of these allegations, Dirks passed along the information to a number of his institutional clients, who sold large amounts of EFC stock. Subsequently, the allegations were confirmed and EFC went into bankruptcy. The SEC brought a disciplinary proceeding against Dirks, alleging that he had violated Rule 10b–5 by giving the information to his clients. The Supreme Court held that Dirks had not acted illegally, since (a) he owed no duty to purchasers of EFC stock, and (b) he could not be found to have aided and abetted a violation by the insider from whom he obtained the information, since the insider had not acted from an improper motive in giving the information to him.

The scope of the prohibition, as it emerges from these decisions, seems roughly as follows:

Which Clause Is Violated? The opinions have not been terribly clear as to which clause of the rule prohibits insider trading. Since all of the cases involved total nondisclosure, they presumably did not violate clause (b), which requires some "statement." In *Cady Roberts,* above, the Commission said that the broker's conduct "at least violated clause (c) as a practice which operated as a fraud or deceit upon the purchasers" and that there was therefore no need to decide the scope of clauses (a) and (b). Subsequent decisions have not significantly clarified this question.

To Whom Is the Duty Owed? If clause (c) is violated, is it because of a "fraud or deceit" on the company or on persons on the other side of the market? In *Cady Roberts,* the Commission indicated that there were elements of both: "[T]he obligation rests on two principal elements; first, the existence of a relationship giving access, directly or indirectly, to information intended to be available only for a corporate purpose and not for the personal benefit of anyone, and second, the inherent unfairness involved where a party takes advantage of such information knowing it is unavailable to those with whom he is dealing."

In *Chiarella,* above, the Supreme Court sharply limited the second element, holding that "[w]hen an allegation of fraud is based upon nondisclosure, there can be no fraud absent a duty to speak * * * ," which "aris[es] from a relationship of trust and confidence

between parties to a transaction" and that the lower
courts had "failed to identify a relationship between
[Chiarella] and the sellers that could give rise to a
duty." Stating that "not every instance of financial
unfairness constitutes fraudulent activity under
§ 10(b)," the Court stated flatly that "[a] duty to
disclose under § 10(b) does not arise from the mere
possession of nonpublic market information." With
respect to the first element, the Court declined to
pass on the question whether Chiarella's breach of
duty to his employer and to the corporations making
the tender offers would support a conviction under
1934 Act Rule 10b–5, since this "misappropriation"
theory had not been properly submitted to the jury.
The Supreme Court returned to the question in
United States v. O'Hagan, 521 U.S. 642 (1997), and
held that misappropriation does constitute a
violation of 1934 Act § 10(b) because it involves
"deception" of the person from whom the information
was obtained and to whom the defendant does not
disclose his intention to trade.

What Is "Material" Information? There was no
question that the dividend cut, in *Cady Roberts,* the
reduced earnings, in *Investors Management,* and the
proposed tender offers, in *Chiarella,* were "material"
in the sense that they would affect the willingness of
an investor to buy or sell the stock at the current
price. In *Texas Gulf Sulphur*, however, the
defendants argued that the information about the ore
discovery did not become "material" until further
drilling established the existence of a commercially
mineable ore body. They pointed to the SEC's own
rules under Regulation A, prohibiting a company

from making any statement about the existence of an ore body unless it was sufficiently tested to be properly classified as "proven" or "probable." The court held, however, that the test of "materiality" for Rule 10b–5 purposes was not whether the company would be permitted to disclose the information if it were selling securities, but whether it was the kind of information that might affect the judgment of reasonable investors, including "speculative" as well as "conservative" investors. On this question, the court found that the size and timing of the purchases, by the defendants, some of whom had never owned TGS stock, were "highly pertinent evidence and the only truly objective evidence of the materiality of the discovery."

When Is Information "Nonpublic"? Under *Texas Gulf Sulphur*, an insider may not act at the moment the company makes a public announcement of the information, but must wait "until the news could reasonably have been expected to appear over the media of widest circulation." In *Investors Management*, above, defendants argued that the information about the company's reduced earnings was already "public" because it was the subject of rumors circulating in the financial community. The Commission held, however, that the information they received was different from the information previously circulating, since it was (1) more specific and (2) more trustworthy, having come from a firm known to be acting as underwriter for the company. Information is public when it is available to the public generally whether in SEC filings, the media, or other publicly available sources. See U.S. v.

Contorinis, 692 F.3d 136, 143 (2d Cir. 2012). For insider trading purposes, publicly available information is considered public even if known by only a few people. Id. It is not always easy to draw the line between public and nonpublic information

Who Is an "Insider"? *Cady Roberts* held that 1934 Act Rule 10b–5, unlike 1934 Act § 16(b), extends beyond officers, directors, and major stockholders to anyone who receives information from a corporate source. *Texas Gulf Sulphur* established that a person who passes on inside information to another person who effects a transaction is as culpable as a person who utilizes it for his own account, and *Investors Management* established the liability of the indirect "tippee," no matter how many links there are in the chain of information.

"Outsider Trading" and Misappropriation. In *Chiarella,* the Supreme Court implicitly recognized "a relationship of trust and confidence between the shareholders of a corporation and those insiders who have obtained confidential information by reason of their position with that corporation" and a resulting "duty to disclose because of the necessity of preventing a corporate insider from taking unfair advantage of the uninformed minority stockholders." The Court also indicated that the liability of a "tippee" could be "viewed as arising from his role as a participant after the fact in the insider's breach of a fiduciary duty." The decision in *Dirks* and subsequent lower court cases limit tippee liability further by holding that the tippee can be held liable only if the information was passed to the tippee for

the personal benefit of the tipper, and if the tippee knew or had reason to know that the tipper had satisfied all the elements of tipper liability.

The Supreme Court in *Dirks* indicated that the personal benefit to the tipper does not have to be financial in nature. It can include a desire to provide a gift to the tippee of the nonpublic information so the tippee can trade on the basis of the information. Dirks v. SEC, 463 U.S. 646, 103 S. Ct. 3255 (1983). It can also include an associational benefit. See, e.g., SEC v. Yun, 327 F.3d 1263, Fed. Sec. L. Rep. (CCH) ¶ 92408, 14 A.L.R. Fed. 2d 819 (11th Cir. 2003) (ongoing business relationship between tipper and tippee could be sufficient to establish insider trading liability). It may also include a reputational benefit. However, according to a three-judge panel of the Second Circuit in United States v. Newman, 773 F.3d 438 (2d Cir. 2014), *cert denied,* 2015 WL 4575840 (2015), the mere existence of a friendship between the tipper and tippee is not sufficient to establish insider trading liability. As explained by the Second Circuit, proof of "a relationship between the insider and the recipient that suggests a *quid pro quo*" or "an intention to benefit the [tippee]" must be established. Id. The three judge panel ruling by the Second Circuit in *Newman* narrows the approach to personal benefit that had been applied previously. The SEC took issue with the court's interpretation of personal benefit, maintaining that the Supreme Court in *Dirks* and other courts support the conclusion that friendship can provide the basis for an inference of a personal benefit. Id. However, the Supreme Court denied certiorari. In contrast to the Second Circuit in

Newman, the Ninth Circuit indicated that a broader view of personal benefit is appropriate. United States v. Salman, 792 F.3d 1087 (9th Cir. 2015), *cert. granted* 2016 WL 207256 (2016). The Supreme Court granted certiorari in the Ninth Circuit case differing with *Newman* and thus will have the opportunity to clarify the scope of the personal benefit requirement for tipper liability.

A tippee will be guilty of insider trading only if the tippee had knowledge of the personal benefit to the tipper that creates liability for the improper tip. United States v. Newman, 773 F.3d 438 (2d Cir. 2014), *cert denied,* 2015 WL 4575840 (2015) (reversing convictions where jury instructions did not require a finding that tippee knew of the personal benefit to the tipper). It is possible, however, that the federal Mail and Wire Fraud statutes may provide a way to lessen or avoid this requirement under Rule 10b–5. See William S. Wang, Application of the Federal Mail and Wire Fraud Statutes to Criminal Liability for Stock Market Insider Trading and Tipping, 70 U. Miami L. Rev. 220 (2015).

1934 Act Rule 10b5–2, adopted in 2000, sets forth "three non-exclusive bases for determining that a duty of trust or confidence was owed by a person receiving information: (1) when the person agreed to keep information confidential; (2) when the persons involved in the communication had a history, pattern, or practice of sharing confidences that resulted in a reasonable expectation of confidentiality; and (3) when the person who provided the information was a spouse, parent, child, or sibling of the person who received the information, unless it were shown affirmatively, based on the facts and circumstances of that family relationship, that there was no reasonable expectation of confidentiality." Sec. Exch. Act Rel. No. 34–42259 (1999). Rule 10b5–2 thus clarifies three situations in which the misappropriation theory applies but leaves it open to the courts to apply the doctrine in other contexts as well. At least one court has held that an expectation of confidentiality is not sufficient to trigger Rule 10b–5's disclose or abstain rule. See United States v. Kim, 184 F.Supp.2d 1006 (N.D.Cal.2002) (also questioning whether at least in criminal cases Rule 10b5–2 goes beyond the scope of the statute). A theft of information has been held insufficient to trigger Rule 10b–5's disclose or abstain rule. See SEC v. Dorozhko, 606 F.Supp.2d 321 (S.D.N.Y. 2008) (computer hacker who traded on stolen information did not violate Rule 10b–5). The Second Circuit reversed, agreeing that the hacker was not under a fiduciary or other duty that triggered the disclose or abstain rule. SEC v. Dorozhko, 2009 WL 2169201 (2d Cir. 2009). However, the hacker could nevertheless be held accountable for the trades to the extent he acquired the nonpublic information through misrepresentation. Id. The Second Circuit sent the case back to the district court to determine whether the hacker obtained the information in a deceptive manner through a misrepresentation such as misrepresenting his identity.

Rule 10b5–2 indicates that a contractual or other relational basis for an expectation of confidentiality may be sufficient to trigger Rule 10b–5. Although the

SEC maintains that a contractual confidentiality obligation is sufficient, this has been challenged as too broad a view. Critics of the SEC view contend that the obligation must be fiduciary in nature. The SEC prevailed on this issue in Cuban, 2009 WL 2096166 (N.D. Texas 2009), to the extent that breach of an express or implied agreement not to use the information can support an insider trading claim. The court, however, found a distinction between a non-use agreement and a confidentiality agreement, which standing alone will not support the disclose or abstain obligation. It has also been questioned whether the marital relationship can trigger the Rule 10b–5 obligation since it is not ordinarily considered to be one that is fiduciary in nature.

The *Chiarella* decision also raised the question whether there can be any liability under Rule 10b–5 for trading on the basis of nonpublic "market information," such as a prospective tender offer, where the source of the information has no connection with the company whose shares are being traded. With respect to tender offers, the SEC adopted 1934 Act Rule 14e–3, which makes it illegal for any person to purchase or sell a security while in possession of material nonpublic information about a prospective tender offer if the purchaser or seller knows or has reason to know that such information emanates from either the offering person or the issuer or persons acting on their behalf. Defendants accused of violating the Rule challenged its validity on the ground that 1934 Act § 14(e) prohibits only "fraudulent, deceptive, or manipulative" acts and that Rule 14e–3 reaches uses of nonpublic information that could not be deemed "fraudulent" under the Supreme Court decision in *Chiarella*. When the issue reached the Supreme Court in the *O'Hagan* case, above, the Court upheld the validity of the Rule on the ground that, "under § 14(e), the Commission may prohibit acts, not themselves fraudulent under the common law or § 10(b), if the prohibition is 'reasonably designed to prevent * * * acts and practices [that] are fraudulent.'"

Scienter. In *Investors Management,* above, the Commission rejected the contention that, in order to violate Rule 10b–5, a tippee must have "actual knowledge that the information was disclosed in a breach of fiduciary duty," and held that it was sufficient that the tippee "know or have reason to know that it was non-public and had been obtained improperly by selective revelation or otherwise." The Commission indicated that liability would also attach where the tippee "knew or had reason to know that the information was obtained by industrial espionage, commercial bribery or the like." As far as the "tipper" is concerned, "[o]ne who deliberately tips information which he knows to be material and non-public to an outsider who may reasonably be expected to use it to his advantage has the requisite scienter." Elkind v. Liggett & Myers, 635 F.2d 156, 167 (2d Cir.1980).

Causation. In *Investors Management*, above, the Commission held that where various factors might have affected a tippee's decision to buy or sell, it is only necessary to show that the inside information was "*a* factor" in the decision, and that "where a

transaction of the kind indicated by the information
* * * is effected by the recipient prior to its public
dissemination, an inference arises that the
information was such a factor." As a general
proposition, it must be shown that the defendant
actually used the nonpublic information to his or her
advantage but such use can be presumed from the
mere possession of the information. United States v.
Smith, 155 F.3d 1051 (9th Cir.1998); SEC v. Adler,
137 F.3d 1325 (11th Cir.1998). 1934 Act Rule 10b5–1
sets forth a safe harbor from the inference that
trading while in possession of nonpublic information
was based on improper use of the information. In
essence, Rule 10b5–1 provides that there is no
liability if the transaction is made pursuant to a bona
fide arrangement made prior to the possession of the
nonpublic information.

Countervailing Fiduciary Obligations. In *Texas
Gulf Sulphur,* above, defendants argued that they
could not disclose the information about the ore
discovery because the corporation was engaged in
acquiring options to purchase the land surrounding
the exploration site. The court, while considering this
a "legitimate corporate objective" (itself an
interesting commentary on the differing standards in
land transactions and securities transactions), held
that it was "no justification" for trading; if the
insiders could not disclose, they "should have kept
out of the market until disclosure was accomplished."

In *Cady Roberts,* above, defendant argued that he
had a fiduciary obligation to his customers to sell for
their account when he came into possession of

adverse information. The Commission rejected this defense: "clients may not expect of a broker the benefits of his inside information at the expense of the public generally." This may create a dilemma for brokers. In Slade v. Shearson, 1974 WL 376 (S.D.N.Y.), plaintiff alleged that Shearson had solicited customer purchases of Tidal Marine stock at a time when it was in possession of material non-public adverse information, which it had received from Tidal Marine in its capacity as an investment banker for that company. Shearson moved for summary judgment, arguing that under the SEC's interpretations of Rule 10b–5, "even if Shearson's corporate finance department had known this non-public information, it was precluded from using it to prevent the solicitation of purchases by its retail sales force until the information was made public." The court denied the motion, holding that prior decisions under Rule 10b–5 held only that inside information could not be disclosed to favored customers, and that its fiduciary obligations to its customers required it to refrain from making affirmative recommendations under the circumstances.

To deal with this problem, many commercial banks and broker-dealers have established "firewalls" barring communication between their commercial banking or underwriting departments, on the one side, and their investment advisory or sales departments, on the other, to prevent the transmission of "inside" information and the liabilities that may result from its use or non-use.

(B) CIVIL LIABILITY

As noted above, a violation of Rule 10b–5 has been held to give rise to a private right of action by a person who can show that the violator invaded an interest of his which the rule was designed to protect. As applied to insider trading, this doctrine has raised difficult questions. The nature of the questions differs depending on (1) whether the transaction involves direct dealings or is effected through the impersonal facilities of an exchange, and (2) whether the right is being asserted by the person on the other side of the transaction or by or on behalf of the corporation.

Claims by the Seller (Purchaser). The operative provisions of Rule 10b–5 are worded in terms of "fraud or deceit." A common law action for deceit requires a showing of (1) false representation of fact, (2) knowledge by defendant that it is false (scienter), (3) intention to induce plaintiff to act, (4) justifiable reliance by plaintiff, and (5) damage to plaintiff. The decisions involving civil liabilities for violation of Rule 10b–5 have evidenced a progressive dilution of these requirements.

Direct Dealings. In List v. Fashion Park, 340 F.2d 457 (2d Cir.1965), plaintiff authorized his broker to sell shares at not less than $18 a share. Defendant, acting through his own broker, purchased the shares at $18.50 and plaintiff subsequently sued him, alleging that defendant had failed to disclose (1) that he was a director of the company and (2) that negotiations were pending that eventually resulted in a merger of the company that caused the stock to be worth $50 a share. The court held, first, that, in order to recover, plaintiff was not required to show an affirmative misrepresentation; non-disclosure of a material fact was sufficient under clause (c) of Rule 10b–5. Second, to show reliance, plaintiff need only show that the undisclosed facts would have affected his judgment (i.e., the "materiality" test, with plaintiff substituted for the "reasonable investor"). However, the court found that the facts as known to the defendant at the time of the transaction would not have affected the plaintiff's judgment, and denied him recovery. (The court was obviously impressed by the fact that the defendant had resold most of the shares at a profit of only $1 a share.)

In Affiliated Ute Citizens v. United States, 406 U.S. 128 (1972), the Supreme Court collapsed the requirements still further. Defendants had purchased shares of the Ute Development Corporation from members of the tribe without telling them that the shares were then trading at higher prices in another market. The Court held that defendants had no right to remain silent:

> "Under the circumstances of this case, involving primarily a failure to disclose, positive proof of reliance is not a prerequisite to recovery. All that is necessary is that the facts withheld be material in the sense that a reasonable investor might have considered them important in the making of this decision. This obligation to disclose and this withholding of a material fact establish the requisite element of causation in fact."

Open Market Transactions. When an "insider" buys or sells on a stock exchange without disclosing material facts, there is an additional problem. Not only will there be nobody on the other side of the market who can show "reliance" in the traditional sense; there will normally be nobody who is able to trace the shares he or she had sold or bought to the defendant.

In 1952, the Second Circuit affirmed a decision that plaintiffs who purchased shares on an exchange in November and December could not recover damages from insiders who had sold on the exchange between March and October and had failed to disclose material adverse information. The court said that a "semblance of privity" between the seller and the buyer was required. Joseph v. Farnsworth, 99 F.Supp. 701 (S.D.N.Y.1951), aff'd, 198 F.2d 883 (2d Cir.1952).

In 1974, the Second Circuit reversed this position and held that privity was not required in an insider trading case under Rule 10b–5. It held that a class action could be brought on behalf of all persons who purchased stock of a company on an exchange during the period that defendants were selling that stock on the basis of inside information. Shapiro v. Merrill Lynch, 495 F.2d 228 (2d Cir.1974). With respect to defendant's argument that their sales could not be said to have "caused" plaintiffs' losses, the court simply cited *Affiliated Ute* for the proposition that the nondisclosure of material information established the requisite element of causation in fact.

The *Shapiro* decision of course raised a difficult question of damages. The court recognized that if damages were measured by the "losses" suffered by all members of the class, the liability would be "Draconian" and left to the district court "the fashioning of appropriate relief, including the proper measure of damages."

This problem of "Draconian liability" led the Sixth Circuit to reject the idea of any civil liability in this situation. In Fridrich v. Bradford, 542 F.2d 307 (6th Cir.1976), the court held that insiders who bought in the open market on the basis of nonpublic information were not liable to persons selling in the open market during the same period on the ground that "defendants' act of trading with third persons was not causally connected with any claimed loss by plaintiffs who traded on the impersonal market and who were otherwise unaffected by the wrongful acts of the insider." *Affiliated Ute* was distinguished on the basis of the face-to-face dealings and the pre-existing relationship between the parties.

The Second Circuit, however, dealt with the damage question in a different way. In Elkind v. Liggett & Myers, 635 F.2d 156, 172 (2d Cir.1980), the court adopted a "disgorgement" approach. Under that approach, any uninformed investor may sue for the difference between what the investor paid (or received) for his stock and the market value that it reached a reasonable time after public disclosure of the inside information, but the total recovery by all such persons is limited to "the amount gained by the [insider] as a result of his selling [or purchasing] at the earlier date rather than delaying his sale [or purchase] until the parties could trade on an equal informational basis." This approach, adapted from the proposed Federal Securities Code, seems to be the most reasonable compromise between imposing "Draconian" liability or no liability at all. As discussed more fully below, 1934 Act § 20A adopted the disgorgement measure of damages for private suits. See also 1934 Act § 21A (permitting disgorgement and penalties in actions brought by the SEC).

Recovery by the Company. One element of the obligation under Rule 10b–5 to refrain from trading on inside information is "the existence of a relationship giving access to information intended to be available only for a corporate purpose and not for the personal benefit of anyone." Cady Roberts, *supra.* It would therefore seem that the company (or a shareholder suing derivatively on its behalf) should have a right of action under Rule 10b–5 to recover the insider's trading profits, at least where the information he or she used was intended solely for corporate purposes. However, one significant court-imposed limitation on private rights of action under Rule 10b–5 (see § 18(b) above) is that the person bringing the action must be a "purchaser" or "seller" of securities in the transaction in question. The courts have accordingly held that the issuer may not sue to recover an insider's trading profits under Rule 10b–5. See, e.g., Davidge v. White, 377 F.Supp. 1084 (S.D.N.Y.1974).

There are, however, three alternative ways in which the insider's profits may be recovered by the corporation. First, they may be recoverable under 1934 Act § 16(b). However, this will only apply if the insider is an officer, director, or 10% shareholder, and if there was a matching purchase and sale within a six-month period.

Second, where the SEC brings an injunctive action against an insider for trading in violation of Rule 10b–5, it may request, and the court may grant, as "ancillary relief," a decree ordering the defendant to turn over his or her profits to the company, "subject to disposition in such manner as the court may direct." See SEC v. Texas Gulf Sulphur, 312 F.Supp. 77 (S.D.N.Y.1970), aff'd, 446 F.2d 1301 (2d Cir.1971); SEC v. Golconda, 327 F.Supp. 257 (S.D.N.Y.1971). See also 1934 Act § 21A.

Third, in certain states, a corporation may be able to recover insider trading profits of its officers or directors under common law agency principles of fiduciary duty. See Diamond v. Oreamuno, 24 N.Y.2d 494, 301 N.Y.S.2d 78, 248 N.E.2d 910 (1969); Brophy v. Cities Service, 31 Del.Ch. 241, 70 A.2d 5 (1949); Rest.2d, Agency § 388, Comment c. However, other courts have rejected the approach taken in these cases, holding that the corporation has no right to recover unless it suffered actual damage. Freeman v. Decio, 584 F.2d 186 (7th Cir.1978); Schein v. Chasen, 313 So.2d 739 (Fla.1975).

In view of the prevailing uncertainty as to the availability of a private damage remedy for insider trading and as to the adequacy of existing penalties in deterring insider trading, the SEC urged Congress to enact stiffer sanctions. Congress responded with two pieces of legislation, the Insider Trading Sanctions Act of 1984 (ITSA) and the Insider Trading and Securities Fraud Enforcement Act of 1988 (ITSFEA), adding §§ 20A and 21A to the 1934 Act.

Under 1934 Act § 21A, if any person violates the 1934 Act or any rule thereunder by trading while in possession of material nonpublic information or by communicating such information in connection with a securities transaction, the SEC can go to court to seek a civil penalty equal to three times the amount of the profit gained or the loss avoided by the illegal transaction. "Profit" or "loss" is defined as the difference between the purchase or sale price and the value of the security a reasonable period after public dissemination of the nonpublic information. The SEC may seek such a penalty both against the person who committed the violation and on any person who "controlled" the violator (which, in most cases, will mean the firm with which the violator is associated). The penalty imposed on the "controlling person" cannot exceed $1 million and can only be imposed if the SEC establishes that such person knowingly or recklessly failed to take appropriate steps or establish adequate procedures to prevent such violations. The amount of the penalty is reduced by any amount the defendant is required to disgorge in an injunction action brought by the Commission under 1934 Act § 21(d).

To provide an incentive for people to "blow the whistle" on insider trading, 1934 Act § 21A(e) provides that up to 10% of any civil penalty recovered by the SEC may, in the SEC's discretion, be paid as a bounty to any person or persons who provide information leading to the imposition of the penalty.

Under 1934 Act § 20A, any person who violates the 1934 Act or any rule thereunder by trading while in possession of material nonpublic information is liable to any person who was "contemporaneously" trading the same security on the other side of the market. Liability under this Section also extends to any person who communicates material nonpublic information and to any person who "controls" the violator, and is similarly reduced by the amount of any disgorgement in an injunction action brought by the SEC.

An action under either 1934 Act § 20A or § 21A may be brought up to five years after the last violation, a considerably longer statute of limitations than that which is found in other specific civil liability provisions of the federal securities laws (see § 37(b) below).

During the hearings on ITSA, Congress was urged to define more precisely the kind of insider trading that would give rise to liability. However, faced with irreconcilable differences between the SEC and industry views, Congress finally opted to define the offense simply by reference to existing law.

The 1988 amendment also modified 1934 Act § 32 to increase the maximum criminal penalty for violation of the Act from $100,000 to $1 million, in the case of individuals, and from $500,000 to $2.5 million, in the case of other entities.

§ 20.   CORPORATE MISSTATEMENTS

The specific disclosure requirements of 1934 Act §§ 13 and 14 apply only to reports, proxy statements, and other documents filed with the SEC by companies that have securities registered under 1934 Act § 12. The provisions of 1934 Act § 10(b) and Rule 10b–5, however, are applicable to any statement, in the form of a report, press release, or other document, made by any issuer.

(A)   ELEMENTS OF THE VIOLATION

The "In Connection with" Requirement. In SEC v. Texas Gulf Sulphur, 401 F.2d 833 (2d Cir.1968), the Commission argued that TGS had violated Rule 10b–5(b) by issuing a press release which described the current status of its exploration of a potential ore body in an unduly pessimistic manner. TGS argued that the press release was not subject to Rule 10b–5 because it was not issued "in connection with the purchase or sale of any security," since the company was not engaged in buying or selling any securities at the time. The court held, however, that the requirement was satisfied if there was a connection between the statement and transactions by and among members of the public, i.e., if it was "of a sort that would cause reasonable investors to rely thereon, and, in connection therewith, so relying, cause them to purchase or sell a corporation's securities." See also Basic, Inc. v. Levinson, 485 U.S. 224 (1988).

Scienter. An inaccurate corporate statement could be alleged to violate clause (2) of Rule 10b–5, which speaks in terms of "untrue statements or omissions" rather than in terms of "fraud." In *Texas Gulf Sulphur,* the court said that the first question in determining whether a corporate statement violated Rule 10b–5 was whether it was "misleading to the reasonable investor." If the statement was found to be misleading, the court held that the company would have violated 1934 Act Rule 10b–5 if "its issuance resulted from a lack of due diligence," importing the affirmative defense found in 1933 Act § 11 (see § 11(b) above). In light of the Supreme Court's subsequent decisions in *Hochfelder* and *Aaron* (see § 18 above), however, it is clear that neither the corporation nor any other person involved in the issuance of a misleading statement can be held to have violated Rule 10b–5 unless they acted with *scienter.*

Failure to Make a Statement. Can a company be held liable under Rule 10b–5 for failing to make a statement correcting prior statements that are no longer accurate? In Financial Industrial Fund v. McDonnell Douglas, 474 F.2d 514 (10th Cir.1973), a mutual fund sued for losses of $700,000 on its purchase of Douglas stock, alleging that the company had withheld an announcement of reduced earnings beyond the point in time at which the relevant facts were available to it. The court of appeals reversed a jury verdict for the plaintiff, holding that there was no proof that Douglas had unduly delayed its announcement. Similarly, in State Teachers v. Fluor, 654 F.2d 843 (2d Cir.1981), the court held that a company had not violated Rule 10b–5 by (a) withholding announcement of a pending contract until all facts were available and (b) failing to request the New York Stock Exchange to suspend trading in the stock until an announcement could be made.

A company has no obligation to correct erroneous projections of its earnings being made by analysts or other outsiders, unless it "so involve[s] itself in the preparation of reports and projections by outsiders as to assume a duty to correct material errors in those projections," Elkind v. Liggett & Myers, 635 F.2d 156, 163 (2d Cir.1980). With regard to projections made by the company itself, courts have generally found no duty to correct or update a projection which has become inaccurate because of events occurring after the projection was made. Stransky v. Cummins, 51 F.3d 1329 (7th Cir.1995); Backman v. Polaroid, 910 F.2d 10 (1st Cir.1990).

A number of cases have raised the question of what disclosure a company must make concerning pending merger negotiations, particularly when rumors circulating in the market are causing heavy trading and price increases in the company's stock. In Basic v. Levinson, 485 U.S. 224 (1988), the Supreme Court rejected the view, espoused in some lower court decisions, that merger negotiations do not become "material" until there is an "agreement in principle" as to the price and structure of the transaction, and that companies are therefore free to deny the existence of any negotiations prior to that time. The Court held that merger discussions are subject to the same test of materiality as other types of contingent or speculative information, namely "a balancing of both the indicated probability that the event will occur and the anticipated magnitude of the event in light of the totality of the company activity."

It formerly was a practice of many companies to disseminate information into the public realm by selectively disclosing information to analysts and then letting that information trickle into the market. This practice gave an informational advantage to those select analysts who could then profit from the information before it became known to the public generally. In 2000, the SEC adopted Regulation FD in order to level the playing field concerning access to information about a company that comes from the company. Sec. Exch. Act Rel. 34–43154 (2000). Under Regulation FD, selective disclosure by a company to analysts or other third parties is no longer permitted. Regulation FD requires companies who make disclosures to analysts to make prompt public announcements so that all investors can have access to the same information.

(B) CIVIL LIABILITY

If a company issues a misleading report or press release, and is found to have acted with the requisite degree of "scienter," it may be held liable in damages to people who purchased or sold its securities before corrected information was made public. The questions are: to whom can it be held liable, and for how much?

Reliance. One important question is whether a plaintiff must show that he or she actually relied on the misleading statement when the plaintiff purchased or sold. In 1975, the Ninth Circuit held that the issuance of a misleading statement constitutes a "fraud on the market." Under this approach, plaintiff need not show that he or she actually relied on the misleading statement; the plaintiff need only show that he or she bought or sold at a price which was affected by the statement. Blackie v. Barrack, 524 F.2d 891 (9th Cir.1975). In 1988, the Supreme Court, in a 4–2 decision with 3 justices not participating, upheld the application of the "fraud on the market" theory to establish a rebuttable presumption of reliance. Halliburton Co. v. Erica P. John Fund, Inc., 134 S. Ct. 2398 (2014); Basic v. Levinson, 485 U.S. 224 (1988).

Causation. In Dura Pharmaceuticals, Inc. v. Broudo, 544 U.S. 336 (2005), the Supreme Court held that change in the stock price following the allegedly misleading disclosures may not be sufficient to show the loss causation necessary to establish a private remedy. The Court thus held that a plaintiff cannot establish loss causation merely by alleging that security price was inflated because of misrepresentation.

Damages. Since the corporation being sued in these cases has generally not engaged in transactions with the plaintiff, courts have held that an "out of pocket" measure of damages, rather than a "rescission" measure of damages, (see § 41 below), is appropriate. Huddleston v. Herman, 640 F.2d 534 (5th Cir.1981); Green v. Occidental, 541 F.2d 1335 (9th Cir.1976) (Sneed, J., concurring).

Overlap with Other Provisions. If the alleged misstatement is made in a 1933 Act registration statement or a 1934 Act report, can a purchaser (or seller) sue for damages under 1934 Act Rule 10b–5 instead of pursuing his remedies under 1933 Act § 11 or 1934 Act § 18? In Herman & MacLean v. Huddleston, 459 U.S. 375 (1983), the Supreme Court held that a purchaser could sue under Rule 10b–5 for misstatements in a registration statement covered by § 11 of the 1933 Act, provided the plaintiff is able to prove that the defendant acted fraudulently or with *scienter.* Courts of appeals have reached the same result with respect to misstatements in documents filed under the 1934 Act. See Ross v. A.H. Robins Co., Inc., 607 F.2d 545 (2d Cir.1979).

1995 Reform Act. Congressional concern about the potential for abuse in class action litigation against publicly-held corporations for alleged misstatements led to the enactment of the Private Securities Litigation Reform Act of 1995 (PSLRA). The procedural reforms adopted in PSLRA are described in § 38(a) below. The Act also stiffened the standards for pleading fraud (see § 18(a) above) established a new causation standard (see § 18(b) above) and limited the liabilities of defendants who are not specifically found to have acted willfully (see § 39 below).

§ 21. CORPORATE MISMANAGEMENT

One of the most important and controversial applications of Rule 10b–5 has been in the area of abuses by corporate management or controlling shareholders that may also constitute violations of their fiduciary duties under state corporation law. Minority shareholders, suing individually, in class actions, or derivatively on behalf of the corporation, have brought actions under Rule 10b–5 to avoid substantive or procedural obstacles in state law. Among the types of transactions which have been attacked are sales of controlling stock interests at a premium, mergers or reorganizations, and sales and purchases by corporations of their own or other securities.

A recurrent type of claim under Rule 10b–5 is a derivative suit by a minority shareholder alleging that the corporation was caused to issue its own securities for an inadequate consideration, usually for the benefit of a controlling person. As far back as 1960, it was held that a corporation which was fraudulently induced to issue its own stock for inadequate consideration was a defrauded "seller" within the protection of the rule. Hooper v. Mountain States, 282 F.2d 195 (5th Cir.1960). However, this left the question of how one defrauds a corporation. If the board of directors makes the decision to issue the securities, and if some or all of the directors are participants in the alleged fraudulent scheme, who can be said to be defrauding whom?

In a pair of 1964 decisions, the Second Circuit drew the distinction that if material information is

withheld from any of the directors, there can be said
to be a fraud on the corporation under 1934 Act Rule
10b–5, but that if all the directors were in on the
scheme, there could be no deception, and the only
available remedy was under state law. Compare
Ruckle v. Roto American, 339 F.2d 24 (2d Cir.1964)
with O'Neill v. Maytag, 339 F.2d 764 (2d Cir.1964).

This distinction did not make much sense, and in
1968 it was rejected in favor of a rule that fraud could
be shown even where all the directors were involved.
"In order to establish fraud it is surely not necessary
to show that the directors deceived themselves. It
must be enough to show that they deceived the
shareholders, the real owners of the property with
which the directors were dealing." Schoenbaum v.
Firstbrook, 405 F.2d 200, 215 (2d Cir.1968); see also
Pappas v. Moss, 393 F.2d 865 (3d Cir.1968).

While *Schoenbaum* and *Pappas* established that
fraud on the "independent" shareholders constituted
fraud on the corporation, they did not establish
whether fraud could be alleged simply by asserting
that the terms of the transaction were substantively
unfair, or whether it was necessary to allege that
there was a misstatement or withholding of material
information. The Supreme Court put the issue to rest
in Santa Fe v. Green, 430 U.S. 462 (1977). In that
case, defendant, owning more than 90% of the stock
of Kirby, merged Kirby into itself by a "short-form
merger" under Delaware law, requiring action only
by defendant's board of directors. Plaintiffs, minority
shareholders in Kirby, alleged that the merger was a
"fraud" on them within the meaning of Rule 10b–5

since (a) there was no justifiable business purpose for the merger, and (b) they were paid only $150 a share in the merger, whereas their pro rata share of Kirby's assets amounted to $772 per share. The Supreme Court held that the essence of any action under 1934 Act § 10(b) was "deception" or "manipulation," and that the type of management overreaching alleged in this case was not the kind of "fraud" covered by that section or any rule adopted under it.

It is unclear to what extent the *Santa Fe* decision undercuts the rationale of the *Schoenbaum* and *Pappas* decisions, which the Supreme Court cited in *Santa Fe* as decisions involving "deception" of the shareholders. It appears that if the transaction is submitted to and approved by a technically "disinterested" quorum of the board of directors, the knowledge of those directors will be imputed to the corporation and there is no "fraud." Maldonado v. Flynn, 597 F.2d 789 (2d Cir.1979). If the transaction is not approved by a disinterested board, and if no disclosure is made to the outside shareholders, they may sue under Rule 10b–5 if the information withheld from them would probably have led them to sue to enjoin the transaction under state law and if "there was a reasonable probability of ultimate success in securing an injunction had there been no misrepresentation or omission." Healey v. Catalyst Recovery, 616 F.2d 641 (3d Cir.1980); see also Goldberg v. Meridor, 567 F.2d 209 (2d Cir.1977); Kidwell v. Meikle, 597 F.2d 1273 (9th Cir.1979).

CHAPTER V

REGULATION OF THE
SECURITIES BUSINESS

As discussed more fully in § 25, below, the securities industry operates under a system of self-regulation. This means that in addition to regulation by the SEC, securities brokers and the securities markets are regulated by self-regulatory organizations organized under the auspices of the SEC and the 1934 Act. The primary regulator of broker dealers is the Financial Industry Regulatory Authority (FINRA) that resulted from the merger of the regulatory arms of the NASD and the NYSE.

A substantial portion of the SEC's activity is devoted to regulation of firms engaged in the securities business. The three principal capacities in which firms act in that business are as broker, dealer, and investment adviser. The 1934 Act defines a "broker" as a "person engaged in the business of effecting transactions in securities for the account of others," 1934 Act § 3(a)(4), while a "dealer" is a "person engaged in the business of buying and selling securities for his own account," 1934 Act § 3(a)(5). An "investment adviser" is defined in § 202(a)(11) of the Investment Advisers Act of 1940 (IAA) as a "person who, for compensation, engages in the business of advising others * * * as to the advisability of investing in, purchasing, or selling securities * * * ."

Under 1934 Act § 15(a), no person may engage in business as a broker or dealer (unless doing exclusively intrastate business or dealing only in exempted securities) unless that person is registered with the Commission. Under 1934 Act § 15(b), the Commission may revoke or suspend a broker-dealer's registration, or impose a censure, if the broker-dealer is found to have violated any of the federal securities laws or committed other specified misdeeds. 1934 Act § 15B, added in 1975, and IAA § 203 contain comparable provisions with respect to municipal securities dealers and investment advisers, respectively.

Broker-dealers are subject to regulation by all of the states in which they operate, as well as by the SEC. However, in 1996, Congress preempted all state regulation of SEC-registered broker-dealers with respect to capital, custody, margin, financial responsibility, record-keeping, bonding, and financial or operational reporting requirements. 1934 Act § 15(h).

§ 22. BROKER-DEALER SALES PRACTICES

In spelling out the substantive obligations of these securities "professionals" in dealing with public investors, the Commission has proceeded largely under the general antifraud provisions of 1934 Act §§ 10(b) and 15(c), 1933 Act § 17(a), and IAA § 206. Its attention has been focused on two broad areas: (a) conflicts between the professional's obligations to his or her customers and the professional's own financial interests, and (b) trading in or recommending securities in the absence of adequate information about the issuer. Violation of the antifraud provisions in these two areas has given rise to lawsuits by aggrieved customers as well as disciplinary actions by the SEC.

In construing the terms "fraud" and "deceit," as applied to securities professionals, the Supreme Court has held that Congress did not use them "in their technical sense," which would require a showing of intent to injure and actual injury to clients. At least in SEC enforcement proceedings, the Court held, they should be interpreted liberally to reach all practices which create a conflict of interest between the firm and its clients. SEC v. Capital Gains, 375 U.S. 180 (1963).

(A) CONFLICTS OF INTEREST

Conflicts of interest in the securities business arise from the fact that what is best for the broker-dealer or investment adviser is not always best for the customer. They are complicated by the fact, noted above, that securities firms often engage in several different types of activities, with differing responsibilities. In particular, many broker-dealer firms act as brokers, or agents, for their customers in purchasing or selling securities listed on a stock exchange, but also act as dealer, or principal, selling to or buying from, their customers, securities traded in the over-the-counter (OTC) and NASDAQ markets. This tends to confuse customers, since the legal obligations of an agent to act in the best interests of his or her principal do not apply to a dealer who is theoretically dealing with the customers at arm's length.

In Charles Hughes v. SEC, 139 F.2d 434 (2d Cir.1943), the court accepted the position urged by the SEC, that a broker-dealer firm which solicited business on the basis of "the confidence in itself which it managed to instill in its customers," was under a duty not to overreach its customers even when dealing with them as "principal." This has come to be known as the "shingle theory," under which a broker-dealer which hangs out its "shingle" as an expert in securities and offers advice to customers on their transactions will be held to violate the antifraud provisions of the 1933 and 1934 Acts when it deals with customers without making full disclosure of its possible conflicts of interest or other facts material to the customer's investment decision.

Excessive Prices. The particular violation alleged by the SEC in the *Hughes* case was the sale of OTC securities to unsophisticated customers at markups ranging from 16% to 40% above their current market value, without any disclosure of that fact. The problem of excessive charges was subsequently dealt with by the National Association of Securities Dealers (NASD), which was the self-regulatory organization for the OTC market.

In 1943, the NASD adopted an "interpretation" to the effect that a markup of not more than 5% would ordinarily be considered a "fair spread or profit" within the meaning of its Rules of Fair Practice. A large number of disciplinary proceedings based wholly or partly on excessive markups have been brought against broker-dealers by both the NASD and the SEC. Although the decisions generally refer to the "5% policy," markups between 5% and 10% may be justified in some circumstances. Markups above 10% are generally considered unjustifiable.

Disclosure of Status. 1934 Act Rule 10b–10 requires a broker-dealer to furnish its customers with a written confirmation of each transaction, indicating, among other things, whether it is acting as broker for the customer, as dealer for its own account, or as broker for another person.

"Churning." Where a broker-dealer is the sole, or dominant, market-maker in a particular security, and creates a market in that security by repeated purchases from, and resales to, its individual retail customers at steadily increasing prices, its course of conduct will be held to violate the antifraud provisions if it does not make full disclosure to the customers of the nature of the market. SEC v. First Jersey, 101 F.3d 1450 (2d Cir.1996); Norris & Hirshberg v. SEC, 177 F.2d 228 (D.C.Cir.1949). But a firm can also be held in violation of the antifraud provisions for "churning" a customer's account (i.e., causing the customer to engage in an excessive number of transactions in order to accumulate a higher commission) where it is acting solely as broker for the customer on a commission basis.

1934 Act Rule 15c1–7 makes it illegal for any broker or dealer to effect transactions in securities, for any customer's account over which such broker or dealer has investment discretion, "which are excessive in size or frequency in view of the financial resources and character of the account." Even where the broker does not technically have discretion over the customer's account, churning may violate the general antifraud provisions. "In order to establish a claim of churning, a plaintiff must show (1) that the trading in his account was excessive in light of his investment objectives; (2) that the broker in question exercised control over the trading in the account; and (3) that the broker acted with the intent to defraud or with the willful and reckless disregard for the interests of his client." Mihara v. Dean Witter, 619 F.2d 814 (9th Cir.1980). A broker can be held liable for the excessive commissions obtained by churning a customer's account, even if the customer's account increased in value during the period in which the churning took place. Nesbit v. McNeil, 896 F.2d 380 (9th Cir.1990).

"Scalping." Another practice which the SEC has attacked as a fraud is "scalping"—a situation in which an investment adviser publicly recommends the purchase of securities without disclosing its practice of purchasing such securities before making the recommendation and then selling them at a profit when the price rises after the recommendation is disseminated. In SEC v. Capital Gains, 375 U.S. 180 (1963), the Supreme Court agreed with the SEC and held such conduct to violate the antifraud provisions of the Investment Advisers Act of 1940, even though there was no allegation that the investment adviser's actions had injured its clients or that it did not believe in the recommendations it was making. However, the fact that the Supreme Court in 1988 split 4–4 in Carpenter v. United States, 484 U.S. 19 (1987), involving the application of the antifraud provisions of 1934 Act § 10(b) to a very similar set of

facts, cast doubt on the continuing vitality of the theory underlying the *Capital Gains* decision. That cloud was removed by the decision in United States v. O'Hagan, 521 U.S. 642 (1997) (see § 19(a) above).

(B) INADEQUATE BASIS FOR RECOMMENDATIONS

An important objective of the disclosure provisions of the federal securities laws, discussed in earlier chapters, is to assure that investors, and the broker-dealers who advise them, have adequate information about the issuer to make rational investment decisions. In furtherance, or rather extension, of this approach, the SEC has taken the position that it is a violation of the antifraud provisions for a broker-dealer to recommend the purchase of a security unless it has enough reliable information about the issuer to form a sound basis for its recommendations.

The Commission initially applied this approach to "boiler-room" operations—firms set up for the sole purpose of aggressively peddling the stock of one or a few highly speculative issuers, by means of long distance telephone calls and high-pressure sales techniques. See Berko v. SEC, 316 F.2d 137 (2d Cir.1963) (holding a "boiler-room" operator violated the Act by making unwarranted predictions that the price of a particular stock would rise to $15 a share within a year, even though the stock did subsequently rise to that level).

This approach was subsequently extended beyond the "boiler-room" situation to apply to all broker-dealers. In Hanly v. SEC, 415 F.2d 589 (2d Cir.1969), the court held that a broker-dealer which made unsubstantiated recommendations was subject to SEC sanctions since, under the "shingle" theory, "by his position he or she implicitly represents he or she has an adequate basis for the opinions he renders." And in a notable SEC proceeding, the nation's largest brokerage firm was required to pay $1.6 million to its customers, and sanctions were imposed on 28 of its salesmen, for making unsubstantiated recommendations of the stock of an electronics company. Merrill Lynch, Sec. Exch. Act Rel. 34–14149 (1977). In 2009, FINRA proposed Rule 2111 which, among other things, would codify the "reasonable basis" (or know your security) obligation.

Supplementing its proceedings against individual broker-dealers, the SEC in 1971 adopted 1934 Act Rule 15c2–11, which prohibits a broker-dealer from making a market in any security unless (a) the issuer has recently made a public offering under the 1933 Act or Regulation A, or (b) the issuer is currently filing reports under the 1934 Act, or (c) the broker-dealer has in its files specified current financial and other information about the issuer and its securities. The purpose, and effect, of this rule is to prevent the creation of public trading markets in securities which have not been registered under either the 1933 Act (including Regulation A) or the 1934 Act. In 1991, the Commission strengthened Rule 15c2–11 by requiring broker-dealers to review the information specified in the rule before initiating or resuming quotations for any security, and to have a reasonable basis to believe that the information is true and accurate and obtained from reliable sources.

Concerned about the widespread incidence of high-pressure sales tactics in the peddling of low-priced speculative stocks to unsophisticated investors, the SEC in 1989 adopted 1934 Act Rule 15c2–6, applicable to dealers in "designated securities" (defined as non-NASDAQ OTC equity securities whose issuers have less than $2 million in net tangible assets and which sell for less than $5 a share). The rule requires that a dealer, before selling "designated securities" to any customer, must obtain the customer's written authorization for the purchase, determine that the securities are suitable for the customer, and provide the customer with a written statement setting forth the basis for such determination of suitability. In 1990, Congress followed up with the enactment of the Penny Stock Reform Act, applicable to essentially the same types of securities, expanding the SEC's authority to regulate their sale, and directing the SEC to facilitate the establishment of an automated system to disseminate last sale and quotation information for them. See 1934 Act §§ 15(g), 17B. In April 1992, the SEC adopted rules to implement these penny stock provisions, requiring dealers in penny stocks to provide their customers with a standardized document disclosing the risks of such investments, the customer's rights in the event of fraud or abuse, and the compensation received by the broker-dealer and the salesperson in connection with the transaction. See 1934 Act Rules 15g–1 through 15g–6.

FINRA and Recommendations. In June 2009, FINRA proposed consolidating the NASD suitability rule and the NYSE "know your customer" rule into a single Rule. *See* FINRA Reg. Notice 09–25, Suitability and "Know Your Customer," http://www. finra.org/file/regulatory-notice-09-25 (FINRA June 2009). FINRA Rule 2111 as proposed follows the former NASD suitability rule more closely than its former NYSE counterpart in that the new FINRA obligation is linked to a broker's recommendations rather than a more generalized know your customer obligation. However, as noted below, a separate FINRA rule incorporates the know your customer obligation independent of a recommendation.

As adopted, FINRA Rule 2111 addresses three distinct suitability issues. First, the rule codifies the "reasonable basis" (or know your security) obligation by providing that in making a recommendation with respect to a security, the firm must have a reasonable basis for believing, based on a due diligence investigation, that the recommendation is suitable for at least some investors. Second, the FINRA rule requires that the firm must have reasonable grounds to believe that a recommendation is suitable for the specific investor to whom the recommendation is made. Third, there is a quantitative approach to recommendations in that the rule requires that firms have a reasonable basis for believing that the number of recommended transactions with a certain time frame is not excessive. This quantitative limitation is aimed at helping to prevent churning and excessive trading issues.

FINRA's suitability rule contains an exemption, subject to specified conditions for recommendations to institutional customers. Under the rule, the firm's suitability obligation would be deemed to be fulfilled if the institutional customer has affirmatively indicated its willingness to waive the protection of the brokerage firm's customer-specific suitability obligation. The firm (or associated person) must have a reasonable basis for believing that the institutional customer is capable of analyzing investment risks— both generally and with respect to the specific investments or investment strategy being recommended. The recommending firm must also have a reasonable basis for believing that the institutional customer in fact exercises independent judgment in evaluating the recommendations.

FINRA Rule 2090 carries forward the NYSE know your customer obligation. Rule 2090 as proposed and subsequently adopted requires brokerage firms to know and to retain the "essential facts" regarding each customer and any person acting on behalf of that customer. See Accelerated Approval of FINRA Rules 2090 and 2011, Sec. Exch. Act Rel. No. 34– 63325, 2010 WL 4663180 (SEC Nov. 17, 2010); FINRA Reg. Notice 09–25, Suitability and "Know Your Customer," http://www.finra.org/file/ regulatory-notice-09-25 (FINRA June 2009). FINRA points out that this obligation is already implicit in other NASD and FINRA rules but is now made explicit.

§ 23. FINANCIAL RESPONSIBILITY OF BROKER-DEALERS

Since many broker-dealers maintain custody of funds and securities belonging to their customers, safeguards are required to assure that the customers can recover those funds and securities in the event the broker-dealer becomes insolvent. The three principal techniques that have been utilized are (a) financial responsibility standards for broker-dealers, (b) requirements for segregation of customers' funds and securities, and (c) maintenance of an industry-wide fund to satisfy the claims of customers whose brokerage firms become insolvent.

(A) NET CAPITAL RULES

The basic financial responsibility standards for broker-dealers are found in the "net capital" rules adopted by the SEC under authority of 1934 Act § 15(c)(3). Prior to the financial debacle suffered by the securities industry in 1968–70, securities firms belonging to exchanges which had "net capital" rules deemed to be more stringent than those of the SEC were exempt from the SEC's requirements. However, after SEC and Congressional investigations showed how flexibly the exchanges had interpreted their rules to allow member firms to continue in business with inadequate capital, the SEC revoked this exemption and made all broker-dealers subject to its requirements.

Under the SEC net capital rule, 1934 Act Rule 15c3–1, which was substantially revised in 1975, see Sec. Exch. Act Rel. 34–11497, a broker-dealer must maintain "net capital" of at least $25,000 ($5,000 in the case of broker-dealers that do not hold any customers' funds or securities and conduct their business in a specified manner). "Net capital" is defined as "net worth" (excess of assets over liabilities), subject to many special adjustments prescribed in the Rule. In addition, a broker-dealer may not let its aggregate indebtedness exceed 1500% of its net capital (800% during its first year of business).

A broker-dealer can alternatively qualify under 1934 Act Rule 15c3–1(f), which is designed to test its general financial integrity and liquidity and its ability to meet its continuing commitments to its customers. Under this alternative, which was significantly liberalized in 1982, a broker-dealer must maintain net capital equal to the greater of $100,000 or 2% of the aggregate debit balances attributable to its transactions with customers.

(B) CUSTOMERS' FUNDS AND SECURITIES

Customers leave large amounts of cash and securities with their brokers. The securities are of two types. The first type is securities purchased "on margin" (i.e., with the broker advancing part of the purchase price to the customer), which (under the standard margin agreement) the broker is entitled to hold as security for the loan and to repledge to secure its own borrowings. The second type is "fully-paid" securities, which the broker holds solely as a convenience for the customer and is supposed to "segregate" from the broker's own securities. The cash "free credit balances" arise principally from two sources: a deposit of cash by a customer prior to giving the broker a purchase order, and receipt by the broker of proceeds of a sale of securities, or interest or dividend income, which has not yet been reinvested or delivered to the customer.

With respect to fully-paid securities, investigators of the securities industry's operational crises in 1968–70 discovered that many firms had lost control of their records. These firms did not have in their possession many of the securities which they were supposed to be holding as custodians for their customers. Accordingly, the SEC in 1972 adopted 1934 Act Rule 15c3–3, which requires that all brokers "promptly obtain and * * * thereafter maintain the physical possession or control of all fully-paid securities" and prescribes daily determinations of compliance with the rule.

With respect to cash free credit balances, brokers have traditionally mingled the cash belonging to customers with their own assets used in their business. Since 1964, 1934 Act Rule 15c3–2 has required brokers to notify their customers at least quarterly that such funds (a) are not segregated and may be used in the business, and (b) are payable to the customer on demand. In the wake of the 1968–70 debacle, which revealed that many firms had been using customers' free credit balances as their own working capital, there were demands for complete segregation of these cash balances. The industry argued, however, that it should continue to have interest-free use of these moneys to finance customer-related transactions (principally margin loans). The result was 1934 Act Rule 15c3–3, adopted by the SEC in 1972, which requires each broker to maintain a "Special Reserve Bank Account for the Exclusive Benefit of Customers" in which it holds cash or U.S. government securities in an amount equal to (a) free credit balances in customers' accounts (plus other amounts owing to customers) less (b) debit balances in customers' cash and margin accounts.

(C) THE SECURITIES INVESTOR PROTECTION ACT

Following the financial collapse of one of its large member firms in 1963, the NYSE established a "trust fund," financed by assessments on its members, to pay the claims of customers of member firms which failed. This trust fund proved inadequate to deal with the financial crisis of 1969–70, however, and the industry turned to Congress to establish a more secure system of customer protection. Congress responded by passing the Securities Investor Protection Act of 1970 (SIPA).

SIPA § 3(a) created a non-profit membership corporation, called Securities Investor Protection Corporation (SIPC), and requires every broker-dealer registered under 1934 Act § 15 (with certain limited exceptions) to be a member. The corporation is managed by a seven-person board of directors, of which one is appointed by the Secretary of the Treasury, one by the Federal Reserve Board, and five by the President. Of the five appointed by the

President, three are to be representatives of different segments of the securities industry and two are to be from the general public. SIPA § 3(c).

In order to accumulate the funds necessary to enable SIPC to meet its responsibilities, each member of SIPC is required to pay an annual assessment equal to ½ of 1% of the member's gross revenues, until SIPC has accumulated a fund of $150 million, and to pay such further assessments as are necessary to maintain the fund at that level. SIPA § 4(c), (d). If this fund proves insufficient, SIPC is authorized to borrow up to $1 billion from the Treasury (through the SEC). The SEC, if it determines that assessments on members will not satisfactorily provide for repayment of the loan, may levy a charge of not more than 1/50 of 1% of all transactions in the exchange and OTC markets to provide for repayment. SIPA § 4(g).

Operation of SIPC. If the SEC or a self-regulatory organization determines that a broker or dealer is in or approaching financial difficulty, it must notify SIPC. If SIPC determines that the member has failed or is in danger of failing to meet its obligations to customers, or that certain other conditions exist, it may apply to a court for a decree adjudicating that the customers of the member are in need of the protection provided by the Act. SIPA § 5(a). A customer of a SIPC member has no right to apply to a court for an order directing SIPC to take action with respect to that member. SIPC v. Barbour, 421 U.S. 412 (1975).

If the court makes the requisite findings and issues the requested decree, it must then appoint as trustee, and attorney for the trustee, "disinterested" persons designated by SIPC. SIPA § 5(b)(3). The functions of the trustee are (a) to return "specifically identifiable property" to customers and to satisfy their other claims out of available funds, (b) to complete the "open contractual commitments" of the firm, and (c) to liquidate the firm's business. If the firm's assets are insufficient to satisfy the claims of all customers, SIPC must advance to the trustee moneys sufficient to satisfy all such claims, up to a maximum of $500,000 for each customer (but not more than $100,000 in respect of claims for cash). SIPA § 6(a), (f). In general, the liquidation proceeding is to be conducted as if it were being conducted under Chapter X of the Bankruptcy Act. SIPA § 6(c).

In light of problems in the administration of the Act, particularly with respect to prompt settlement of customers' claims, the Act was amended in 1978 to permit the trustee to purchase securities for delivery to customers, to transfer customers' accounts in bulk to another broker-dealer, and to make direct payments to customers without judicial supervision in small liquidations. See S.Rep. 95–283 (1978).

§ 24. MARKET REGULATION

In addition to its provisions for the regulation of individual broker-dealers, the Securities Exchange Act regulates the overall operations of the markets in which securities are traded. The principal regulatory provisions included in the original act in 1934 were

1934 Act §§ 7 and 8, governing the extension of credit on listed securities, and 1934 Act § 11, regulating trading by exchange members for their own account. These provisions have been substantially modified over the years. In the Securities Acts Amendments of 1975, Congress also added 1934 Act §§ 11A and 17A, directing the SEC to facilitate the establishment of a "national market system" and a national system for clearing and settlement of transactions.

(A) MARKET STRUCTURE

The fixed minimum commission rates maintained by the New York Stock Exchange (NYSE) prior to 1975 resulted in the diversion of a substantial portion of institutional trading to the "regional" exchanges or to the "third market" (an over-the-counter market in NYSE-listed stocks, maintained by non-member market makers). This "fragmentation" results in orders for a single stock being routed to different markets, with customers in some cases receiving less favorable prices than they would have received if all orders met in a single place.

Accordingly, in the Securities Acts Amendments of 1975, Congress directed the SEC to "use its authority to facilitate the establishment of a national market system" to link all markets for particular securities. 1934 Act § 11A. The first result of this effort was the 1976 replacement of the old NYSE "tape" with a "consolidated tape" which records all transactions in a listed security, wherever effected. In 1978, the exchanges introduced an "intermarket trading system" (ITS) which permits electronic transfer of orders from one exchange floor to another when a better price is available on the other exchange.

The exchanges continued to resist the development of a competing over-the-counter market in listed stocks by barring their members from "effect[ing] any transaction in any listed stock in the over-the-counter market, either as principal or agent." NYSE Rule 390. But that rule was repealed in 2000. Although the markets remain divided between the exchanges and the over the counter markets, there is increased competition and a blurring of the distinctions for many purposes. 1934 Act Rules 11Ac1–1 and 11Ac1–4 permit electronic communications networks ("ECN"s) for providing electronic quotations and facilitating transactions in the over-the-counter markets and also for exchange-listed securities. The existence of these alternative trading platforms has increased competition and heightened the obligations of market participants in finding the best execution of transactions for their customers. For example, in executing transactions, it is no longer sufficient to limit the search for the best price to traditional market makers, quotations available through the ECNs must also be considered. See, e.g., Newton v. Merrill, Lynch, Pierce, Fenner & Smith, 135 F.3d 266 (3d Cir.1998); Exch. Act Rel. No. 34–40760 (1998). Similar obligations apply to specialists on the exchanges who must look beyond their own order books to determine a security's price. See § 24(b) below.

In 2006, the New York Stock Exchange (NYSE) expanded its electronic order execution capabilities when it merged with Archipelago which had been one of the largest electronic communications networks (ECNs). Subsequently, the NYSE eyed international expansion when it merged with Euronext, a major offshore trading facility.

(B) CLEARING AND SETTLEMENT

Congressional and SEC investigations of the securities industry's "paperwork crisis" during the period from 1968 to 1970 revealed that a substantial cause of the problem was the obsolete and inefficient method of completing transactions by the delivery (and, in some cases, cancellation and reissuance) of stock certificates. Accordingly, in the Securities Act Amendments of 1975, Congress directed the SEC to "use its authority to facilitate the establishment of a national system for the prompt and accurate clearance and settlement of transactions in securities." 1934 Act § 17A(a). In furtherance of this objective, the SEC was given direct regulatory power over clearing agencies and transfer agents, 1934 Act § 17A(b), (c), as well as the power to prescribe the format of securities registered under the 1934 Act. 1934 Act § 12(*l*).

Since the crisis, transfers of certificates have been reduced substantially by the establishment of a depository through which certain major brokers and banks can effect transfers among themselves without movement of certificates. Also the SEC in 1977 prescribed a set of minimum performance standards for transfer agents. See 1934 Act Rules 17Ad–1 *et seq.*

(C) TRADING BY EXCHANGE MEMBERS

The principal function, and purpose, of a national securities exchange is to provide a marketplace in which member firms, acting as brokers, can purchase and sell securities for the account of their customers. The question addressed in 1934 Act § 11 is the extent to which stock exchange members and their firms should be permitted to trade in listed securities for their own account, in view of the possibly unfair advantages they may have over public customers when engaging in such trading.

1934 Act § 11(a), as amended in 1975, prohibits an exchange member from effecting any transactions on the exchange for its own account, or any account with respect to which it exercises investment discretion, with certain specified exceptions, including transactions as a market maker (specialist) or odd-lot dealer, stabilizing transactions in connection with distributions (see § 17(a) above), bona fide arbitrage transactions, and other transactions which the SEC concludes should be exempt from the prohibition.

Traditionally, the inquiry has focused on three special categories of transactions: (a) "floor trading" and "off-floor trading" by members and their firms, (b) transactions by "odd-lot dealers," and (c) transactions by specialists. More recently, the increasing domination of NYSE trading by institutional customers has focused attention on two additional categories: (d) "block positioning" by member firms, and (e) transactions for "managed institutional accounts."

"Floor Trading" and "Off-Floor Trading." The principal purpose of 1934 Act § 11(a), as originally enacted, was to authorize the SEC to write rules (1) "to regulate or prevent floor trading" by exchange members, and (2) to prevent excessive off-floor trading by members if the Commission found it "detrimental to the maintenance of a fair and orderly market."

"Floor trading" was the specialty of a small percentage of NYSE members who maintained their memberships for the sole or primary purpose of roaming around the exchange floor and trading for their own account in whatever securities caught their fancy. The SEC adopted some mild restrictions on floor trading in 1945, but nothing significant was done until 1963, when the Commission's Special Study of the Securities Markets concluded that floor trading was a vestige of the pre-1934 "private club" atmosphere of the exchanges, and should be abolished. In 1964, the Commission adopted a rule prohibiting all floor trading by members, unless conducted in accordance with a plan adopted by an exchange and approved by the Commission. 1934 Act Rule 11a–1. The NYSE simultaneously adopted a plan, which was then approved by the Commission, requiring floor traders to register with the exchange, to maintain minimum capital and pass a qualifying examination, and to comply with special restrictions on their trading activity. See NYSE Rules 110–112. In 1978, the NYSE established a new category of "registered competitive market makers" with certain responsibilities to assist the specialist in maintaining an orderly market. NYSE Rule 107. As floor traders have switched over to this new category, traditional floor trading has continued to diminish in importance.

"Off-floor" trading by member firms (i.e., transactions initiated by decisions at the firm's offices, rather than on the floor), accounts for a much greater proportion of activity than floor trading. This type of activity has not been thought to give rise to the same kind of problems as floor trading, and the SEC has never undertaken to impose any direct restrictions on it. However, after an SEC study of off-floor trading in 1967, the NYSE adopted rules designed to prevent member firms from transmitting orders to the floor ahead of their customers at times when they might be privy to "inside information."

Specialists and Designated Market Makers. For most of its existence, the NYSE operated under a trading system led by specialists. The NYSE started to phase out the traditional specialist system in 2008. The discussion that follows explains trading by specialists and the move towards replacing the specialist with designated market makers.

The specialist firm occupies a unique dual role in the operation of the NYSE and other exchanges. First, it acted as a "broker's broker," maintaining a "book" on which other brokers could leave customers' "limit orders" (i.e., orders to buy or sell at a price at which they could not currently be executed). Second, it acts as the exclusive franchised dealer, or "market maker" in its assigned stocks, buying and selling shares from other brokers when there are no customer orders on its book against which they can be matched. In 1975, Congress amended 1934 Act § 11(b) to make clear that the SEC had authority to limit specialists to acting either as brokers or dealers, but not both, but the Commission has not yet taken any action pursuant to this authority.

The functions of the specialist can be illustrated by the following example. A firm is the specialist in an actively-traded stock, in which the market is $40–$40.10. This means that customer orders are on the specialist's book to buy specified numbers of shares at $40 or less, and other orders are on the specialist's book to sell at $40.10 or more (formerly, shares were quoted in halves, quarters and eighths, rather than cents, and the minimum unit was 1/8 point, or 12½ cents; in 2000, the markets moved to a decimal system.) A broker who comes to the specialist with an order to sell "at the market" will sell to the customer with the first buy order on the book at $40, and a broker who comes with a market order to buy will buy from the customer with the first sell order on the book at $40.10. The specialist acts solely as a subagent, receiving a portion of the "book" customer's commission to the customer's broker. The monopoly created by the specialist's book has been diluted. The emergence of alternative trading platforms such as the over-the-counter markets and electronic communications networks and their ability to trade exchange-listed securities have increased competition. The specialist must pair matchable orders that arrive at the specialist's trading post through various media "generally either through the NYSE's Super Designated Order Turnaround System ('DOT') to an electronic display book (the

'Display Book'), or by floor brokers gathered in front of the specialists' trading posts ('the crowd')." See, e.g., In the Van Der Moolen Specialists USA, Sec. Exch. Act Rel. No. 34–49502 (2004).

Now assume the same firm is also specialist in an inactively traded stock. The only orders on the book are an order to buy at $38 and an order to sell at $42. If the specialist acted solely as agent, a broker who came in with a market order to sell would receive $38, and another broker who came in an hour later with a market order to buy would pay $42. The report of these two trades on the "tape" would indicate the stock had risen 4 points, or 10%, in an hour. The exchange therefore imposes an obligation on the specialist to maintain an "orderly market" in the specialist's assigned stocks, buying and selling for his or her own account to even out swings which would result from buyers and sellers not appearing at his post at the same time. In this case the specialist might make the market at $40–$40.25, trading for his or her own account as long as necessary, but yielding priority to customers' orders on the specialist's book whenever they provide as good a price to the party on the other side.

While this combination of functions has obvious advantages, it also offers possibilities for abuse. With the monopoly trading position and knowledge of the "book," the specialist, by moving the price of the specialty stocks up and down, can guarantee himself or herself profits in both the specialist's "broker" and "dealer" functions. The SEC from time to time studied, and expressed its concern about, this problem, but has never undertaken direct regulation of specialists' activities. In 1965, it adopted 1934 Act Rule 11b–1, requiring the principal exchanges to maintain and enforce rules designed to curb abuses by specialists, but SEC and Congressional studies have expressed continuing dissatisfaction with NYSE surveillance and regulation of specialist activities. Starting in 1976, however, the NYSE has disciplined a number of specialists for improper trades or reports of trades, failure to maintain orderly markets, and other violations. In 2003, the SEC instituted proceedings against the specialist firms that uncovered a raft of abuses and led to the imposition of more than $240 million in penalties.

In 2008, the NYSE replaced the conventional "specialist" system with a new system centered on the "designated market maker" (DMM). Sec. Exch. Act Rel. No. 34–58845 (SEC Oct. 29, 2008). This official name change reflects important policy modifications implemented by the NYSE regarding the role of the firms that were typically referred to as specialists. The new system was set up to be implemented in phases. When fully implemented, the designated market maker system will result in a number of significant changes to the ways in which these firms operated under the specialist system. Three systemic changes were identified in the applicable SEC release: "(i) the phasing out of the specialist system and adopting a Designated Market Maker ('DMM') structure; (ii) the alteration of NYSE's priority and parity rules, most significantly to allow DMMs to trade on parity with orders on NYSE's Display Book® ('Display Book'); and (iii) the introduction of new order functionality, including the DMM Capital Commitment Schedule ('CCS') and hidden orders." Id.

In order to achieve parity between DMMs and other market makers, unlike specialists, DMMs will no longer have access to exclusive advanced looks at incoming trade orders. Instead, the DMMs receive the same information, at the same time, that is made available to other market participants. Due to this new parity, DMMs are no longer subject to the specialist's "negative obligation" regarding trading in their own accounts and now are allowed to trade for their own account. This change was implemented to provide more equality among all trading parties and thus to help accomplish better pricing and more efficiency overall in the trading process.

As a result of the phasing out of the specialist system, the NYSE now allows for more integration between the upstairs and downstairs operations of trading firms. Previously, the specialist operation was required to be a separate unit of the firm; the new DMM units may now interact with the upstairs operations provided certain specific procedures are followed. This integration of operations should allow DMMs access to more capital and create more cost-effective operations and overall efficiencies, resulting in a deeper and broader market. Along with these recent major policy shifts, the NYSE rules still impose an affirmative obligation on DMMs to commit their own capital when necessary to combat pricing problems due to imbalances or illiquidity. The overall result of these comprehensive NYSE policies is designed to improve the speed, liquidity, and fairness of trading for all market participants.

"Block Positioning." Institutional investors (principally pension funds, mutual funds, and insurance companies) have increased their investments in common stocks to the point that they currently account for 60–70% of the trading on the New York Stock Exchange. Institutions often trade in large blocks (10,000 shares or more) which put special strains on exchange market-making mechanisms. If a member firm which specializes in institutional business has a customer which wishes to sell 100,000 shares of a particular stock, but can only find buyers for 80,000, the firm itself will "position" the remaining 20,000 shares, and then sell them off over a period of time as the market can absorb them. 1934 Act § 11(a)(1)(A) recognizes this "market making" function as a legitimate exception to the prohibition against trading by members for their own account.

(D) DEALER "SPREADS"

As noted in § 24(c), above, shares have traditionally been quoted and traded in halves, quarters, and eighths of a dollar, rather than in cents. The minimum "spread" between bid and asked prices traditionally had been one-eighth of a dollar, or 12½ cents (one-sixteenth, or 6¼ cents, in the case of very low priced stocks). A study published by two economists in 1996 purported to show that dealers in the OTC market were conspiring to refuse to quote shares in eighths, thus assuring themselves a spread of at least a quarter, or 25 cents, per share on their trades. The ensuing outcry led to decisions by both the exchanges and the NASDAQ system in 1997 to begin trading all stocks in sixteenths, as well as an announcement by the NYSE that it planned to switch to decimal pricing (i.e., quoting shares in dollars and cents) by the year 2000. Decimalization was implemented by 2001 and thus the minimum spread is now 1 cent.

(E) EXTENSION OF CREDIT— MARGIN REGULATION

"For the purpose of preventing the excessive use of credit for the purchase or carrying of securities," 1934 Act §§ 7 and 8 authorize the Federal Reserve Board to limit "the amount of credit that may be initially extended and subsequently maintained on any security," and to regulate borrowing by brokers and dealers. Pursuant to this authority, the Federal Reserve Board has promulgated regulations governing the extension of credit by broker-dealers (Regulation T), banks (Regulation U), and the obtaining of credit by purchasers (Regulation X). See 12 C.F.R. pts. 220, 221, 207, 224.

While 1934 Act § 7 authorizes the Federal Reserve Board to regulate both the initial extension and the subsequent maintenance of credit, the Federal Reserve Board rules, or "margin regulations," as they are generally known, in fact regulate only the initial extension of credit on a new purchase. See 12 C.F.R. § 220.7(b). This is done by specification of a "maximum loan value" of securities, expressed as a percentage of current value, which the Federal Reserve Board changes from time to time in response to increases and decreases in the amount of speculative activity and the availability of credit. For example, if the current "maximum loan value" is 50%, a customer who wants to buy securities with a current market value of $4,000 must put up $2,000 in cash and may borrow the remaining $2,000 from the broker "on margin." If the securities subsequently decline in value to $2,500, the Federal Reserve Board margin regulations would not require the customer to pay an additional $750 to the broker to reduce the customer's debt to $1,250. However, certain stock exchanges do impose "margin maintenance" rules on their members, requiring that customers maintain a "margin," or equity, in their accounts equal to at least 25% of current market value. See, e.g., NYSE Rule 431(b). Thus, if the broker in this example was an NYSE member, it would be required to make a "margin call" on the customer to reduce the customer's loan by $125, thus raising the customer's "margin" to $625, or 25% of current market value. If the customer then wanted to buy another $2,500 worth of securities, the Federal Reserve Board margin regulations would require the customer to put up $1,875 in cash, since she could only borrow an additional $625 from the broker—the difference between the maximum loan value of the account ($2,500) and the customer's outstanding obligation to the broker ($1,875).

The Federal Reserve Board restrictions apply only to extension of credit on equity securities; there are no limitations on the amount of credit that may be extended for the purchase of U.S. government bonds, state and local government bonds, or nonconvertible corporate debt securities. 1934 Act § 7(a); 12 C.F.R. § 220.4(i). As originally enacted, § 7 permitted extension of credit only on equity securities listed on a stock exchange; over-the-counter stocks had no "loan value." However, the statute was amended in 1968 to permit extension of credit on OTC stocks meeting criteria established by the Federal Reserve Board. The Federal Reserve Board now provides for the automatic marginability of stocks that are part of the NASDAQ System.

1934 Act § 11(d) bars broker-dealers from extending any credit to customers for the purchase of newly-issued securities with respect to which the broker-dealer is acting as an underwriter or selling group member.

While the power to regulate extensions of credit under 1934 Act §§ 7 and 8 is vested in the Federal Reserve Board, enforcement of the rules with respect to broker-dealers is the responsibility of the SEC and the self-regulatory organizations. A large number of proceedings have been brought against broker-dealers for violations of the margin rules, which bar them not only from extending credit in violation of Federal Reserve Board limitations but also from arranging for the extension of such credit by others. 1934 Act § 7(c); 12 C.F.R. § 220.7(a).

Although the basic purpose of the margin regulations is to restrict stock market speculation, rather than to protect individual customers, some courts have allowed customers to sue their brokers

for losses on transactions in which the brokers
extended credit in violation of the rules, even where
the illegal extension of credit was not shown to have
induced the customer to enter into the transaction.
Pearlstein v. Scudder, 429 F.2d 1136 (2d Cir.1970),
modified at 527 F.2d 1141 (2d Cir.1975). However,
the addition in 1970 of 1934 Act § 7(f), prohibiting
customers from obtaining credit in violation of the
Federal Reserve Board rules, coupled with the
Supreme Court's current reluctance to imply new
private rights of action, has led the courts in the more
recent cases to deny customers any right to recover
in these circumstances. See Utah State v. Bear
Stearns, 549 F.2d 164 (10th Cir.1977); Gilman v.
FDIC, 660 F.2d 688 (6th Cir.1981).

Disclosure. Loans by securities firms to their
customers are specifically exempted from the federal
Truth in Lending Act, which requires creditors to
make clear disclosures to loan applicants. 15 U.S.C.
§ 1603(2). However, the exemption was premised on
a Congressional understanding that the SEC would
promulgate substantially similar disclosure rules
under its existing authority. 1934 Act Rule 10b–16,
adopted by the SEC in 1969, requires broker-dealers
to disclose to their margin customers (a) the rate and
method of computing interest on their indebtedness,
and (b) the nature of the firm's interest in the
customer's securities and the circumstances under
which additional collateral may be required.
Customers have generally been held to have an
implied private right of action to sue their brokers for
violations of these disclosure requirements, since the
rule was adopted under 1934 Act § 10(b), as to which

the Supreme Court has continued to recognize such a right. See Angelastro v. Prudential-Bache, 764 F.2d 939 (3d Cir.1985).

§ 25. "SELF-REGULATION"

The scheme of regulation of the securities business is complicated by the fact that regulatory authority is not lodged solely in the SEC, but is divided between the SEC and a number of "self-regulatory organizations" (SROs). These are private associations of broker-dealers to which Congress has delegated (a) authority to adopt and enforce rules for the conduct of their members, and (b) responsibility to assure compliance by their members with provisions of the federal securities laws.

Stock Exchanges. When Congress created the SEC in 1934, stock exchanges, as private associations, had been regulating their members for up to 140 years. Rather than displace this system of "self-regulation," Congress superimposed the SEC on it as an additional level of regulation. 1934 Act § 5 requires every "national securities exchange" to register with the SEC. Under 1934 Act § 6, an exchange cannot be registered unless the SEC determines that its rules are designed, among other things, to "prevent fraudulent and manipulative acts and practices, to promote just and equitable principles of trade," and to provide for appropriate discipline of its members for any violations of its own rules or the securities laws.

Under this authority, the various exchanges, of which the New York Stock Exchange (NYSE) is by far the largest and most important, have maintained and enforced a large body of rules for the conduct of their members. These rules fall into two categories: (1) rules relating to transactions on the particular exchange and (2) rules relating to the internal operations of the member firms and their dealings with their customers.

Rules in the first group govern: criteria for listing securities on the exchange and provisions for delisting or suspension of trading in particular securities; obligations of issuers of listed securities; bids and offers on the exchange floor; activities of "specialists" (designated market-makers in listed securities); transactions by members in listed securities for their own account; conditions under which transactions in listed securities may be effected off the exchange; clearing and settlement of exchange transactions; and rules for the governance and operation of the exchange itself.

Rules in the second category govern: the form of organization of member firms and qualifications of their partners or officers; qualifications of salesmen and other personnel; handling of customers' accounts; advertising; and financial statements and reports. In the case of firms that are members of more than one exchange, there is a kind of "pecking order" with respect to regulatory responsibility: the NYSE has principal responsibility for regulation of the internal affairs of all of its members (which includes almost all of the largest firms in the industry), the American Stock Exchange has principal responsibility for those of its members that are not also NYSE members, and the various "regional" exchanges in cities other than New York have responsibility over their "sole" members.

1934 Act § 19, as originally enacted, gave the SEC power to suspend or withdraw the registration of an exchange, to suspend or expel any member of an exchange, to suspend trading in listed securities, and to require changes in exchange rules with respect to a wide range of matters. However, it did not require SEC approval for changes in stock exchange rules, nor did it provide for SEC review of disciplinary actions by exchanges against their members.

National Association of Securities Dealers. When Congress decided to extend federal regulation over the non-exchange, or over-the-counter (OTC) market, it followed the pattern already established with respect to exchanges. 1934 Act § 15A, added by the "Maloney Act" of 1938, authorized the establishment of "national securities associations" to be registered with the SEC. Like an exchange, any such association must have rules designed "to prevent fraudulent and manipulative acts and practices [and] to promote just and equitable principles of trade" in transactions in the OTC market. 1934 Act § 15A(b)(6). Only one such association was established, the National Association of Securities Dealers (NASD). As explained below, the NASD as a self-regulator has been replaced by the Financial Industry Regulatory Authority (FINRA).

The NASD adopted a substantial body of "Rules of Fair Practice," dealing with various problems in the OTC and NASDAQ markets. Among the most

important are: its rule that a dealer may not
recommend a security unless the dealer has reason
to believe it is "suitable" to the customer's financial
situation and needs; its interpretation of its "fair
spread or profit" rule to bar markups in excess of 5%
on principal transactions (see § 22(a) above); its
procedures for reviewing underwriting compensation
and provisions for assuring that members make a
bona fide public offering of underwritten securities;
and its rules with respect to execution of orders in the
OTC and NASDAQ markets and disclosure in
confirmations to customers.

Prior to 1971, the NASD was a purely regulatory
organization, since the OTC market had no central
facility comparable to an exchange floor. Trading was
effected by telephone calls between dealers on the
basis of quotations published in commercial "sheets"
by broker-dealers who chose to make markets in
particular securities. However, in 1971, the NASD
put into operation an electronic automated quotation
system (NASDAQ) for selected OTC securities. In
this system, dealers can insert and instantaneously
update bid and asked quotations for securities in
which they are registered with the NASD as market
makers. The NASD thus combined the dual functions
of an exchange: regulating access to and operation of
NASDAQ, and regulating the internal affairs of those
of its members which are not members of any
exchange (generally the smaller firms). At the
beginning of the twenty-first century, the NASD
spun-off its NASDAQ market as a separate for-profit
entity. NASD Regulation (NASDR) is now a separate
entity that handled the NASD's regulatory functions.

In 2006, the NASDAQ national market became registered under 1934 Act § 6 as a national securities exchange.

Prior to 1983, a firm was not required to join the NASD in order to trade in OTC securities. However, in that year, 1934 Act § 15(b)(8) was amended to provide that no broker or dealer may effect transactions in any security (other than commercial paper, bankers' acceptances, or commercial bills) unless it became an NASD member.

FINRA. Following demutualization, it was necessary to separate the profit centers from the regulatory functions. As a result, the regulatory functions that formerly belonged to the NASD and the NYSE were transferred to new SROs—NASD Regulation (NASDR) and New York Stock Exchange Regulation (NYSER). In 2007, NASDR merged with NYSER to form the Financial Industry Regulatory Authority (FINRA) that carries out the functions formerly handled by NASDR and NYSER. As this book went to press, FINRA continued to work on a consolidated rulebook of regulations.

Securities Acts Amendments of 1975. Between 1968 and 1970, the securities industry passed through an operational and financial crisis, which ultimately led to extensive Congressional modification of the self-regulatory scheme. The Securities Acts Amendments of 1975 made important changes in the powers of the SRO's and the SEC's role in supervising them. 1934 Act § 19, as amended in 1975, expanded and consolidated the SEC's authority over *all* self-regulatory organizations. The

SEC's authority with respect to exchanges and FINRA is roughly comparable to, but even broader than, its previous authority over the NASD. In particular, the SEC must give advance approval for any exchange rule changes and has review power over exchange disciplinary actions. The 1975 amendments also confirmed the SEC action terminating the power of exchanges to fix minimum rates of commission (which both Congress and the SEC found to have been a major cause of market distortion) and directed the SEC to eliminate any other exchange rules which imposed unwarranted restraints on competition.

(A) CIVIL LIABILITY UNDER SRO RULES

In addition to the questions of policy discussed above, the authority delegated by Congress to non-governmental entities to adopt rules having the force of law has given rise to two difficult questions of civil liability. The first question is whether a self-regulatory organization can be held liable in damages for failure to enforce its rules. The second question is whether a customer of a broker-dealer has an implied private right of action against the firm for damages resulting from its violation of an exchange or NASD rule, as may exist in the case of violation of an SEC rule.

Exchange or NASD and FINRA Liability. While an exchange cannot be held liable for failing to *adopt* a rule which would have prevented injury to a plaintiff, see Cutner v. Fried, 373 F.Supp. 4 (S.D.N.Y.1974), courts have stated that there may be liability for damages resulting from its failure to *enforce* a rule which it has adopted. In the early case of Baird v. Franklin, 141 F.2d 238 (2d Cir.1944), the court held that 1934 Act § 6, under which the rules of an exchange must provide for appropriate sanctions against members who engage in conduct inconsistent with just and equitable principles of trade, "places a duty upon the Stock Exchange to enforce the rules and regulations prescribed by that section." (That duty is now explicitly imposed by 1934 Act § 19(g)(1), added in 1975.)

However, the approach taken by the Supreme Court since 1975 of not implying a private right of action under any section of the law in the absence of evidence of a congressional intent to create one (see § 36 below) has changed the situation. In Walck v. American Stock Exchange, 687 F.2d 778 (3d Cir.1982), the court found "a clear congressional intent not to create a private damages remedy" against an exchange under 1934 Act § 6 and thus held that no such right existed. See also Spicer v. CBOE, 977 F.2d 255 (7th Cir.1992).

Limited Immunity from Suit. A number of courts have recognized a doctrine of "absolute immunity" for SROs when they act in a quasi-public prosecutorial or adjudicatory activity pursuant to regulatory authority delegated to them under the Exchange Act. MFS Securities Corp. v. New York Stock Exchange, Inc., 277 F.3d 613 (2d Cir.2002); D'Alessio v. New York Stock Exchange, Inc., 258 F.3d 93 (2d Cir.2001); Partnership Exchange Securities Co. v. NASD, 169

F.3d 606 (9th Cir.1999). A similarly immunity exists
with respect to arbitration proceedings.

Liability for Violation of SRO Rules. The other
question is whether an SRO member who violates
one of the rules of the organization is liable in
damages to a person injured by the violation. In
Colonial v. Bache, 358 F.2d 178 (2d Cir.1966), the
court declined to hold either that there would always
be, or that there would never be, a private right of
action for violation of an exchange or NASD rule. The
question, said Judge Friendly, was "the nature of the
particular rule and its place in the regulatory
scheme." The case for implying a private right of
action would be strongest where a rule "provides
what amounts to a substitute for regulation by the
SEC itself" and "imposes an explicit duty unknown to
the common law"; it would be weakest in a case, like
Colonial, where plaintiff was claiming that failure to
comply with an alleged oral understanding violated
the exchange's "catch-all" prohibition against
"conduct inconsistent with just and equitable
principles of trade."

Courts began to reject the *Colonial* approach in
light of the Supreme Court's more restrictive attitude
toward implied private rights of action (see § 36
below), and held that there is no right of action for
violation of any exchange or NASD (and now FINRA)
rules, since there is no evidence that Congress
intended to create one. See also Spicer v. Chicago
Board Options Exchange, 977 F.2d 255 (7th
Cir.1992); Craighead v. E.F. Hutton, 899 F.2d 485
(6th Cir.1990); Jablon v. Dean Witter, 614 F.2d 677

(9th Cir.1980); Klitzman v. Bache, 499 F.Supp. 255 (S.D.N.Y.1980). However, since those rules constitute an industry expression of what constitutes proper conduct, a willful violation of the rules may give rise to a claim under 1934 Act Rule 10b–5. Clark v. John Lamula Investors, 583 F.2d 594 (2d Cir.1978).

(B) ANTITRUST LIMITATIONS ON SRO ACTIONS

As noted above, an SRO may be held civilly liable for failure to enforce its rules. On the other hand, it may also be held civilly liable for action taken to enforce those rules, if a member or nonmember injured by the action can show that the SRO lacked legal authority for the action it took.

Prior to the 1975 amendments, there was no statutory means of obtaining SEC or court review of an exchange disciplinary action, although NASD disciplinary actions were subject to SEC review. The principal vehicle for attacking exchange actions in the courts, therefore, was federal antitrust law, particularly the prohibition in § 1 of the Sherman Act against contracts, combinations, or conspiracies in restraint of trade. The theory of such attacks was that, since an exchange is an association of competing broker-dealers, any action it takes which limits the ability of members to compete with one another, or the ability of non-members to compete with members, is a *per se* violation of the Sherman Act, unless the exchange is exempted from the antitrust laws by the provisions of the federal securities laws.

Silver v. NYSE, 373 U.S. 341 (1963), involved an
NYSE order to its members to terminate their wire
connections with plaintiff, a broker-dealer who dealt
solely in unlisted securities. The district court held
that the NYSE action was a *per se* violation of the
antitrust laws, since the NYSE had no statutory
power to regulate trading in unlisted securities. The
court of appeals reversed, holding that the NYSE had
statutory power to regulate all transactions by its
members, including their transactions in unlisted
securities, and that since the NYSE action was
"within the general scope of its authority" under the
1934 Act, that action was exempt from the antitrust
laws. The Supreme Court rejected both extremes. It
held that the NYSE did have statutory authority to
regulate its members' transactions in unlisted
securities but that the 1934 Act did not automatically
repeal the antitrust laws with respect to any action
which the Exchange had authority to take. "Repeal is
to be regarded as implied only if necessary to make
the [Act] work, and even then only to the minimum
extent necessary. This is the guiding principle to
reconciliation of the [antitrust laws and securities
laws]." The implied repeal analysis applies in other
contexts as well. For example, the Sherman Antitrust
Act's restraint of trade provisions were held to have
been impliedly repealed with respect to a claim
challenging listing of options on securities exchanges.
In re Stock Exchanges Options Trading Antitrust
Litigation, 317 F.3d 134 (2d Cir.2003).

With respect to the specific situation before it, the
Court said that since the SEC had no power to review
Exchange disciplinary actions, there was "nothing

built into the regulatory scheme which performs the antitrust function of insuring that an exchange will not in some cases apply its rules so as to do injury to competition which cannot be justified as furthering legitimate self-regulative ends." And since the NYSE had refused to tell the plaintiff the nature of the charges against him or afford him an opportunity to explain or refute them, the NYSE had no basis for justifying its action in that case as "necessary to make the Exchange Act work."

This "antitrust-due process" approach has been followed in a number of subsequent cases, see, e.g., Zuckerman v. Yount, 362 F.Supp. 858 (N.D.Ill.1973), and also held applicable to the NASD, Harwell v. Growth Programs, Inc., 451 F.2d 240 (5th Cir.1971). However, the need to resort to antitrust law to attack SRO disciplinary actions is substantially lessened by 1934 Act § 19(d), added in 1975, which makes all SRO disciplinary actions reviewable by the SEC (and thus ultimately by the courts).

The more significant question raised by the decision in *Silver* was whether the antitrust laws applied to exchange *rules* which operated to restrict competition, particularly the exchange rules which required members to charge fixed minimum rates of commission on all transactions. In 1975, *after* the SEC had ordered an end to fixed commission rates and *after* Congress had confirmed that decision in the 1975 amendments, the Supreme Court held that the pre-existing rules fixing commission rates were not subject to antitrust attack. The Court said that, "given the expertise of the SEC, the confidence the

Congress has placed in the agency, and the active roles the SEC and the Congress have taken, permitting courts throughout the country to conduct their own antitrust proceedings would conflict with the regulatory scheme authorized by Congress." Congress." Gordon v. NYSE, 422 U.S. 659 (1975).

Since the 1975 Amendments confirm the termination of fixed commission rates, and direct the SEC to "review existing and proposed rules of the self-regulatory organizations and to abrogate any present rule or to disapprove any proposed rule imposing a competitive restraint neither necessary nor appropriate in furtherance of a legitimate regulatory objective," H.Rep. No. 94–229, at 94 (1975), future application of antitrust laws and principles to exchange and NASD (and now FINRA) actions will most likely arise in the course of SEC review of those actions, rather than in separate proceedings in the courts.

In 1979, in the course of considering proposed amendments to NASD rules governing fixed-price underwritings, the SEC ordered public hearings to determine, among other things, whether the rules unduly restricted price competition. Upon conclusion of the hearings, the SEC approved the rule changes, which continue to sanction fixed-price offerings and which purport to restrict underwriters from using portions of the underwriting discount to reward dealers and others for unrelated services. Sec. Exch. Act Rel. 34–17371 (1980). The SEC regulation of IPO practices serves as an implied repeal of the antitrust laws, leading the Second Circuit to hold that purchasers in public offerings lacked antitrust standing to challenge price fixing by the underwriters. Friedman v. Salomon/Smith Barney, Inc., 313 F.3d 796 (2d Cir.2002). The Supreme Court in another case subsequently held that IPO practices, including "laddering" were immune from antitrust attack because of their regulation under the securities laws. Credit Suisse Securities (USA) LLC v. Billing, 551 U.S. 264 (2007).

CHAPTER VI

REGULATION OF INVESTMENT COMPANIES AND INVESTMENT ADVISERS

In § 30 of the Public Utility Holding Company Act of 1935, Congress directed the SEC to make a study of investment trusts and investment companies, their corporate structure, their investment policies, and their influence on the companies in which they invest. The resulting SEC study, submitted to Congress in 1938–39, detailed a number of serious abuses in the operation of these investment vehicles. The exposure of these abuses led to the passage of the Investment Company Act of 1940 (ICA), which provided for SEC regulation of investment company activities.

Following World War II, investment companies (particularly mutual funds) experienced a period of rapid growth. A Wharton School "Study of Mutual Funds" (1962) for the SEC, and the SEC's own report on "Public Policy Implications of Investment Company Growth" (1966) suggested the need for modification of the 1940 Act, particularly with respect to the controls over management and sales compensation. After four years of hearings, reflecting serious disagreements between the SEC and the industry, Congress passed the Investment Company Act Amendments of 1970, significantly revising the law. Further minor changes were made in the Securities Acts Amendments of 1975.

§ 26. COVERAGE OF THE 1940 ACT

The Investment Company Act (i) requires every investment company to register with the SEC, (ii) imposes substantive restrictions on the activities of a registered investment company and persons connected with it, and (iii) provides for a variety of SEC and private sanctions.

Under ICA § 3(a), an investment company is an entity which (a) "is * * * engaged *primarily* * * * in the business of investing, reinvesting, or trading in securities" (emphasis added), or (b) is "engaged" in that business and more than 40% of its assets consist of "investment securities" (i.e., all securities other than government securities and securities of majority-owned subsidiaries).

(A) TYPES OF INVESTMENT COMPANIES

Most investment companies are organized as corporations, although they may also be set up in trusts, partnerships, or other forms. Most of the regulatory provisions use corporate terms such as "directors" and "shareholders," so appropriate modifications must be made when other forms are used.

The Act divides investment companies into three classes: "face-amount certificate companies," which issue fixed-income debenture-type securities; "unit investment trusts," which offer interests in a fixed portfolio of securities, and the most important class, "management companies," which includes all other types of investment companies. ICA § 4.

"Management companies" are further divided into "open-end" and "closed-end" companies, ICA § 5(a), and into "diversified" and "non-diversified" companies, ICA § 5(b). "Open-end companies," commonly known as "mutual funds," are those which offer redeemable securities. They generally offer shares on a continuous basis, at a price related to current net asset value (i.e., the current market value of the fund's portfolio divided by the number of shares of the fund outstanding), and stand ready to redeem shares at any time at the shareholder's request, also at net asset value or at a price related to it. "Closed-end companies" are more similar to other types of corporations; at any time, they have a fixed number of shares outstanding, which are traded either on an exchange or in the over-the-counter market, at prices which reflect supply and demand and may be substantially above or below the net asset value.

An investment company is "diversified" if, with respect to at least 75% of its portfolio, the securities of any single issuer do not account for (a) more than 5% of the investment company's assets, or (b) more than 10% of the outstanding voting securities of that issuer. (These diversification requirements are similar to those which permit an investment company to qualify for special tax treatment under § 851(b)(4) of the Internal Revenue Code.) Since diversification depends on the amount of investment in a single issuer, an investment company which invests solely in a single industry or geographical area is still considered "diversified."

Although money market funds are not classified as a separate type of investment company under the statute, the SEC has adopted special rules applicable to these funds. For example, the Commission has imposed limits on the amount of money that money market funds can invest in debt instruments of any one issuer. ICA Rule 2a–7. One of the unique aspects of money market funds was that the per share value remained constant. Variations in net asset value will thus, if anything, affect the dividends on the shares, rather than the price of the shares. In July 2104, the SEC amended its applicable Investment Company Act Rules to permit floating net asset values, which thus allows funds to "break the buck" as it has been called colloquially. Under the rules as amended, institutional money market funds may have a floating net asset value rounded to the fourth decimal place. Money Market Fund Reform; Amendments to Form PF. Sec. Act Rel. No. 33–9616, Inv. Adv. Act Rel. No. IA–3879, Inv. Co. Act Rel.90.10 No. IC–31166 (SEC July 23, 2014). Money market funds can impose a liquidity fee of up to two percent and/or a redemption gate, which temporarily suspends redemptions, in the event that weekly liquidity levels fall below the threshold set forth by the SEC in the rules. Id. The rules also enhanced disclosure requirements and increased portfolio diversification requirements.

"Inadvertent" Investment Companies. Because of the broad definition of "investment company" in ICA § 3(a), an operating company that sells a significant part of its assets and reinvests the proceeds in securities of other companies that it does not control

may find itself in the position of an "inadvertent" investment company. This means the company is subject to serious restrictions on its activities if it registers with the SEC or to severe sanctions if it does not. Compounding this dilemma in many cases is the difficulty of determining what the company's "principal" business is or how to value its "investment securities" and other assets for the purpose of determining whether it meets the 40% test. See SEC v. Fifth Ave., 289 F.Supp. 3 (S.D.N.Y.1968).

Even if more than 40% of a company's assets are "investment securities," it is not considered an investment company if either (i) it is primarily engaged in other businesses, directly or through wholly-owned subsidiaries, or (ii) it applies for and obtains an SEC order declaring it to be primarily engaged in other businesses, directly or through majority-owned subsidiaries or "controlled companies conducting similar types of businesses." ICA §§ 3(b)(1), (2). While the former exemption is self-executing, the latter provides a broader exemption where the company can convince the SEC that its relationships with its "controlled companies" take it outside the purposes of the Act.

(B) EXEMPTIONS

Closely-Held Companies. ICA § 3(c)(1) excludes from the definition of "investment company" any issuer which has not more than 100 beneficial security holders and which is not making any public offering of securities. Relying on this exemption, a large number of private "hedge funds" have been established, usually in partnership form, to engage in short selling, margin transactions, option trading, and other types of aggressive investment practices barred to registered investment companies.

Hedge Funds. A hedge fund is a variety of an investment company that typically is offered to a limited number of investors with high net worth requirements. These funds were generally formed as limited partnerships but have increasingly been organized as limited liability companies, which have become the more popular form of doing business over the years. Hedge funds tend to be high-risk investments since they are based on leveraging and hedging techniques. These funds frequently engage in short selling, margin transactions, and generally participate in the derivatives markets.[3]

---

[3]   As explained in an NASD investor advisory:

To get positive investment performance, hedge fund managers use sophisticated investment strategies and techniques that may include, among other techniques:

- short selling (sale of a security you do not own)
- arbitrage (simultaneous buying and selling of a security in different markets to profit from the difference between the prices)
- hedging (buying a security to offset a potential loss on an investment)
- leverage (borrowing money for investment purposes)
- concentrating positions in securities of a single issuer or market
- investing in distressed or bankrupt companies
- investing in derivatives, such as options and futures contracts
- investing in volatile international markets

As noted above, ICA § 3(c)(1) provides an exemption for funds that have fewer than 100 beneficial owners, and § 3(c)(7) exempts funds of which all shareholders are qualified purchasers. The exemptions from registration in §§ 3(c)(1) and 3(c)(7) of the Investment Company Act were often used to provide an exemption for hedge funds from the Act's registration provisions. According to the SEC, in 2003 only sixty of the more than 5,700 hedge funds in this country were registered under the Investment Company Act. As with other exempt funds, although these unregistered hedge funds are subject to general antifraud provisions, they are not subject to the Investment Company Act's specific disclosure requirements.

In the fall of 2004, the SEC, by a three-to-two vote of the Commissioners, in essence eliminated the exclusion that had shielded hedge fund managers from registration. The rule amended provides a "look through" approach in counting the number of advisory clients so as to limit the exclusion for advisers providing services to a limited number of clients. See Rule 203(b)(3)–2 (2004). As a result of the SEC's "look through" calculation method, many hedge fund managers that were formerly exempt were to be subject to registration as investment advisers under § 203 of the Investment Advisers Act.

- investing in privately issued securities

NASD Investor Alert, http://www.nasdr.com/alert_hedgefunds. htm (Aug. 23, 2002). *See, e.g.,* NASD Reminds Members of Obligations When Selling Hedge Funds, http://www.nasdr.com/ pdf-text/0307ntm.pdf (NASD Feb. 2003).

In 2006, the D.C. Circuit Court of Appeals struck down the SEC's Investment Adviser Act hedge fund rule. Goldstein v. SEC, 451 F.3d 873 (D.C. Cir. 2006). The SEC's eventual response to *Goldstein* was to abandon attempts to require registration under the Investment Advisers Act. Instead, in December 2006, the Commission proposed an antifraud rule aimed at hedge funds and also heightened sophistication and wealth requirements for investors qualifying for Investment Company Act and Securities Act exemptions. The proposed new antifraud rule under ICA § 206(4), which has since been adopted, prohibits an investment adviser from defrauding investors in a hedge fund or certain other pooled investments. The SEC also proposed two new 1933 Act rules to require individuals investing in hedge funds and other private funds relying on an exemption under ICA § 3(c)(1) to have a minimum of $2.5 million in certain types of investments at the time of their investment in the fund. The SEC adopted the proposed rule in July 2007. Rule 206(4)–8. The pooled investment fraud rule avoids identifying certain acts that amount to "fraud," which would leave room for would-be fraudsters to argue that unenumerated acts are not prohibited; instead, the rule contains a broad definition of fraud that is open to interpretation by the SEC. The rule, which does not require a showing of scienter, does not provide a private right of action. IAA Rule 206(4)–8. As a result of these rules, even though the SEC abandoned the proposed registration requirement for hedge funds, there has been an increase in transparency and regulation of some hedge funds. An increasing number of hedge funds have been listed on securities exchanges.

"Business Development Companies." The Small Business Investment Incentives Act of 1980, 94 Stat. 2275, established a class of "business development companies," which are exempt from many of the provisions of the Act. ICA § 6(f). A "business development company" is one which invests in, and "makes available significant managerial assistance" to, companies which (a) do not have any securities eligible for margin credit under 1934 Act § 7 (see § 24(a) above), or (b) are controlled by the business development company. ICA § 2(a)(46), (48). A business development company that invests at least 70% of its assets in "eligible portfolio companies" is exempt from all of the regular substantive restrictions of the Act and is subject instead to a separate body of rules contained in a group of sections added to the Act, which in many respects are less restrictive than the rules applicable to other classes of investment companies. ICA §§ 6(f), 54–65.

Specialized Investment Media. The Act excludes from coverage banks, insurance companies, savings and loan associations, finance companies, oil and gas drilling funds, charitable foundations, tax-exempt pension funds, and other special types of institutions. ICA §§ 3(c)(3)–(13). However, insurance companies and banks have been held to be subject to the Act when they publicly offer investment plans or services in which the rate of return varies depending on the performance of a separate fund of securities. Thus, for example, money market funds that are not pure banking products offered by commercial banks will be subject to the ICA.

In Prudential v. SEC, 326 F.2d 383 (3d Cir.1964), the court accepted the SEC position that a separate account established by an insurance company to fund "variable annuities" was itself an investment company required to register under the Act, even though the company that operated the account was clearly engaged primarily in the business of insurance. The 1970 amendments subsequently exempted separate accounts used to fund certain types of employee pension plans. ICA § 3(c)(11). When insurance companies began to develop "variable life insurance" in the early 1970s, the SEC first took the position that the separate accounts used to fund such insurance should be exempt from the Act because of the possible conflicts with state insurance laws. ICA Rel. IC–7644 (1973). However, the SEC subsequently reversed this position, withdrew the blanket exemption, and adopted rules to exempt such accounts only from specified provisions of the Act. ICA Rel. IC–9482 (1976).

Common trust funds, and collective funds maintained by banks for investment of pension fund assets, are specifically excluded from the definition of "investment company." ICA §§ 3(c)(3), (11). In 1962, the Comptroller of the Currency authorized national banks to establish commingled funds for "managing agency accounts," in effect permitting them to offer their customers interests in a bank-managed "mutual fund." However, the Supreme Court held that a bank's operation of such a fund involved "underwriting" of securities in violation of the Glass-Steagall Act. Investment Co. Inst. v. Camp, 401 U.S. 617 (1971). Ten years later, the Supreme Court upheld a regulation of the Federal Reserve Board permitting bank holding companies to manage closed-end investment companies. Federal Reserve Board v. Investment Co. Inst., 450 U.S. 46 (1981). Since that time, lower courts have permitted banks to engage in a wide range of investment company-related activities. See, e.g., Investment Co. Inst. v. Conover, 790 F.2d 925 (D.C.Cir.1986). The Gramm-Leach-Bliley Act, enacted in 1999, permits banks to engage in securities activities, thus expanding banks' potential interaction with the ICA.

§ 27.   REGULATION OF FUND ACTIVITIES

Registration and Reporting Requirements. An investment company registers with the SEC by filing a notification of registration setting forth a statement of its investment policy and other specified information. ICA § 8. A registered company must file annual reports with the Commission, ICA § 30, and maintain specified accounts and records, ICA § 31.

Protection of Assets. As a safeguard against looting of investment company assets, all securities must be held in the custody of a bank or stock exchange member, or under strict procedures laid down by the SEC. ICA § 17(f), ICA Rule 17f–2. Larceny or embezzlement from an investment company is a federal crime, ICA § 37, and officers and employees who have access to the company's cash or securities must be bonded. ICA § 17(g), ICA Rule 17g–1.

Capital Structure. An open-end company (mutual fund) may not issue any "senior security" (debt or preferred stock) other than notes to evidence bank borrowings. ICA § 18(f). A closed-end company may issue not more than one class of debt securities and not more than one class of preferred stock, provided that it has an asset coverage of at least 300%, in the case of debt, or 200%, in the case of preferred stock. ICA §§ 18(a), (c). No registered management company may issue any rights or warrants to purchase any of its securities. ICA § 18(d). An investment company may not make any public offering of its securities until it has a net worth of at least $100,000. ICA § 14(a).

Dividends. No dividends may be paid from any source other than accumulated undistributed net income, or net income for the current or preceding fiscal year, unless accompanied by a written statement disclosing the source of such payment. Under the tax laws, an investment company must pay dividends to its shareholders amounting to at least 90% of its taxable ordinary income each year to avoid double taxation of its income to itself and its shareholders. IRC § 852(a)(1).

Investment Activities. An investment company may not purchase securities on margin, sell short, or participate in joint trading accounts. ICA § 12(a). It may not incur underwriting commitments aggregating more than 25% of the value of its total assets. ICA § 12(c). Unless authorized by the vote of a majority of the holders of its voting securities, it may not borrow money, issue senior securities, underwrite any securities, purchase or sell real estate or commodities, make loans, change its investment policy with respect to concentration or diversification, change its subclassification, or change the nature of its business so as to cease to be an investment company. ICA § 13(a).

Investment companies, unlike trusts, insurance companies, and other types of institutional investors, are not limited to a "legal list" in making investments, nor are they subject to the "prudent man" rule. The managers, therefore, cannot be held liable for losses resulting from investments which turned out badly or might have been deemed "imprudent" by a conservative investor. The managers are subject to SEC sanctions, however, if they fail to provide the kind of investment management and supervision that they advertised in their sales literature or statements of policy. Managed Funds, Sec. Act Rel. 33–4122 (1959); Financial Programs, Sec. Exch. Act Rel. 34–11312 (1975); Chase, Inv. Adv. Act Rel. IA–449 (1975). In such situations, the directors of the fund may also be held civilly liable, under state law, for damages caused by the mismanagement. Lutz v. Boas, 39 Del.Ch. 585, 171 A.2d 381 (1961). In Brouk v. Managed Funds, 286 F.2d 901 (8th Cir.1961), the court held that such mismanagement did not give rise to an implied right of action against the directors under the Investment Company Act, but subsequent decisions have recognized such a right of action. See Fogel v. Chestnutt, 668 F.2d 100 (2d Cir.1981).

Fund Investments in Other Funds. As a result of its unpleasant experience in the 1960s with The Fund of Funds, a large European-based mutual fund which invested heavily in the shares of American mutual funds, the SEC urged Congress to prohibit any investment company from acquiring shares of any other investment company. The 1970 amendments, however, did not impose a complete prohibition. Instead, they limited such investment so that no investment company can own more than 3% of the stock of another investment company nor invest more than 5% of its assets in any one investment company or more than 10% of its assets in other investment companies generally. ICA § 12(d).

§ 28.   MANAGEMENT AND CONTROL

(A)   SHAREHOLDERS, DIRECTORS AND OFFICERS

All shares of stock issued by an investment company must have equal voting rights, and voting trusts, where shareholders transfer their title and voting rights to a trustee to consolidate shareholders' voting power, are prohibited. ICA §§ 18(i), 20(b). Solicitations of proxies from investment company shareholders are subject to approximately the same rules that apply under 1934 Act § 14 to solicitations of shareholders of listed companies. ICA § 20(a), Rules 20a–1, 2, 3.

In addition to their voting rights under the laws of an investment company's state of incorporation, shareholders are entitled to vote on: changes in investment policy or status, ICA § 13(a), approval or assignment of investment advisory contracts, ICA § 15(a), filling of more than a specified number of vacancies in the board of directors, ICA § 16(a), sale of stock of a closed-end company below net asset value, ICA § 23(b), and appointment of independent public accountants, ICA § 32(a).

The Act contains a number of provisions designed to insure the integrity of directors and officers and the independence of the board of directors. Under ICA § 9(a), no person who has been convicted within 10 years of a securities-related felony or is enjoined from securities-related activities may serve as a director or officer or in certain other specified capacities. And ICA § 17(b) prohibits any provisions indemnifying directors or officers against liabilities to the company arising out of their willful misfeasance, bad faith, gross negligence, or reckless disregard of duty.

To assure the existence of independent voices on the board of directors, ICA § 10(a) provides that no more than 60% of the members of the board may be "interested persons" of the company. (There is an exception for "no-load" funds managed by registered investment advisers, which are required to have only one "non-interested" director. ICA § 10(d).) The term "interested person" was introduced by the 1970 amendments, and represents a significant broadening of the category of "affiliated persons" which was the standard prior to 1970. In addition to "affiliated persons," who are persons in a direct control relationship with the investment company or its adviser, ICA § 2(a)(3), the term "interested person" includes any broker-dealer or affiliate of a broker-dealer, any person who has served as legal counsel to the company within the past two years, any member of the immediate family of an affiliated person, and any other person whom the SEC determines to have had "a material business or professional relationship" with the company or its principal executive officer within the past two years, ICA § 2(a)(19).

In 1999, the SEC proposed rules, which were adopted in 2001, designed to enhance the independence of investment company directors. ICA Rel. No. IC–24082 (1999). Under the rules as amended, the independence requirements, which are a precondition for various amendments from the ICA, require that (1) independent directors constitute either a majority or a super-majority (two-thirds) of the fund's board of directors, (2) independent directors select and nominate other independent directors, and (3) any legal counsel for the fund's independent directors be an independent legal counsel. The SEC has also been moving toward requiring boards and chairmen to be independent of the fund manager.

(B) MANAGEMENT COMPENSATION

Most business corporations are managed by their own officers, who act under the supervision of the board of directors. In contrast, investment companies, particularly mutual funds, normally contract with a separate entity known as the "investment adviser" to provide all management and advisory services to the investment company for a fee. In fact, the normal procedure is for the investment advisory organization (which may be a partnership or a privately or publicly held corporation) to create one or more mutual funds as "corporate shells" to serve as vehicles for pooling the investments of a large number of small customers.

In an effort to protect the shareholders of an investment company from overreaching by the adviser, ICA § 15(a) provides that an investment adviser must serve under a written contract approved initially by a vote of the shareholders and thereafter approved annually by the board of directors of the investment company. The typical investment advisory contract calls for compensation of the adviser on the basis of a percentage of the fund's net assets. As mutual funds developed, the most common arrangement was to set the annual advisory or management fee at ½ of 1% of the average net assets of the fund during the year. As some funds grew in size during the 1950s to $1 billion or more, the annual fees charged by their advisers increased correspondingly to $5 million or more a year. Critics of the industry, subsequently joined by the SEC, attacked these fees on the grounds that they bore no relation to the value of the services provided by the adviser, and were grossly out of line with fees charged for the management of pension funds and other portfolios of comparable size and investment objectives. Derivative suits were brought by shareholders on behalf of a number of funds alleging that the high fees constituted a waste of corporate assets and a breach of the directors' fiduciary duties to the funds under state corporation law and the Investment Company Act. In the fully litigated cases, the plaintiffs were unsuccessful. The courts, while finding the fees "high," held that they were not so "unconscionable" or "shocking" as to constitute "waste." Acampora v. Birkland, 220 F.Supp. 527 (D.Colo.1963); Saxe v. Brady, 40 Del.Ch. 474, 184 A.2d 602 (1962); Meiselman v. Eberstadt, 39 Del.Ch. 563, 170 A.2d 720 (1961). However, a number of other cases were settled, with the adviser agreeing to scale down the fee to a lower percentage of assets as the fund reached a certain size or making other adjustments.

In its 1966 report to Congress on mutual funds, the SEC recommended that the Act be amended to subject advisory fees to a statutory standard of "reasonableness," with a listing of factors to be taken into account in determining whether a particular fee was "reasonable." The industry vehemently opposed this recommendation, and the 1970 amendments to the Act took a different approach. A provision was added to ICA § 36, under which an investment adviser is "deemed to have a fiduciary duty with respect to the receipt of compensation for services" from an investment company. This duty is specifically made enforceable in the courts, either by the SEC or in a suit by a fund shareholder, which does not require prior demand on the directors. Daily Income Fund v. Fox, 464 U.S. 523 (1984).

While the Congressional reports on this amendment refer to the developments which led up to the legislation, they do not define the content of the adviser's "fiduciary duty." It has been held, however, to bar an adviser from increasing its fees, even with shareholder approval, where the increase was of no benefit to the investment company. See Galfand v. Chestnutt, 545 F.2d 807 (2d Cir.1976).

Shareholder actions brought under ICA § 36(b) have tended to focus on the money market funds because of the high fees generated by their dramatic growth (see § 26(a) above). In the first fully litigated case, the court upheld the fairness of an annual management fee of $33 million on a fund with assets of $11 billion, after consideration of all the factors mentioned in the legislative history of the amendment. Gartenberg v. Merrill Lynch, 694 F.2d 923 (2d Cir.1982), 740 F.2d 190 (2d Cir.1984). Subsequent cases have consistently rejected challenges to management fees under ICA § 36(b). See, e.g., Jones v. Harris Associates L.P., 527 F.3d 627, 633 (7th Cir. 2009), *cert. granted* 556 U.S. 1104 (2009), *reversed* 559 U.S. 335 (2010).; Krinsk v. Fund Asset Management, 875 F.2d 404 (2d Cir.1989); Kalish v. Franklin Advisers, 742 F.Supp. 1222 (S.D.N.Y.1990), aff'd, 928 F.2d 590 (2d Cir.1991). *But cf.* Gallus v. Ameriprise Financial Inc., 561 F.3d 816 (8th Cir. 2009) (remanding judgment for defendant).

The Supreme Court in Jones v. Harris Associates L.P., 559 U.S. 335 (2010), unanimously upheld consideration of a fiduciary standard in reviewing compensation under the investment advisory contract. The Supreme Court held that limiting the inquiry to disclosure was not consistent with the Act nor with the congressional intent. The burden of proving that the fee arrangement violates the Act's standards falls on the plaintiff. In evaluating the fee arrangement, the reviewing court should consider all relevant factors, not just the adequacy of the disclosures. The benchmark for judging the advisory fee whether the fees are within a range that likely would result from arm's length bargaining. As explained by the Court "[t]he essence of the test is whether or not under all the circumstances the transaction carries the earmarks of an arm's length bargain." The Supreme Court agreed with the Seventh Circuit that courts should not second guess the directors' collective judgment and that some measure of deference is appropriate. Nevertheless, the courts will examine fees in light of the fiduciary obligation imposed by the Act while at the same time giving deference to the board's decision if such deference is warranted by all of the relevant surrounding circumstances. It is not sufficient that the plaintiff's establish the possibility of lower fees by comparison with comparable fee arrangements. Instead, the plaintiffs must carry a heavier burden of showing a "large disparity" in fees. In rejecting the Seventh Circuit's approach, the Supreme Court gave its approval to the following factors set forth by the Second Circuit in *Gartenberg*. In reviewing fees under the advisory contract courts should consider "the adviser-manager's cost in providing the service, . . . the extent to which the adviser-manager realizes economies of scale as the fund grows larger, and the volume of orders which must be processed by the manager" in addition to "(1) the nature and quality of the services provided to the fund and shareholders; (2) the profitability of the fund to the adviser; (3) any 'fall-out financial benefits,' those collateral benefits that accrue to the adviser because of its relationship with the mutual fund; (4) comparative fee structure (meaning a comparison of the fees with those paid by similar funds); and (5) the independence, expertise, care, and conscientiousness of the board in evaluating adviser compensation."

As an additional measure to assure adequate consideration of advisory fees by an investment company's board of directors, the 1970 amendments also added ICA § 15(c), under which any amendment or renewal of the advisory contract must be approved by a majority of the *disinterested* directors, who are under a duty to request "such information as may reasonably be necessary to evaluate the terms of [the] contract."

(C) TRANSFER OF MANAGEMENT

One of the evils at which the 1940 Act was aimed was "trafficking" in advisory contracts, in which the adviser to an investment company would assign its rights under the contract to another person or entity. Accordingly, ICA § 15(a)(4) required that every advisory contract with an investment company automatically terminate upon its assignment. The term "assignment" was defined to include any transfer of a controlling interest in the management organization, ICA § 2(a)(4), so that any such transfer would also require approval by the shareholders of the investment company.

In its 1966 report, the SEC proposed the addition of a provision to the Act which would bar transfer of control of a management organization where it was "likely to impose additional burdens on the investment company or to limit its freedom of future action." In view of uncertainty as to the purpose and scope of this recommendation, no such provision was added in the 1970 amendments. However, in Rosenfeld v. Black, 445 F.2d 1337 (2d Cir.1971), a shareholder's derivative action attacking the payment of a fee to the former adviser in connection with a change of advisers, the court adopted the position originally urged by the SEC in the *Insurance Securities* case, and held that the transaction, under the circumstances presented, was a breach of the adviser's implied fiduciary duty under the ICA.

This decision created great uncertainty as to when, if ever, the stock of a management organization could be sold at a premium over net asset value. Congress therefore added § 15(f) to the ICA in 1975, providing that no attack could be made on the amount received on such a sale, provided that (a) for a period of three years after the sale, at least 75% of the directors of the investment company must be disinterested (instead of the normal 40%), and (b) no unfair burdens (in the form of compensation for anything other than bona fide services) are imposed on the investment company as a result of the transaction. Stockholders have an implied private right of action for a violation of ICA § 15(f). Meyer v. Oppenheimer, 764 F.2d 76 (2d Cir.1985).

§ 29.   TRANSACTIONS WITH AFFILIATES

One obvious possibility for abuse by the persons in control of an investment company is to cause the investment company to buy securities from them, or to sell securities to them, at a price which is more favorable to them than to the investment company. Under ICA § 17(a), therefore, it is illegal for any affiliated person, promoter, or principal underwriter of an investment company to sell securities or other property to the company, or buy them from the company, or to borrow from the company, subject to certain limited exceptions. However, under ICA § 17(b), the SEC is authorized, upon application, to exempt a proposed transaction from the prohibition of ICA § 17(a) if it finds that the transaction (1) is fair and reasonable and does not involve overreaching on the part of any person concerned, (2) is consistent with the policy of the investment company, and (3) is consistent with the general purposes of the Act. Under this standard, the SEC must be satisfied that the transaction is fair, not only to the investment company, but to all other parties to the transaction. E.I. du Pont v. Collins, 432 U.S. 46 (1977).

(A)   JOINT TRANSACTIONS

In addition to the prohibition on transactions between an investment company and an affiliate, ICA § 17(d) bars affiliates and underwriters from entering into any transaction in which the investment company is a "joint participant," in contravention of SEC rules designed to prevent the investment company from participating "on a basis different from or less advantageous than" the other participant. Under the authority of this section, the SEC adopted ICA Rule 17d–1, requiring all joint arrangements to be approved by the Commission before any transactions are consummated. A pattern or practice under which officers or directors repeatedly make investments in enterprises in which the investment company is also investing has been held to be a "joint arrangement" within the meaning of these provisions. SEC v. Midwest, CCH ¶ 91,252 (D.Minn.1963).

The "Portfolio Affiliate" Problem. The term "affiliated person," as defined in ICA § 2(a)(3), includes not only any person who "controls" an investment company or owns more than 5% of its stock, but also any corporation or other entity more than 5% of the stock of which is owned by the investment company. Any understanding between an investment company and one of these "portfolio affiliates" (for example, with respect to acquiring substantial interests in the stock of another corporation in connection with a take-over bid) may constitute a "joint arrangement" requiring SEC approval. SEC v. Talley, 399 F.2d 396 (2d Cir.1968).

(B)   BROKERAGE TRANSACTIONS

ICA § 17(e) bars an affiliated person from receiving any compensation for acting as an agent or broker in any transaction by the investment company, except that such a person may receive a brokerage commission for effecting securities transactions for the investment company, provided it does not exceed "the usual and customary broker's commission" for such transactions. This exception permits brokerage firms which act as advisers to investment companies also to act as brokers for those companies. However, the elimination of fixed minimum commissions on stock exchange transactions in 1975 (see § 25(b) above) complicated the problem of determining when a commission exceeds the "usual and customary commission." The SEC in 1979 adopted a rule specifying the conditions to be met in order for commissions to satisfy the statutory standard. ICA Rule 17e–1. In addition, in 2004, the SEC amended ICA Rule 12b–1 (relating generally to distribution of open-end management company shares) to prohibit mutual funds from paying securities brokers an added commission for directing customers purchases to their mutual fund shares.

The most difficult problem with respect to brokerage commissions, however, has not been the direct payment of commissions to affiliated brokers, but the routing of commissions to brokerage firms which provided other services to the investment company or its adviser. Prior to 1975, the rules of the various stock exchanges specified minimum commissions to be paid on all transactions. Investment companies tend to trade in larger-than-average transactions which, under the existing commission rate schedules, were highly profitable to the brokerage firms which executed them. Investment company managers therefore began to direct their brokerage business to firms which also performed other services, particularly those which sold mutual fund shares to the public, thus increasing the size of the fund and consequently the fee received by the adviser. Under stock exchange rules, it was not necessary to direct the actual orders to the firms which sold fund shares; a large order could be directed to a firm skilled in executing such orders, with instructions to "give up" a portion of the commission (often as much as 75%) to other firms which sold fund shares.

The termination of fixed commission rates in 1975 substantially eliminated the "give-up" problem. However, in the 1975 Securities Acts Amendments, Congress added § 28(e) to the 1934 Act, under which an adviser to an investment company or any other institution is deemed not to have breached any fiduciary duty under state or federal law by causing the institution to pay a broker a higher commission than other brokers would charge for the same transaction if the adviser determines in good faith that the commission is reasonable "in relation to the value of the brokerage and research services" provided by the broker to all accounts under the adviser's management. This provision, designed to permit institutional managers to use commission dollars paid by managed accounts to acquire research as well as execution services, encouraged the allocation of brokerage to high-cost brokers through what are known as "soft dollar" arrangements. In 1976, the SEC issued a release designed to limit these arrangements by providing that they could not be used to acquire "products and services which are readily and customarily available and offered to the general public on a commercial basis." Sec. Exch. Act Rel. 34–12251 (1976). Ten years later, however, the

Commission concluded that that standard was "difficult to apply and unduly restrictive in some circumstances" and stated that the "principle to be used to determine whether something is research is whether it provides lawful and appropriate assistance to the money manager in the performance of his investment decision-making responsibilities." Sec. Exch. Act Rel. 34–23170 (1986). This liberalization led to an explosion in these arrangements, so that by 1990 it was estimated that one-third to one-half of all trades on the NYSE were paid for in part with "soft dollars."

§ 30. SALE OF FUND SHARES

As noted above, investment companies are divided into "closed-end" and "open-end" companies. Closed-end companies, like other corporations, issue a fixed number of shares to the public in a one-shot underwritten offering. Open-end companies, or "mutual funds," make a continuous offering of shares at a price related to the current "net asset value" (i.e., the current market value of the fund's portfolio, divided by the number of shares outstanding). Mutual funds are in turn divided into "load" and "no-load" funds. Load funds distribute their shares to the public either through securities dealers or (in the case of a few large fund complexes) through their own "captive" sales forces, charging a sales commission, or "load," ranging up to 8.5% of the public offering price. No-load funds sell shares directly to the public through the mail, charging the current net asset value, with no sales charge added. The principal underwriter of a fund's shares must operate under a written contract renewed at least annually by the shareholders or directors of the fund. ICA § 15(b).

A number of problems with investment company sales practices came to light in recent years. A number of funds offer "breakpoint" pricing for their shares depending either upon the class of shares being offered or the amount of money investment. An SEC study indicated that many firms have not been offering many investors the breakpoint discounts that could have been applicable. These findings resulted in increased focus on disclosures relating to and the pricing of investment company shares.

Other improper mutual fund practices have recently been uncovered. Investigations by the SEC and the New York Attorney General revealed that many reputable mutual funds were engaging in fraudulent practices. The two most visible practices were late trading schemes and market timing.

Late trading involves insiders using their positions to take advantage of forward pricing. Open-end mutual fund shares are based on forward pricing. Open-end fund shares are priced each day based on the net asset value of the fund's assets at the close of regular trading in the securities markets (4:00 p.m. Eastern Standard Time). Late trading occurs when a trade is entered after the markets closed but is priced at the level fixed by the 4:00 calculation. This allows late traders to take advantage of events taking place after 4:00 that will move the net asset value either up or down. This allows the late trader to guarantee a profit by trading on news available to everyone but at a price available only to those who have access to late trading. All other investors desiring to trade on the news get to trade at the price fixed at 4:00 on the *next* trading day, after that news has affected the price of the securities in the fund's portfolio. Late trading thus operates just like insider trading. A group of insiders are able to take advantage of their access based on their position. In the case of insider trading, the violation consists of taking advantage of information not generally available at a transaction price available to the investing public. Conversely, late trading allows an insider to take advantage of pricing not available to the investing public in order to take advantage of price movements resulting from information that is generally available. Late trading practices unfairly advantage participating investors and have been the subject of SEC enforcement actions. In late 2003, the SEC proposed a 4:00 p.m. cut-off for mutual fund trading in order to eliminate late trading issues.

Market timing of transactions in mutual fund shares is another way to take advantage of the forward pricing mechanism of open-end mutual fund shares. It provides another way for traders to take advantage of prices that have become stale because the mutual fund share price is fixed notwithstanding events and news that will affect the fund share price once the next net asset valuation is made at the close of trading. Market timing permits traders to trade during the course of business one day and then lock in a mutual fund price based on the previous day's close and then sell the mutual fund shares the next day once the fund shares are trading at the price that reflects the new information. The mutual fund industry segments engaging in this practice claim that although it may have been questionable, it is not illegal. Nevertheless, the SEC and the states have been pursuing certain market timing practices as securities law violations. There are at least two instances in which institutional market timing of mutual fund shares is clearly improper. In the first instance, if a mutual fund, as it should, discourages short-term investment strategies but then enters into arrangements with market timers that encourage timing, the fund has breached obligations to the other fund shareholders. The second situation involves off-shore funds where the varying time zones allow market timers to take advantage of forward pricing of mutual fund shares in much the same was as late traders in the United States. Improprieties also occur when a fund fails to charge redemption fees in order to facilitate undisclosed or otherwise improper market timing by the account holder.

(A) DISCLOSURE REQUIREMENTS

The disclosure requirements of the Securities Act of 1933 apply to investment companies, but with certain modifications. Under ICA § 24(a), an investment company's registration statement, instead of containing the information required by Schedule A to the 1933 Act, may set forth certain of the information contained in the company's reports under ICA § 30. And ICA § 24(b) requires that any sales literature used by a mutual fund to supplement the information contained in its prospectus must be filed with the SEC. In addition, since mutual funds make continuous offerings of their shares, ICA § 24(e)(3) modifies 1933 Act §§ 11 and 13 to provide that the effective date of the most recent amendment to a fund's registration statement is deemed to be the effective date of the registration statement and the date of commencement of the fund's public offering. (In the absence of this provision, people who purchased fund shares several years after the commencement of the fund's public offering would have no right of action under 1933 Act §§ 11 and 12.)

The SEC was strongly criticized for imposing unduly strict limitations on what mutual funds can say in their advertising. Accordingly, in 1979 it took three steps which drastically reduced the restrictions: (a) it adopted Rule 482 under the 1933 Act, under which an advertisement in the print or broadcast media which contains only information that could be included in a statutory prospectus (but not necessarily all of such information) satisfies the prospectus delivery requirements of 1933 Act § 5; (b) it rescinded its detailed "Statement of Policy" governing the contents and method of presentation of investment company sales literature; and (c) it adopted Rule 156 under the 1933 Act, specifying the factors which would be taken into account in determining whether investment company sales literature would be considered false or misleading under the general antifraud provisions. See Sec. Act Rels. 33–6034, 6116, 6140 (1979). In 1996, Congress further liberalized these provisions by authorizing the SEC to permit investment companies to use prospectuses that include information not found in the prospectus filed as part of the statutory registration statement. ICA § 24(g).

To enhance the ability of mutual fund investors to compare the costs of different funds, the SEC in 1988 revised its disclosure forms to require all funds to feature prominently in their prospectuses a standardized fee table showing how large of a bite management fees, sales charges, and other expenses will take out of a $1,000 investment over various periods of time.

(B) CONTROLS ON PRICES

Closed-End Companies. To prevent "dilution" of the interests of existing shareholders, ICA § 23(b) prohibits closed-end companies from issuing shares at a price below their current net asset value without the consent of a majority of their shareholders. Since the shares of closed-end companies normally trade in the market at substantial discounts from net asset value, this provision makes it extremely difficult for existing closed-end companies to make additional offerings of their shares.

Open-End Companies. ICA § 22 contains a complicated set of provisions governing the prices at which shares of open-end companies, or "mutual funds," can be sold to the public. ICA § 22(a) authorizes the NASD to adopt rules prescribing the methods of computing the price at which its members may purchase shares from the fund and resell them to the public, for the purpose of preventing dilution or unfair discrimination between different purchasers or holders of fund shares.

ICA § 22(d) provides that no fund shares may be sold to the public "except at a current offering price described in the prospectus." If a particular fund states in its prospectus that its shares are offered at current net asset value plus a sales load of 8.5%, no dealer may sell shares of that fund to the public at any other price. The price-fixing provisions of ICA § 22(d), like other "retail price maintenance" statutes, have been defended by the industry on the ground that they are essential to the maintenance of an "orderly distribution system." In its 1966 Mutual Fund Report to Congress, the SEC pointed out how the statutory restraint on competition had produced uneconomically high sales charges for mutual fund shares, but stopped short of recommending that ICA § 22(d) be repealed. Instead, it persuaded Congress to modify ICA § 22(b) (which had previously contained a prohibition against "unconscionable or grossly excessive" sales loads) to give the NASD (now FINRA) authority to fix maximum sales loads so that the public offering price "shall not include an excessive sales load but shall allow for reasonable compensation for sales personnel, broker-dealers, and underwriters, and for reasonable sales loads to investors." The NASD, operating under this "reasonable" standard, eventually adopted rules, effective June 1, 1976, under which sales loads may not exceed 8.5% (the previously prevailing figure). However, most funds that sell shares on a "load" basis currently charge sales loads averaging about 5%.

Payment of Distribution Costs by Fund. ICA § 12(b) prohibits a mutual fund from acting as distributor of its own securities, except in compliance with SEC rules. Prior to 1980, this provision effectively barred the funds themselves from bearing any part of the cost of selling fund shares, meaning that these costs had to be paid out of the sales loads received by the underwriter or, in the case of funds sold on a "no-load" basis, by the management company. In 1980, the Commission adopted ICA Rule 12b–1, under which a fund can act as distributor of its own shares and bear all or part of the cost of distribution, provided it does so pursuant to a plan approved by the directors and shareholders of the fund. Abuses soon developed with respect to these "12b–1 plans." The SEC has brought a number of proceedings against fund managers for using fund assets for expenses unrelated to sales, and the NASD has barred funds which impose ICA 12b–1 charges from advertising themselves as "no-load" funds.

(C) EXCHANGE TRADED FUNDS

In recent years, a new type of mutual fund has become increasingly popular. A number of closed-end funds are now traded like stocks on the exchanges, including the New York Stock Exchange. These exchange traded funds (ETFs) allow investors to buy into a large basket of stocks. The selection of stocks in the ETF may be in order to recreate a widely followed stock index such as is done with Standard and Poor's Depositary Receipts (SPDRS). ETFs can also be sector or industry funds allowing investors to diversity within identified industries, stocks, and/or markets. ETFs are not limited to securities. If the funds include derivative investments such as swaps or more traditional commodity futures contracts, they will also be subject to the jurisdiction of the Commodity Futures Trading Commission under the Commodity Exchange Act.

§ 31. REGULATION OF INVESTMENT ADVISERS

Definitions and IAA Coverage

IAA § 203(a) requires registration of all investment advisers doing business through an instrumentality of interstate commerce unless exempted under section 203(b). The Investment Advisers Act defines "investment adviser" to include "any person who, for compensation, engages in the business of advising others, either directly or through publications or writings, as to the value of securities or as to the advisability of investing in, purchasing, or selling securities * * * ." IAA § 202(a)(11). As discussed below, there are significant exclusions from the definition of investment adviser. Some of the more important exclusions are banks, lawyers, accountants, engineers, or teachers rendering such advice incidental to their professions. Broker-dealers who render advice incidental to their broker-dealer operations are excluded from the definition of investment adviser. There is another exclusion for publications that render impersonal investment advice. Also excluded from the definition are financial planners and other professionals who may render generalized advice as to how people should manage their money—including their investment activities but do not render advice on individual securities or mutual funds. When the activities of an entity are purely administrative and do not involve rendering investment advice, the Act's definition of investment adviser will not be implicated. However, the fact that an entity's primary function is not the rendering of investment advice will not preclude application of the Investment Advisers Act.

As evidenced by the exclusions from the definition of investment adviser, simply because someone renders investment advice as part of their profession does not put them within the Investment Advisers Act's definition of investment adviser. This is true even for the professions not expressly listed in the exclusions from the Act. Thus, for example, a sports agent who advises professional athletes on investment matters does not necessarily fall within the definition of investment adviser. See Zinn v. Parrish, 644 F.2d 360, 364 (7th Cir.1981). A number of factors will be considered in determining whether someone who renders investment advice as part of their profession will fall within the definition of investment adviser.

The more individualized the investment advice that is given, the more likely it is that someone will be classified as an investment adviser. As pointed out above, one of the considerations is whether the person rendering the investment advice is in the business of rendering such advice. Whether someone who renders advice is considered to be in the business of rendering investment advice depends on a number of factors. A significant factor is whether the person rendering advice holds himself or herself out as an investment adviser or someone providing investment advice. A second factor weighing in favor of classifying someone as an investment adviser is whether he or she receives any separate or additional compensation representing "a clearly definable charge" for those advisory services. See United States v. Elliott, 62 F.3d 1304, 1309–1311 (11th Cir.1995). The SEC takes a broad view of what constitutes compensation for advisory services. Rendering of investment advice without compensation is likely to take the person rendering the advice out from under the purview of the Investment Advisers Act. As a third factor, if the person rendering specific investment advice does so other than on "rare, isolated and non-periodic" occasions, he or she is not likely to be considered to be in the business of rendering investment advice. See id.

The definition of investment adviser depends upon the advice being rendered with regard to securities as opposed to some other type of investment. However, it is to be recalled that the definition of security is expansive and is not limited to traditional securities, such as stocks and bonds. Thus, for example, someone who offers clients advice with regard to investment vehicles, such as tax-exempt repurchase agreements, stock income agreements, or collateral loan agreements can fall within the Act's definition of investment adviser. See id.

The use of the Internet has raised all sorts of challenging regulatory issues under the securities laws. One such issue relates to its use for investment advice. Investment advice can be rendered through web sites as well as through chat rooms. The use of the Internet for the rendering of investment advice will classify the person rendering the advice as an investment adviser, unless he or she can fit within the exclusion for publications that render impersonal investment advice. See SEC v. Park, 99 F.Supp.2d 889 (N.D.Ill.2000) (holding defendants did not fall within the exclusion from the definition of investment adviser for general publications). The SEC has indicated that providing a "passive" electronic bulletin board to facilitate the posting of information about securities will not qualify as rendering investment advice for the purpose of having to register under the Investment Advisers Act. In order to avoid having to register, the providers of passive bulletin boards (1) may not be involved in any purchase or sale negotiations arising from the bulletin board and (2) may not give advice regarding the merits or shortcomings of any particular trade. See, e.g., Internet Capital Corp., 1998 WL 9357 (SEC No Action Letter Jan. 13, 1998).

Following the wake of scandals in the mutual fund industry, the SEC adopted a series of new compliance requirements for investment companies and investment advisers. IAA Rule 206(4)–7 requires registered investment advisers to adopt and implement written policies and procedures, reasonably designed to prevent violations of the Advisers Act. These policies and procedures at a minimum, to the extent that they are relevant, must address portfolio management processes, including (1) allocation of investment opportunities and compliance with clients' investment objectives and restrictions; (2) trading practices, including best execution and soft dollar arrangements; (3) proprietary trading of the adviser and personal trading activities of its employees; (4) accuracy of disclosures; (5) safeguarding of client assets; (6) creation and maintenance of required records; (7) marketing services, including the use of solicitors; (8) valuation of client assets and the assessment of fees based on those valuations; (9) safeguards for client privacy protection; and (10) business continuity plans.

IAA Rule 206(4)–7 further requires that registered investment advisers review their policies and procedures annually to determine their adequacy and the effectiveness of their implementation. The rule also requires registered investment advisers to designate a chief compliance officer to administer its compliance policies and procedures. This chief compliance officer should have sufficient seniority and authority to (1) be competent and knowledgeable regarding the Advisers Act and (2) be empowered with full responsibility and authority to develop and enforce appropriate policies and procedures.

Exclusions from the Definition of Investment Adviser

The definition of investment adviser excludes banks, lawyers, accountants, engineers, or teachers rendering such advice incidental to their professions. IAA § 202(a)(11)(B). Also excluded are advises who render advice solely with respect to government securities of the United States government. IAA § 202(a)(11)(E).

Exclusions   Generally;   Exemptions Distinguished. An exclusion from the definition of Investment Adviser means that there is no regulation under any of the provisions of the Investment Advisers Act. In contrast, an exemption provides only an exemption from the Act's registration provisions.

Exclusion for Broker-Dealers. IAA § 202(a)(11)(C) excludes from the definition of investment adviser is any broker-dealer whose advisory service "is solely incidental to the conduct of his business as a broker or dealer" and without special compensation. Once it is established that someone is a broker, the burden falls on the SEC (or other plaintiff) to show that the investment advice given was more than incidental to the brokerage activities and that special compensation was received for that advice. See, e.g., SEC v. Kenton Capital, Ltd., 69 F.Supp.2d 1, 13 (D.D.C.1998). Absent proof of such special compensation, a broker-dealer will not be classified as an investment adviser. A broker-dealer's holding himself or herself out as a financial planner will not in itself implicate the Investment Advisers Act registration provisions. See Inv. Adv. Act Rel. No. IA–770 (Aug. 13, 1981). When dealing with investment advice furnished by brokerage firms, a critical issue is whether the customer is paying specially for the advice or whether the advice is simply part of the brokerage service. Although excluded from the Investment Advisers Act, brokers and dealers furnishing such incidental advice are subject to the suitability, "know your customer," and "know your merchandise" requirements when making investment recommendations to customers (see chapter 14 above).

Publications. Bona fide news media including financial publications of general circulation and persons limiting such advice to securities issued or guaranteed by the federal government are not subject to the Investment Advisers Act registration requirements, as are other persons excluded by SEC rule. IAA § 202(a)(11)(D)–(F). However, the SEC has indicated that registration may be required for a computer-generated financial planning service, although not recommending specific securities, which would nevertheless offer a service developed by an unaffiliated organization where the service identifies investments that would affect the generalized investment recommendations. See In re Computer Language Research, Inc., [1985–1986 Transfer Binder] Fed.Sec.L.Rep. (CCH) ¶ 78,185 (SEC No Action Letter Dec. 26, 1985). In Lowe v. SEC, 472 U.S. 181 (1985), the Supreme Court interpreted the exclusion for publications and investment newsletters, explaining that the exclusion is limited to publications that render impersonal investment advice. The Court then held that the publication in question, a semimonthly newsletter, did fall within the exclusion, which meant the publisher was not an investment adviser. Regardless of whether the publisher is an investment adviser, recommendations in publications that contain materially misleading factual information can run afoul of 1934 Act Rule 10b–5.

Financial Planners. The past several decades have witnessed the growth of financial planning as an industry. The emergence of the financial planning industry necessarily raises questions concerning the applicability of the Investment Advisers Act's registration provisions. Financial planners who render only generalized investment advice do not have to register under the Investment Advisers Act.

Exemptions from the Investment Advisers Act

In addition to the above-mentioned exclusions from the definition of investment adviser, the Act provides exemptions from registration. IAA § 203(b). These exemptions do not immunize the adviser from the Act's antifraud provisions. While securities offerings to sophisticated investors are exempted from registration under the 1933 Act, there is no comparable exemption for investment advisers.

There are three exemptions from investment adviser registration. First, a local adviser—that is, one whose clients are residents of the state of its principal place of business—is exempt so long as the adviser does not furnish advice with regard to exchange-listed securities. IAA § 203(b)(1). This exemption for local advisers became less meaningful after April 10, 1997. As of that date, advisers with less than $25 million in assets under management who are not advisers to registered investment companies are subject to the exclusive regulatory jurisdiction of the states. IAA § 203A.

The second exemption from investment adviser registration applies to advisers whose only clients are insurance companies. IAA § 203(b)(2). The third exemption from investment adviser registration applies to advisers who do not have more than fifteen clients and do not hold themselves out as advisers either to the public or to investment companies. IAA § 203(b)(3).

This third exemption for so-called private investment advisers was used to shield most hedge funds from regulation. Advisers of most hedge funds were not subject to the Act's registration requirements. The SEC tried to subject hedge fund advisers to the registration requirements of IAA § 203. See Registration Under the Advisers Act of Certain Hedge Fund Advisers, Inv. Co. Act Rel. No. IA–2333, 2004 WL 2785492 (SEC 2004). The exclusion for advisers that have a limited number of clients was amended to provide a "look-through" approach that no longer counts a fund as one advisory client but rather looked through to the fund's investors as advisory clients. However, as previously mentioned, the look-through approach was struck down as inconsistent with the statutory scheme. Goldstein v. SEC, 451 F.3d 873 (D.C. Cir. 2006). As discussed below, the SEC now regulates most hedge funds.

Regulation of Private Funds

As part of the Dodd-Frank Act, Congress gave the SEC statutory authority and a mandate to regulate private investment funds. Section 403 of the Dodd-Frank Act eliminated the former exemption for advisers with fewer than fifteen advisory clients that was found in former IAA § 203(b)(3). Under this new regulatory scheme, larger private fund advisers are subject to registration, reporting, and disclosure obligations under the Investment Advisers Act. A private fund is defined as an investment company that is not subject to Investment Company Act registration because the fund has fewer than one hundred shareholders or where all of the shareholders are qualified purchasers under the Investment Company Act. IAA § 202(a)(29). The Dodd-Frank Act directs the SEC to adopt an exemption from the private fund registration requirements for an adviser having less than $150 million in assets under management in the United States and which provides investment advice *solely* to one or more private funds meeting the definition. IAA § 203(m)(1). Also, the Investment Advisers Act now sets forth an exemption for foreign private advisers with fewer than fifteen U.S. clients and less than $25 million aggregate assets attributable to clients in the United States. IAA § 203(b)(3).

The private fund registration, reporting, and record-keeping requirements will be implemented by SEC rulemaking. The Act nevertheless sets standards as to some of the record-keeping and reporting requirements. For example, the required records and reports will include: the amount of assets under management, the extent of leverage, including off-balance sheet leverage; the types of investment assets; credit risk exposure as a counterparty; trading and investment positions; the valuation policies and procedures; any arrangements or understandings that would provide more favorable treatment for some fund investors as compared with others; the firm's trading practices; and such other information and reports as the SEC may require as necessary and appropriate in the public interest and for investor protection or to promote assessment of systemic risk.

SEC Rulemaking

In June 2011, the SEC adopted the rules implementing the Dodd-Frank provisions relating to private investment advisers. See Exemptions for Advisers to Venture Capital Funds, Private Fund Advisers with Less Than $150 Million in Assets Under Management, And Foreign Private Advisers Inv. Adv. Act Rel. No. IA–3222, 2011 WL 2482894 (June 22, 2011). As a result of the Dodd-Frank Act and the implementing rules, a number of formerly exempt private funds advisers must register with the SEC under the Investment Advisers Act. See Rules Implementing Amendments to the Investment Advisers Act of 1940, Inv. Adv. Act Rel. No. IA–3221, 2011 WL 2482892 (June 22, 2011). However, there are some categories of advisers that do not require Investment Adviser Act registration. Those advisers include: advisers solely to venture capital funds; advisers solely advising private funds with less than $150 million in assets under management in the United States; and certain foreign advisers that do not have a place of business in the United States. The discussion below summarizes the private adviser rules.

Division of Federal and State Jurisdiction

As a result of 1996 amendments to the Investment Advisers Act, there is exclusive federal jurisdiction over larger advisers and those advising registered investment companies. Investment advisers managing more than $25 million in assets and advisers to registered investment companies fall under the exclusive jurisdiction of the SEC. All other advisers are subject to the exclusive jurisdiction of the states. The Act further limits the regulation that can be imposed on those advisers by states other than the adviser's principal place of business. There have been attempts by some advisers covered by this exception to retain their registration under the Act. Presumably, such a request is motivated by a preference for the federal rather than state regulatory regime. The SEC rules permit federal registration of some investment advisers even though they do not reach the $25 million threshold. IAA Rule 203A–2 exempts advisers that otherwise would have to be registered in thirty or more states from the prohibition against SEC registration of advisers below the $25 million dollar threshold. Thus, truly national advisers can register with the SEC regardless of the asset value of the accounts they manage. Federal registration is permitted for newly formed investment advisers who reasonably expect that they will satisfy the thirty-state test within ninety days of registration with the SEC. Also, an Internet-based investment adviser that provides all of its investment advice through the Internet may register with the SEC regardless of the amount of funds under management. IAA Rule 203A–2(f).

As a result of the Dodd-Frank amendments, there are now three categories of investment advisers for determining whether state or federal registration is required for non-exempt advisers: small, midsized, and large advisers. The category of small advisers consists of advisers with less than $25 million under management. Non-exempt small advisers must register under state law rather than with the SEC. Large advisers are those with $100 million or more under management. The SEC has the statutory authority to raise the $100 million threshold for federal registration through SEC rulemaking. IAA § 203A(a)(2). Large advisers must register with the SEC absent an applicable exemption. In between these two categories are midsized advisers—those with between $25 and $100 million under management. Non-exempt midsized investment advisers must register either with the states or with the SEC, depending upon how many states require registration of the adviser. For these midsized advisers, state registration is required unless there are at least 15 states that would require registration, in which case the adviser may register with the SEC. Id.

Investment advisers subject to the state registration requirements register electronically through the Investment Adviser Registration Depository (IARD). The registration depository is a joint effort of the SEC and the North American Securities Administrators Association (NASAA).

CHAPTER VII

SANCTIONS FOR VIOLATIONS

The federal securities laws provide for several different types of official sanctions against persons who violate the law and specify the procedures to be followed in utilizing them.

§ 32. SEC INVESTIGATIONS

The SEC has statutory authority to conduct investigations to determine whether there has been a violation of federal securities law. This authority includes power to subpoena witnesses, administer oaths, and compel the production of books and records anywhere in the United States. 1934 Act § 21; 1933 Act §§ 19(b), 20(a). In areas of doubtful jurisdiction, this authority empowers the SEC to conduct an initial inquiry to determine whether the subject of the inquiry is in fact subject to the securities laws. SEC v. Wall St. Transcript, 422 F.2d 1371 (2d Cir.1970); SEC v. Brigadoon, 480 F.2d 1047 (2d Cir.1973). However, where it is alleged that an SEC investigation was commenced because of political pressures, a court may deny enforcement of an SEC subpoena on grounds of abuse of process. SEC v. Wheeling-Pittsburgh, 648 F.2d 118 (3d Cir.1981).

In general, when information comes to the attention of the Commission indicating that a violation may have occurred, the Commission first conducts an informal inquiry, interviewing witnesses but not serving any compulsory process or taking any sworn statements. If this initial inquiry indicates the existence of a violation, the staff will ask the Commission for a formal order of investigation, which delineates the scope of the investigation and designates the staff members entitled to administer oaths and compel the production of witnesses and records.

The procedures to be followed in "formal investigative proceedings" are set forth in the Commission's Rules Relating to Investigations (RRI), 17 C.F.R. Pt. 203. Under these rules, a witness compelled to testify or produce evidence is entitled to see a copy of the formal order of investigation, RRI Rule 7(a), and to be accompanied, represented, and advised by counsel, RRI Rule 7(b), (c). To prevent collusion among witnesses, no witness nor his or her counsel may be present at the examination of any other witness, RRI Rule 7(b); however, the SEC may not bar a witness from being represented by his or her regular counsel, even though that counsel has also represented other witnesses, unless it can establish that the dual representation will "impede its investigation," SEC v. Csapo, 533 F.2d 7 (D.C.Cir.1976). Although the witness has an absolute right to inspect the transcript, the Commission may for good cause deny a witness the right to obtain a copy of the transcript of his or her own testimony. RRI Rule 6. See Commercial Capital v. SEC, 360 F.2d 856 (7th Cir.1966).

The conduct of an SEC investigation is subject to the same testimonial and related privileges as a judicial proceeding, McMann v. SEC, 87 F.2d 377 (2d

Cir.1937), including the attorney-client privilege, the Fourth Amendment prohibition against unreasonable searches and seizures, and the Fifth Amendment privilege against self-incrimination. However, since the securities business is "affected with a public interest" and the securities laws require the maintenance of certain books and records, production of records related to the business may be compelled in spite of Fifth Amendment claims. Shapiro v. United States, 335 U.S. 1 (1948); SEC v. Olsen, 354 F.2d 166 (2d Cir.1965).

The Commission is exempt from the Right to Financial Privacy Act of 1978 where it can show good reason to obtain financial records of a customer from a financial institution. 1934 Act § 21(h). The Commission need not notify the customer of its investigation for up to ninety days.

The SEC's formal investigative proceedings are normally conducted privately to avoid unwarranted injury to the reputations of the persons being investigated. 1934 Act § 21(a) authorizes the Commission to publish information concerning any violations that it uncovers in the course of its investigations. In some cases, the Commission has allowed persons who are under investigation to submit written statements describing their actions and promising to behave better in the future, which the Commission then makes public under 1934 Act § 21(a) "as part of the process of resolving their involvement in the investigation." One member of the Commission strongly criticized this procedure, arguing that the publicity constitutes the imposition of a sanction, and that it "is wrong for a government prosecutor to impose sanctions based on factual admissions, as contrasted to violations of law." Sec. Exch. Act Rels. 34–15664, 15665, 15667 (1979).

If the Commission determines to conduct a public investigation in a particular situation, and the record contains implications of wrongdoing by any person, that person must be afforded a reasonable opportunity for cross-examination and for production of rebuttal testimony or documentary evidence. RRI Rule 7(d). However, in a private investigation, a person who knows himself or herself to be a target of the investigation has no right to appear before the staff or the Commission to rebut charges that may have been made against the target. See SEC v. National Student Marketing, 538 F.2d 404 (D.C.Cir.1976).

An SEC investigation may serve as the prelude to several different types of governmental proceedings.

§ 33. SEC ADMINISTRATIVE PROCEEDINGS

If an SEC investigation uncovers evidence of a violation of the securities laws, the Commission may order an administrative hearing to determine responsibility for the violation and to impose sanctions. An administrative proceeding can only be brought against a person or firm registered with the Commission (such as a broker-dealer, investment adviser, investment company, or other regulated entity) or with respect to a security registered with the Commission. Sanctions available in an administrative proceeding include censure, limitations on the registrant's activities, or revocation of registration.

An SEC suspension proceeding has been held to be subject to the five-year statute of limitations found in 28 USC § 2462, which is applicable to actions "for the enforcement of any civil fine, penalty, or forfeiture." Johnson v. SEC, 87 F.3d 484 (D.C.Cir.1996).

Prior to 1964, the Commission had no direct means of disciplining an employee of a broker-dealer firm who had participated in the firm's illegal activities. The 1964 Securities Acts Amendments gave the Commission direct power to suspend or bar from association with any broker-dealer any person who the Commission finds has violated one or more specified provisions of the 1934 Act.

Additional amendments by Congress significantly expanded the SEC's powers by giving it authority (a) to impose civil penalties of up to $500,000 and/or order disgorgement of profits in administrative proceedings, and (b) to issue cease and desist orders against persons found to be violating or about to violate the securities laws, whether or not such persons are registered with the SEC. See 1934 Act §§ 21B, 21C.

The Dodd-Frank Act expanded the SEC's administrative authority beyond securities professionals. Accordingly, the SEC now has the power to bring administrative cease-and-desist proceedings and to impose monetary penalties against *any* person, rather than the previous limitation to impose fines on broker-dealers, investment advisers and companies, and other regulated enterprises. The Dodd-Frank Act also increased the penalty amounts that the SEC can seek in such administrative proceedings by adopting a three-tier penalty schedule under Section 8A of the Securities Act of 1933. The ability of the SEC to impose administrative sanctions against any person greatly expands the efficiency of many enforcement actions that formerly had to be filed in a federal court. At the same time, targets of administrative enforcement proceedings do not have the extensive rights available to defendants in civil court proceedings, including rights to pretrial discovery, protections of evidentiary rules, access to a jury trial, or a lesser standard for review upon appeal than applies to appeals from administrative orders. In the wake of Dodd-Frank's expansion of SEC administrative proceedings, a number of respondents raised constitutional challenges to the appoint process for administrative law judges (ALJs). See, e.g., Jarksey v. SEC, 803 F.3d 9 (D.C.Cir.2015) (respondent must fully litigate case before SEC prior to raising constitutional challenge). As this book went to press, we are still awaiting a decision on constitutionality.

(A) CONDUCT OF HEARINGS

An administrative hearing is commenced by serving a copy of the Commission's order for the hearing on all named respondents. The hearing is held before an independent Commission employee, known as an "administrative law judge." This hearing is generally conducted in the same manner as a non-jury trial, with the Commission staff and the respondents each having the right to present evidence and testimony and to cross-examine witnesses. The hearing may be either public or private in the Commission's discretion (proceedings under the 1933 Act must be public), with respondents often favoring private proceedings to minimize the adverse publicity.

At the conclusion of the hearing, the administrative law judge must file an "initial decision" containing the ALJ's findings of fact and conclusions of law. This decision may be reviewed by the Commission itself either on petition of one of the parties or on the Commission's own initiative. The Commission is not required to grant a petition for review, but its Rules of Practice provide that it will do so where suspension, denial, or revocation of registration is involved. The Commission decides the matter on the basis of briefs and (if requested) oral argument, and it may modify the initial decision in any way, including an increase in the sanctions imposed. See Hanly v. SEC, 415 F.2d 589 (2d Cir.1969).

It is quite common for respondents to make offers of settlement, consenting to lesser sanctions and SEC publication of its findings of violations in exchange for saving the expense and prolonged adverse publicity of a protracted proceeding. The Commission normally insists, as a condition of settlement, that the respondent agree that the Commission may publish its finding as to respondent's violations. Critics of the SEC have charged that the Commission uses its power to force settlements as a means of making and announcing new "law" in essentially non-adversary proceedings.

Under Rule 102(e) of its Rules of Practice, the SEC has asserted its authority to "deny * * * the privilege of appearing or practicing before it to any person who is found by the Commission after notice of and opportunity for hearing" (a) not to possess the requisite qualifications, (b) to be lacking in character or integrity or to have engaged in unethical or improper professional conduct, or (c) to have willfully violated federal securities laws. Under this Rule, the Commission has disqualified a number of lawyers and accountants from practice before it, despite objections that any person authorized by state law to practice his or her profession is entitled to appear before the SEC. While the courts may overturn an SEC disqualification that is not supported by substantial evidence or is procedurally improper, Kivitz v. SEC, 475 F.2d 956 (D.C.Cir.1973), Rule 102(e) itself has been upheld as a valid exercise of the Commission's power to protect the integrity of its own processes. Touche Ross v. SEC, 609 F.2d 570 (2d Cir.1979).

(B) JUDICIAL REVIEW OF SEC ACTIONS

Any party aggrieved by a final order entered in an SEC administrative proceeding may obtain review of the order in the United States Court of Appeals for the District of Columbia or in the circuit in which the party resides or has its principal place of business. 1933 Act § 9; 1934 Act § 25; ICA § 43. The courts have on occasion been critical of the SEC for its failure to enunciate clearly the legal rules or facts on which it was basing its decisions. See, e.g., Berko v. SEC, 297 F.2d 116 (2d Cir.1961), 316 F.2d 137 (2d Cir.1963). See also Checkosky v. SEC, 23 F.3d 452 (D.C.Cir.1994). Despite claims that the imposition of severe sanctions, based on allegedly fraudulent conduct, should be made only on the basis of "clear and convincing evidence," the Supreme Court has upheld the power of the Commission, under § 7 of the Administrative Procedure Act, to find a violation on the basis of "a preponderance of the evidence." Steadman v. SEC, 450 U.S. 91 (1981).

The Commission has taken the position that certain actions are not "orders" subject to judicial review. These include (a) a decision not to order a company to include a shareholder proposal in its proxy statement, see Medical Committee v. SEC, 432 F.2d 659 (D.C.Cir.1970), vacated as moot, 404 U.S. 403 (1972), (b) a decision not to object to the action of a stock exchange increasing the minimum commission rates to be charged by its members, see Independent Investor Protective League v. SEC, CCH ¶ 93,270 (2d Cir.1971) (summary of SEC brief), and (c) the adoption of a rule disqualifying certain types of entities from membership on a stock exchange, see PBW Stock Exchange v. SEC, 485 F.2d 718 (3d Cir.1973). The effect of these not being classified as orders is that there was no judicial review for these actions.

With respect to Commission "no-action" positions, the courts have taken the position that if the action involves a routine matter which the Commission properly delegated to its staff and declined to re-examine, there is no "order" subject to judicial review. Kixmiller v. SEC, 492 F.2d 641 (D.C.Cir.1974); see Koss v. SEC, 364 F.Supp. 1321 (S.D.N.Y.1973). With respect to SEC rule-making proceedings, the 1975 Securities Acts Amendments reversed the holding in the *PBW Stock Exchange* case, above, and authorized persons "adversely affected" by the adoption of an SEC rule to obtain review in a court of appeals. 1934 Act § 25(b). In addition, courts have held that an SEC rule adoption, while not an "order," is "agency action" subject to judicial review under § 10 of the Administrative Procedure Act. Independent Broker-Dealers' Trade Assn. v. SEC, 442 F.2d 132 (D.C.Cir.1971); Natural Resources Defense Council v. SEC, 389 F.Supp. 689 (D.D.C.1974).

§ 34.   SEC INJUNCTION ACTIONS

In addition to its power to bring administrative proceedings against persons and firms registered with it and to issue cease and desist orders, the Commission has specific statutory authority to bring an action in a federal district court to enjoin violations of the securities laws by any person. See, e.g., 1934 Act § 21(d).

Standards for Granting. In determining whether the SEC has made a "proper showing" for the issuance of an injunction, a court does not apply the "irreparable injury" test applicable to injunction actions by private parties. However, an SEC injunction action is generally commenced some time after the allegedly illegal acts have taken place, and "the current judicial attitude toward the issuance of injunctions on the basis of past violations at the SEC's request has become more circumspect than in earlier days." SEC v. Commonwealth, 574 F.2d 90 (2d Cir.1978). Therefore, an injunction will be granted only where "there is a reasonable likelihood of further violation in the future," id., or where the defendant poses a "continuing menace" to the public, SEC v. Caterinicchia, 613 F.2d 102 (5th Cir.1980).

Scope of Injunction. In appropriate cases, the injunction may prohibit specified kinds of illegal conduct with respect to any securities, not merely those involved in the past violation. However, the injunction may not be so broad as to turn any violation of law into a contempt of court. SEC v. Savoy, 665 F.2d 1310 (D.C.Cir.1981).

Consequences. In addition to giving rise to a possible contempt citation if the defendant commits another violation of the securities laws, the issuance of an injunction has certain direct consequences. A person who has been enjoined from future violations is disqualified from utilizing the exemption from 1933 Act registration provided by Regulation A and by 1933 Act Rule 505, and from being associated with a registered investment company, see ICA § 9(a)(2). More significantly, the Supreme Court has held that a defendant who is found to have violated the law in an SEC injunction action is barred by the doctrine of collateral estoppel from relitigating that issue in a subsequent private damage action based on the same course of conduct. The Court rejected arguments that this holding violated the defendant's constitutional right to a jury trial in the damage action. Parklane v. Shore, 439 U.S. 322 (1979).

Ancillary Relief. In addition to an injunction against further violations, the SEC will often ask the court for ancillary relief appropriate to the type of violation committed. For example, where the defendant has profited from "insider trading" or manipulative activities, the court may require the defendant to make a rescission offer, see SEC v. Bangor Punta, 331 F.Supp. 1154 (S.D.N.Y.1971), aff'd with modifications, 480 F.2d 341, 390–91 (2d Cir.1973), or to turn over his profits to the issuer or to a court-appointed trustee for distribution to persons entitled to them, see SEC v. Texas Gulf Sulphur, 446 F.2d 1301 (2d Cir.1971); SEC v. Golconda, 327 F.Supp. 257 (S.D.N.Y.1971). Where the offense involves pervasive corporate mismanagement, the SEC may obtain appointment of a receiver, SEC v. Fifth Avenue Coach Lines, 289 F.Supp. 3 (S.D.N.Y.1968), or of independent directors and special counsel to pursue claims on behalf of the corporation, SEC v. Mattel, Lit.Rels. 6531, 6532 (D.D.C.1974), or of a "special agent" to supervise defendant's compliance with the law, SEC v. Beisinger, 552 F.2d 15 (1st Cir.1977).

In 1990, Congress expanded the power of the courts in actions brought by the SEC by authorizing them (a) to prohibit any person who is found to have violated 1934 Act § 10(b) from serving as a director or officer of a company registered under the 1934 Act, and (b) to impose civil penalties of up to $500,000 on securities law violators. 1934 Act §§ 21(d)(2), (3).

§ 35.   CRIMINAL PROSECUTIONS

Willful violations of the securities laws or the rules promulgated under them are punishable by fine and imprisonment. See, e.g., 1933 Act § 24; 1934 Act § 32. The Commission does not prosecute criminal cases itself, but it transmits the evidence to the Justice Department, which decides whether to prosecute and handles the prosecution. See 1934 Act § 21(e).

As in criminal prosecutions generally, the "willfulness" requirement means only that the defendant must have intended the act which he or she did, and does not require a showing that the defendant knew the securities laws were being violated. United States v. Schwartz, CCH ¶ 93,023 (E.D.N.Y.1971), affirmed 464 F.2d 499 (2d Cir.1972).

The courts have consistently rejected arguments by defendants that various provisions of the securities laws are unconstitutionally vague when made the basis for criminal prosecutions. See United States v. Wolfson, 405 F.2d 779 (2d Cir.1968).

Conviction of a violation of the securities laws carries with it automatic disqualification from certain benefits or positions, such as the use of the Regulation A exemption, 1933 Act Rule 252(c)(3), (d)(1), or association with a registered investment company, ICA § 9(a)(1).

§ 36.   SRO DISCIPLINARY PROCEEDINGS

In an SEC administrative proceeding against a broker-dealer, one of the sanctions available to the Commission is the suspension or revocation of the respondent's membership in a self-regulatory organization (SRO), such as a national securities exchange or national securities association. In addition, the SROs themselves are specifically authorized, and indeed required, to impose sanctions on their members for violations of the securities laws or the SROs' own rules. 1934 Act §§ 6(b)(6), 15A(b)(7), 19(g)(1).

Originally, SRO disciplinary proceedings were rather informal, with respondents being accorded few of the protective features associated with governmental sanctions. It has been held, however, that SROs are sufficiently involved with the SEC to bring their disciplinary actions "within the purview of Fifth Amendment controls over governmental due process." Intercontinental Industries v. American Stock Exchange, 452 F.2d 935 (5th Cir.1971). On the other hand, SROs have been held not to be subject to the procedural requirements of the Administrative Procedure Act, Shultz v. SEC, 614 F.2d 561 (7th Cir.1980), and a claim that an SRO is "structurally biased" because its disciplinary decisions are made by members of the industry who have a pecuniary interest in putting the respondent out of business has also been rejected, First Jersey v. Bergen, 605 F.2d 690 (3d Cir.1979). Under the 1975 amendments to the Exchange Act, SROs must notify members of the specific charges against them, give them an opportunity to defend themselves, and support any sanctions with a statement setting forth the specific acts in which the member was found to have engaged, the specific rules which the member was found to have violated, and the reasons for the sanction imposed. 1934 Act §§ 6(d)(1), 15A(h)(2).

Prior to 1975, disciplinary actions by the NASD were subject to SEC review, but disciplinary actions by stock exchanges were not. Under the 1975 amendments, reports of all SRO disciplinary actions must be filed with the SEC, and such actions are subject to review by the SEC, either on its own motion or on application of any aggrieved person. If the SEC finds that the respondent engaged in the acts charged, that such acts violated the specified provisions, and that such provisions were applied in a manner consistent with the purposes of the Exchange Act, it is to affirm the sanction; if not, it is to set aside the sanction and, if appropriate, remand the matter to the SRO for further proceedings. The SEC must also set aside the sanction if it is excessive or oppressive or if it imposes any burden on competition not necessary in furtherance of the purposes of the 1934 Act. 1934 Act § 19(e). An SEC order affirming an SRO sanction is subject to court review in the same manner as an SEC sanction imposed in one of its own administrative proceedings.

CHAPTER VIII

CIVIL LIABILITIES

Supplementing the governmental and quasi-governmental sanctions for violations of federal securities law is the possibility of private actions for damages and other relief against alleged violators. The amount of private litigation under federal securities law has grown rapidly in recent years and currently accounts for a substantially greater expenditure of effort and expense than does direct government enforcement. The growth in private litigation was not slowed by the Private Securities Litigation Reform Act of 1995 (PSLRA) nor the Securities Litigation Uniform Standards Act of 1998 (SLUSA).

§ 37. SOURCES OF LIABILITY

There are three different types of provisions in the federal securities laws that may give rise to civil liabilities.

The first type is a provision creating an explicit private right of action. Four of these provisions are of the most importance. First, 1933 Act § 11 gives a right of action to purchasers of securities sold under a registration statement that contains material misstatements or omissions. Second, 1933 Act § 12 gives a right of action to purchasers of securities sold in violation of the registration requirements or by means of misleading statements. Third, 1934 Act § 16(b) gives a right of action to an issuer (or a shareholder suing on its behalf) against officers, directors, and major shareholders who profit from "short-swing" trading in the issuer's stock. And fourth, 1934 Act § 18 gives a right of action to a person who purchases or sells a security in reliance on misleading statements in a report filed under that Act.

The second type of provision that may give rise to civil liability is a provision purporting to affect legal relationships between private parties, but not explicitly creating a right of action. Examples of this type are 1934 Act § 29(b) and ICA § 47(a), which provide that every contract made in violation of the provisions of those respective Acts shall be "void" regarding the rights of specified persons, thus creating an implied private right of action to have the contract declared invalid. ICA § 47 was amended in 1980 to provide that a contract made in violation of that Act will be enforceable if the court finds that "enforcement would produce a more equitable result than non-enforcement and would not be inconsistent with the purposes of" the Act. The legislative history indicates that Congress believed that the change "codifies case law under the present section, and its analogs in other securities laws." H.Rep. 96–1341, at 37 (1980).

The third type, and by far the most important in terms of the volume of litigation, is the many provisions prohibiting certain actions or declaring them "unlawful." Starting with the famous decision in Kardon v. National Gypsum Co., 69 F.Supp. 512 (E.D.Pa.1946), the courts, applying traditional tort principles, implied a private right of action on behalf of persons injured by an alleged violation who were within the class of persons that the statutory prohibition was designed to protect. The provisions which were most extensively used as the basis for private actions of this type were (a) the general antifraud prohibitions in 1934 Act §§ 10(b) and 15(c)(1), 1933 Act § 17(a), and IAA § 206, and (b) the provisions governing proxy solicitations and tender offers in 1934 Act § 14.

The Supreme Court's first decision on the question came in J.I. Case Co. v. Borak, 377 U.S. 426 (1964), where the Court implied a private right of action to sue for a misleading proxy solicitation in violation of 1934 Act § 14(a), on the ground that the statutory purpose of "protection of investors * * * implies the availability of judicial relief where necessary to achieve that result." With respect to the availability of a private right of action under 1934 Act § 10(b) and 1934 Act Rule 10b–5, the Court in Superintendent v. Bankers Life, 404 U.S. 6 (1971), simply noted in a footnote, without discussion, that it was "established" that such a cause of action did exist.

Starting in 1975, the Supreme Court has taken a much more restrictive line. It has specifically refused to imply a private right of action under the Securities Investor Protection Act, SIPC v. Barbour, 421 U.S. 412 (1975), or under the record-keeping requirements of 1934 Act § 17, Touche Ross v. Redington, 442 U.S. 560 (1979), noting the differences between those provisions and the provisions involved in *Borak*. It has indicated in a number of decisions that it no longer adheres to the rationale of *Borak*, and that *Borak* and *Superintendent of Insurance* were "aberrations." See Blue Chip v. Manor, 421 U.S. 723, 730 (1975); Cannon v. University of Chicago, 441 U.S. 677, 692 n. 13, 735–36 (1979); Touche Ross v. Redington, above. Finally, in Transamerica Mortg. Advisors v. Lewis, 444 U.S. 11 (1979), the Court, in a 5–4 decision, refused to imply a private right of action under the antifraud provisions of IAA § 206, a decision which, as the dissenters noted, "cannot be reconciled with our decisions recognizing implied private rights of action for damages under securities laws with substantially the same language," i.e., 1934 Act § 10(b) and Rule 10b–5.

Three years after the *Transamerica Mortg.* decision, however, the Supreme Court held, again in a 5–4 decision, that a private right of action *could* be implied under the antifraud provisions of the Commodity Exchange Act. Merrill Lynch v. Curran, 456 U.S. 353 (1982). While the majority in the *Merrill Lynch* case relied on certain peculiarities in the legislative history of the Commodity Exchange Act, the dissenters found the decision flatly inconsistent with *Transamerica Mortg. Advisors*. Indeed, the only apparent reason for the different result in the two cases is that Justice Blackmun switched sides, since the lineup of the other eight justices remained the same.

The present situation appears to be as follows: (i) The Supreme Court will not overrule its decisions in *Borak* and *Bankers Life,* and will continue to recognize private rights of action for damages under

1934 Act §§ 14(a) and 10(b). (ii) The court will not imply the existence of such rights under any other sections unless it finds evidence in the language of the statute or the legislative history that Congress intended to create a private right of action. See Transamerica Mortg. Advisors v. Lewis, above, at 15–16; Touche Ross v. Redington, above, at 568. (iii) Most lower courts will refuse to recognize private rights of action under other sections. See, e.g., In re Washington Public Power Supply System Securities Litigation, 823 F.2d 1349 (9th Cir.1987) (finding no implied private right of action under 1933 Act § 17(a)). (iv) Congressional committees may start including in their reports specific references to implied private rights of action. See, e.g., H.Rep. 96–1341, at 29 (1980) ("The Committee wishes to make plain that it expects the courts to imply private rights of action under [the Small Business Investment Incentive Act of 1980], where the plaintiff falls within the class of persons protected by the statutory provision in question.").

The elements of a private right of action under the various substantive provisions of the federal securities laws are described under the appropriate headings in the preceding chapters. The following discussion covers problems relating to all private actions under those laws.

§ 38.   JURISDICTIONAL QUESTIONS

Under 1934 Act § 27, federal courts have exclusive jurisdiction over actions to enforce any liability under the 1934 Act. Federal and state courts have

concurrent jurisdiction of claims under the Securities
Act, 1933 Act § 22(a), and the Investment Company
Act, ICA § 44, although most claims under those laws
are also brought in federal courts. Under normal
rules of pendent jurisdiction, plaintiffs can, and often
do, add counts alleging violation of state common law
or statutes to their federal claims under the
securities laws.

(A) VENUE AND SERVICE OF PROCESS

The generous venue and service of process
provisions of the federal securities laws are an
important incentive to plaintiffs to frame their
complaints so as to state a claim under those laws.
Actions can be brought in any district in which the
defendant is found or is an inhabitant or transacts
business, and process can be served on any defendant
in that district or in any other district in which he or
she can be found. 1933 Act § 22; 1934 Act § 27; ICA
§ 44. However, special venue provisions applicable to
certain kinds of defendants may limit the choice
available under the securities laws. For example, the
Supreme Court has held that a national bank can be
sued under the federal securities laws only in a
district in which a suit against that bank is permitted
by the National Bank Act. Radzanower v. Touche
Ross, 426 U.S. 148 (1976).

When a number of private actions involving
common questions of fact are brought in different
judicial districts, the Judicial Panel on Multidistrict
Litigation, pursuant to 28 U.S.C. § 1407, may order
consolidated or coordinated pretrial proceedings for

all of the pending actions. However, under the 1975 amendments, actions brought by private parties may not be consolidated or coordinated under this provision with an action brought by the Commission, unless the Commission consents. 1934 Act § 21(g).

(B) STATUTE OF LIMITATIONS

The specific civil liability provisions of the securities laws contain their own statutes of limitations. An action under 1933 Act § 11 or 12(a)(2) must be brought within one year after discovery of the untruth or omission and not more than three years after the sale, while an action under 1933 Act § 12(a)(1) must be brought within one year after the violation. 1933 Act § 13. An action under 1934 Act § 16(b) must be brought within two years after the insider realized the impermissible profit, and an action under 1934 Act § 18 must be brought within one year after discovery of the true facts and within three years after the violation. An action under 1934 Act § 20A, which was added in 1988, must be brought within five years of the violation.

There is no federal statute of limitations applicable to implied rights of action generally. Prior to 1991, the courts in those cases generally looked to the law of the state in which the court sat, applying either the limitation applicable to actions for fraud or deceit, or the limitation applicable to actions under the state securities law, depending on which bore the closest resemblance to the federal statute involved. However, in 1991, the Supreme Court held, in a 5–4 decision, that where "the claim asserted is one implied under a statute that also contains an express cause of action with its own time limitation, a court should look first to the statute of origin to ascertain the proper limitations period." Lampf v. Gilbertson, 501 U.S. 350 (1991). Accordingly, the Court held that the appropriate limitations period for actions under 1934 Act § 10(b) was one year from discovery of the fraud and three years from the date of the violation, the period specified in §§ 9 and 18 of the 1934 Act. It rejected application to 1934 Act § 10(b) of the five-year limitations period found in 1934 Act § 20A on the ground that that provision was enacted more than 50 years after the original Act and was designed for the "specific problem" of insider trading, not for other more general provisions of the Act. In 2002, as part of the Sarbanes-Oxley Act, Congress enacted a statute of limitations applicable to securities fraud claims, including Rule 10b–5. 28 U.S.C. § 1658(b) does not apply to all claims under the securities laws—only those involving a "claim of fraud, deceit, manipulation, or contrivance" and imposes a statute of limitations of two years from the date of discovery and a repose period of five years, running from the date of the violation.

The Court in *Lampf* also held that the doctrine of "equitable tolling," under which the statute of limitations does not begin to run until the fraud is discovered, was "fundamentally inconsistent" with the one-year, three-year pattern found in the other sections of the Act and was therefore inapplicable to actions under § 10(b). Lampf v. Gilbertson, 501 U.S. 350 (1991).

Courts held that the statute of limitations adopted in *Lampf* also applied to actions under 1934 Act § 14(a), Westinghouse Electric Corp. v. Franklin, 993 F.2d 349 (3d Cir.1993), but does not apply to SEC enforcement actions, SEC v. Rind, 991 F.2d 1486 (9th Cir.1993). It is unclear, however, whether 28 U.S.C. § 1658(b)'s longer limitations periods apply since 1934 Act § 14(a) does not contain the same language as 1934 Act § 10(b), limiting SEC rules to a "manipulative or deceptive device or contrivance." The better view is that 28 U.S.C. § 1658(b)'s limitation period applies to Rule 14a–9 claims.

The equitable defense of laches (prejudice to defendant resulting from plaintiff's undue delay in bringing suit) has been held to be available in an action brought under 1934 Act, even where the action is brought within the time specified in the relevant state statute of limitations and regardless of whether the action is strictly "equitable" in nature. Royal Air v. Smith, 312 F.2d 210 (9th Cir.1962). However, the same court has held that defense unavailable in a suit under the specific civil liability provisions of the Securities Act, since those actions are essentially "legal" in nature and since federal law provides a short and definite standard of limitations. Straley v. Universal, 289 F.2d 370 (9th Cir.1961).

§ 39.   STANDING TO SUE

The express civil liability provisions generally specify the persons entitled to sue, although interpretation of these provisions may cause difficulties. Greater difficulties arise in determining who has standing to assert private rights of actions implied from general prohibitions.

In actions based on 1934 Act § 10(b) and 1934 Act Rule 10b–5, the Supreme Court in 1975 reaffirmed the rule laid down in Birnbaum v. Newport, 193 F.2d 461 (2d Cir.1952), that suit can only be brought by a person who purchased or sold securities in the transaction in question. See Blue Chip v. Manor (§ 18(a) above).

In actions based on the proxy solicitation and tender offer provisions of 1934 Act § 14, the courts have been generous in granting standing. They have held that violations of the proxy rules may be challenged by the corporation itself, Studebaker v. Gittlin, 360 F.2d 692 (2d Cir.1966), or by a shareholder who alleges he or she was damaged by the deceit practiced on other shareholders to obtain their votes, J.I. Case Co. v. Borak, 377 U.S. 426 (1964). In the case of takeover bids, the courts have held that either the target corporation or the bidder has standing to seek an injunction against violations by the other. Electronic v. International, 409 F.2d 937 (2d Cir.1969); Florida Commercial Banks v. Culverhouse, 772 F.2d 1513 (11th Cir.1985). However, the Supreme Court has denied standing to a defeated contestant in a takeover bid to seek damages from the target corporation's management and the successful contestant, on the ground that it was not within the class of persons Congress intended to protect by the enactment of 1934 Act § 14(e). Piper v. Chris-Craft, 430 U.S. 1 (1977).

In some cases, the courts have rested their decision on standing on broad policy issues, rather than the technical relationship of the plaintiff to the transaction in question. For example, in the Second Circuit decision in the *Piper* case, Judge Mansfield, concurring, based his recognition of standing "solely on the ground that vigorous enforcement of the antifraud provisions through private litigation calls for [the] implication of a private right of action." See 480 F.2d at 396. However, the Supreme Court decisions in *Blue Chip* and *Piper* seem to reject that rationale as a basis for standing in any situation in which it has not already been recognized.

(A) CLASS ACTIONS

Since securities law violations frequently involve a large number of potential claimants, the "class action" provisions of the Federal Rules of Civil Procedure (FRCP) are often utilized to permit one or more of the affected persons to bring an action on behalf of the entire class. As a practical matter, a class action is the only remedy when the damage suffered by each individual plaintiff is too small to warrant the expense of bringing suit.

A class action will only be permitted under FRCP Rule 23 if "(1) the class is so numerous that joinder of all members is impracticable, (2) there are questions of law or fact common to the class, (3) the claims of the representative parties are typical of the claims of the class, and (4) the representative parties will fairly and adequately protect the interests of the class." In addition, the plaintiff must establish either that separate actions would create a risk of inconsistent adjudications, or impairment of the rights of non-parties, or that "the questions of law or fact common to the members of the class predominate over any questions affecting only individual members" and that the class action is "superior to other available methods" for adjudicating the controversy.

In situations involving public offers of securities or publication of allegedly misleading statements that affected the price at which a security was traded in the open market, there is normally no difficulty in establishing that joinder of all parties would be impracticable. See Green v. Wolf, 406 F.2d 291 (2d Cir.1968); Cannon v. Texas Gulf Sulphur, 47 F.R.D. 60 (S.D.N.Y.1969). With respect to plaintiff's status as an adequate representative of the class, it is normally not difficult to find a plaintiff who has a "typical" claim and no conflicting interests. A question may be raised as to the competence of the plaintiff's attorney, who is often the moving force in bringing a class action, to represent the interests of the class. However, courts have not been overly sympathetic to defendants' expressions of concern on this question. See Dolgow v. Anderson, 43 F.R.D. 472 (E.D.N.Y.1968).

There is often a more difficult question as to whether the common issues of law or fact predominate over the separate issues. Where the gravamen of the complaint is oral misrepresentations, the court will be reluctant to permit a class action. Moscarelli v. Stamm, 288 F.Supp. 453 (E.D.N.Y.1968). Where misstatements of a similar nature are made in a series of prospectuses or other documents, the court may divide the class of plaintiffs into subclasses pursuant to FRCP Rule 23(c)(4)(B). See Green v. Wolf, above; Blackie v. Barrack, 524 F.2d 891 (9th Cir.1975). Use of the out-of-pocket measure of damages may also create problems in the administration of a class action. See Green v. Occidental, 541 F.2d 1335 (9th Cir.1976) (Sneed, J., concurring).

1995 Reform Act (PSLRA). Congressional concern about the potential for abuse in class action litigation against publicly-held corporations for alleged misstatements led to the enactment of the Private Securities Litigation Reform Act of 1995 (PSLRA). Among the abuses identified by the House and Senate committees were "(1) the routine filing of lawsuits against issuers of securities and others whenever there is a significant change in an issuer's stock price, without regard to any underlying culpability of the issuer, and with only faint hope that the discovery process might lead eventually to some plausible cause of action; (2) the targeting of deep pocket defendants, including accountants, underwriters, and individuals who may be covered by insurance, without regard to their actual culpability; (3) the abuse of the discovery process to impose costs so burdensome that it is often economical for the victimized party to settle; and (4) the manipulation by class action lawyers of the clients whom they purportedly represent." PSLRA attempted to deal with these perceived abuses by adopting the following procedural reforms:

- Requiring the named class plaintiff to file a statement designed to disclose whether he is really a tool of the attorney for the plaintiff class;

- Prohibiting broker-dealers from taking fees for assisting attorneys in identifying class plaintiffs;

- Requiring the court to appoint as lead plaintiff the member of the plaintiff class that "has the largest financial interest in the relief sought by the class." This "lead plaintiff," which would normally be a financial institution, would then be responsible for the selection of counsel to represent the class;

- Barring discovery by plaintiff's attorneys while a motion to dismiss is pending;

- Requiring full disclosure of the terms of any proposed settlement;

- Restricting attorney's fees to "a reasonable percentage of the damages * * * actually paid to the class"; and

- Requiring the losing party to pay the attorney's fees of the winning party where the losing party is found to have violated the pleading requirements of Rule 11 of the Federal Rules of Civil Procedure, and authorizing the court to require the plaintiffs and/or their attorneys to post security for the payment of such expenses.

See 1933 Act § 27; 1934 Act § 21D. The Act also stiffened the standards for pleading fraud (see § 18(a) above), established a new causation standard, see § 18(b) above, and limited the liabilities of defendants who are not specifically found to have acted willfully (see § 40 below).

1998 Uniform Standards Act (SLUSA). Three years after the Litigation Reform Act, Congress significantly preempted the role of state law and state courts with respect to securities class actions. The Securities Litigation Uniform Standards Act of 1998 (SLUSA) mandates that most class actions involving publicly traded securities be brought in federal court. Class actions involving state securities law and common law with regard to "covered securities" are preempted. Covered securities are defined in such a way as to include most publicly traded securities. 1933 Act § 16(f)(3), 1934 Act § 28(f)(5)(E), 1933 Act § 18(b). SLUSA applies only to class actions and thus not to individual or derivative suits. There also is an exclusion for actions brought in the state of incorporation involving certain corporate transactions. SLUSA preemption applies to fraud related claims and thus does not preclude state law claims on other theories such as conversion or breach of contract or breach of fiduciary duty.

(B) DERIVATIVE ACTIONS

In cases involving mergers or acquisitions or alleged management misconduct, the action is often brought by a shareholder suing derivatively on behalf of the corporation. In merger cases, the action may be framed in terms of both individual and derivative claims, with the courts not always being too precise about which form is appropriate. See J.I. Case v. Borak, 377 U.S. 426 (1964).

Any derivative action brought in a federal court must comply with FRCP Rule 23.1. That rule requires, *inter alia,* that the plaintiff have been a shareholder at the time of the transaction complained of and that the plaintiff "allege with particularity" the efforts he or she has made to secure the desired action from the directors and, "if necessary," the shareholders. The requirement of prior demand on the directors is normally waived where the board is under the domination of the defendants in the action. In Kamen v. Kemper, 500 U.S. 90 (1991), the Supreme Court held that the question of whether demand on the directors should be waived in an action brought under the ICA was governed by the law of the state of incorporation, rather than federal law.

The currently favored defense tactic for obtaining dismissal of derivative actions against directors is to refer the action to a committee of "disinterested" directors. If the committee decides that maintenance of the action is not in the best interests of the corporation, it asks the court to dismiss the action. Several state courts have held that the courts in such situations should defer to the "business judgment" of the disinterested directors and dismiss the action. See Auerbach v. Bennett, 47 N.Y.2d 619, 419 N.Y.S.2d 920, 393 N.E.2d 994 (1979); cf. Zapata v. Maldonado, 430 A.2d 779 (Del.1981). In Burks v.

Lasker, 441 U.S. 471 (1979), the Supreme Court held that the federal courts should apply state, not federal, law to determine whether the disinterested directors of an investment company had the authority to discontinue a derivative action alleging violations of the Investment Company and Investment Advisers Acts, unless it found the state law rule inconsistent with the policy of those Acts. In that case, the Supreme Court strongly intimated that it found no such inconsistency, and two subsequent lower court decisions have held that it is not inconsistent with the policies of 1934 Act §§ 10(b) and 14(a) to authorize disinterested directors to discontinue derivative actions alleging violations of those sections. Abramowitz v. Posner, 672 F.2d 1025 (2d Cir.1982); Maldonado v. Flynn, 671 F.2d 729 (2d Cir.1982). However, it may be inconsistent with the policy of 1934 Act § 14(a) to authorize directors to discontinue a derivative action when the directors were named as defendants in the action. Galef v. Alexander, 615 F.2d 51 (2d Cir.1980).

Actions under 1934 Act § 16(b) to recover "short-swing" profits on behalf of a corporation are governed by the specific provisions of that section, which require prior demand on the directors. However, the courts have consistently held, contrary to the normal rule governing derivative actions, that the plaintiff in a § 16(b) action need not have been a shareholder at the time of the transactions involved, either because such a requirement would be inconsistent with the purposes of that section, Blau v. Mission, 212 F.2d 77 (2d Cir.1954), or because the statute creates a distinct primary right of action which is not a derivative action in the traditional sense, Dottenheim v. Murchison, 227 F.2d 737 (5th Cir.1955). In Gollust v. Mendell, 501 U.S. 115 (1991), the Supreme Court held that a person who had been a shareholder of the issuer at the time of bringing an action under § 16(b) could continue to prosecute the action after the issuer had been merged into another company, as long as the plaintiff maintained a "continuing financial interest" in the litigation through ownership of securities of the surviving company.

(C) BARS TO RECOVERY

The general rules of law and equity barring suit by a plaintiff who has waived any rights or otherwise has been estopped, or who is found to be *in pari delicto* ("in equal fault") with the defendant, are applicable in securities cases, but with important limitations.

Waiver and Estoppel. Both the 1933 Act and the 1934 Act provide that "any condition, stipulation, or provision binding any person to waive compliance with any provision of [the Act] shall be void." 1933 Act § 14; 1934 Act § 29(a). Notwithstanding those provisions, the Ninth Circuit held that the common law defenses of waiver and estoppel are available in suits under either Act. Straley v. Universal Uranium & Milling Corp., 289 F.2d 370 (9th Cir.1961); Royal Air v. Smith, 312 F.2d 210 (9th Cir.1962). The Fifth Circuit, on the other hand, held that under 1933 Act § 14, plaintiff could not be held to have waived his rights by refusing defendant's offer to repurchase illegally sold securities, but that his could be estopped if defendant had made an unconditional tender and demand for return of the securities. Meyers v. C & M, 476 F.2d 427 (5th Cir.1973).

Arbitration Agreements. In Wilko v. Swan, 346 U.S. 427 (1953), the Supreme Court held that a customer's agreement with his or her broker to arbitrate any dispute with respect to the customer's account could not be raised as a defense to an action by the customer under 1933 Act § 12(a)(2) for alleged misrepresentations in the sale of stock. The Court said that the agreement to arbitrate was a "stipulation" to waive compliance with the 1933 Act, within the meaning of 1933 Act § 14, and was therefore void. However, 24 years later, in Shearson v. McMahon, 482 U.S. 220 (1987), the Court reached the opposite conclusion in a case involving a customer's suit against a broker under 1934 Act Rule 10b–5. In a 5–4 decision, the majority cited the strong policy favoring arbitration embodied in the Federal Arbitration Act, found no evidence that Congress had intended to override that policy when it enacted the 1934 Act, and noted the improvement in SEC oversight of the industry's arbitration process since 1953.

In the *McMahon* decision, the Supreme Court was not clear as to whether it was overruling or distinguishing *Wilko*. In the subsequent case of Rodriguez v. Shearson, 490 U.S. 477 (1989), the Court, in a 5–4 decision, expressly overruled *Wilko* and held that an arbitration agreement with a broker barred a customer from suing the broker under the express liability provisions of 1933 Act § 12. The Court found there was "no sound basis for construing the prohibition in § 14 on waiving 'compliance with any provision' of the Securities Act to apply to [the] procedural [as distinct from the substantive] provisions" of 1933 Act § 12. The dissenters felt that the Court should not overrule a prior construction of the statute "which Congress [had elected] not to amend during the ensuing 3 ½ decades."

In the wake of the *McMahon* decision, members of Congress put pressure on the SEC to reform industry arbitration procedures. The industry's self-regulatory organizations established a Securities Industry Conference on Arbitration, which worked with the SEC staff over a period of several months to produce a mutually acceptable set of rules. In May 1989, the Commission approved the rules submitted by the NASD and the New York and American Stock Exchanges. See Sec. Exch. Act Rel. 34–26805 (1989). These rules, which have been amended from time to time, among other things, generally provide:

(a) The SRO will prepare a summary of each arbitration proceeding, describing the parties, the issues, and the relief requested and awarded, which will be available for inspection in their public reference rooms;

(b) Each member firm must explain to customers the consequences of signing an arbitration agreement and their rights in arbitration proceedings;

(c) Arbitrators having certain specified connections with the securities industry, including lawyers, accountants, and other professionals, will be considered "industry" rather than "public" arbitrators;

(d) Procedures are established for service of pleadings, discovery of information, and replacement of arbitrators, and requiring that a verbatim record of each proceeding be maintained; and

(e) Member firms may not enter into agreements that restrict customers from filing claims, seek punitive damages or attorneys' fees, or restrict the situs of an arbitration hearing.

There was some consumer dissatisfaction with diversion of customer disputes to arbitration and there were proposals to guarantee brokerage customers their day in court. However, Congress took no action on bills which would have barred broker-dealers from requiring customers to sign an arbitration agreement as a condition of opening an account. Some states have adopted similar laws, but they have not met with much success. For example, in Securities Industry Ass'n v. Connolly, 883 F.2d 1114 (1st Cir.1989), the court held that a Massachusetts statute containing such provisions was preempted by the Federal Arbitration Act. In 2001, the California Code of Civil Procedure was revised to require that, within ten days of the proposed appointment of a neutral arbitrator, the neutral arbitrator disclose in writing "all matters that could cause a person aware of the facts to reasonably entertain a doubt that the proposed neutral arbitrator would be able to be impartial, including * * * [a]ny matters required to be disclosed by the ethics standards for neutral arbitrators adopted by the Judicial Council pursuant to this chapter." Pending court challenges, the NASD, and the New York Stock Exchange circumvented the California ethics rules for arbitrations by permitting parties to move ahead with arbitrations by waiving their rights under the California rules. Thus, despite their efforts to date, the states have not been successful in expanding customer protections beyond the arbitration programs.

The strong policy favoring arbitration under the Federal Arbitration Act continues to favor enforcement of arbitration agreements. This means that courts are overwhelmingly unconvinced that arbitration agreements should be set aside because they are contracts of adhesion or otherwise unconscionable. Courts also are liberal in terms of interpreting the scope of arbitration agreements, which, for example, have been held to apply to transactions not involving securities so long as those transactions are carried out in connection with the broker-customer relationship. Even procedural matters are likely to be determined by arbitrators rather than the courts. Thus, for example, the applicability of the arbitration forum's statute of limitations is to be determined by the arbitrator. Howsam v. Dean Witter Reynolds, Inc., 537 U.S. 79 (2002).

Pari Delicto. Courts have traditionally denied relief to plaintiffs who are found to be *in pari delicto* with defendants or, in cases seeking equitable relief, if the plaintiff does not come into court with "clean hands." In actions under the securities laws, plaintiffs are generally not barred from suit because they participated in the illegal activities, at least where their culpability is less than that of defendants. Can-Am v. Beck, 331 F.2d 371 (10th Cir.1964). The Supreme Court has specifically held that a "tippee" who buys stock on the basis of "inside information," which turns out to be false, is not barred by the "clean hands" doctrine from suing his "tipper" under 1934 Act Rule 10b–5, since the tippee cannot properly be characterized as being "of substantially equal culpability as his tippers." Bateman Eichler v. Berner, 472 U.S. 299 (1985). In Pinter v. Dahl, 486 U.S. 622 (1988), the Court extended this approach to actions under 1933 Act § 12(a)(1), holding that the *in pari delicto* defense is available in such an action only if the role played by the plaintiff in the offering is "more as a promoter than as an investor."

Contributory Negligence. The provisions creating explicit private rights of action for misleading statements bar the plaintiff from recovery only if he or she *knew* of the untruth or omission. 1933 Act §§ 11(a), 12(a)(2); 1934 Act § 18(a). With respect to implied private rights of action under the antifraud provisions, courts have generally held that plaintiff must establish that he or she actually exercised "due diligence" to be entitled to recover. However, in light of the Supreme Court's decision in Ernst & Ernst v.

Hochfelder (see § 18(a) above) that *scienter* on the part of the *defendant* must be shown to maintain an action under the antifraud provisions, some courts have held that a plaintiff is not barred by ordinary negligence, but only if he "intentionally refused to investigate, 'in disregard of a risk known to him or so obvious that he must be taken to have been aware of it, and so great as to make it highly probable that harm would follow.' " Dupuy v. Dupuy, 551 F.2d 1005 (5th Cir.1977).

§ 40.   PERMISSIBLE DEFENDANTS

The primary perpetrators of securities violations are often persons or entities from whom it is impossible to obtain any financial recovery. Plaintiffs will therefore attempt to include as defendants more solvent individuals or entities who have had some connection with the violation—"deep pockets" from which a judgment can be paid. Among the types of parties often named as secondary defendants are the employer of an individual wrongdoer; directors of a corporate wrongdoer; underwriters, broker-dealers, banks, or agents that participated in the transaction; accountants; lawyers; and self-regulatory organizations.

In actions under 1933 Act § 11, the liability of persons having specified relationships to the issuer is spelled out in considerable detail. In actions under other sections, however, the liabilities of secondary defendants must be determined under such doctrines as agency liability, aiding and abetting, conspiracy, tort liability, and contribution and indemnification.

(A) LIABILITY OF PRINCIPAL

There are two independent bases for holding a brokerage firm or other principal liable for securities violations by its employees or agents. Under traditional agency rules, a principal is liable for damages caused to a third party by an agent who had authority, apparent authority, or "agency power" to make representations on the principal's behalf. Rest. (2d), Agency § 257. In addition, 1933 Act § 15 and 1934 Act § 20 make any person who "controls" another person jointly and severally liable to any third party to whom the controlled person incurs liability under those Acts. However, the controlling person can escape liability if he can show that "he acted in good faith and did not induce the act constituting the violation," 1934 Act § 20, or "had no knowledge or reasonable ground to believe in the existence of the facts" giving rise to the violation, 1933 Act § 15. On the question whether the controlling person must be shown to have been a "culpable participant" in the violation to impose liability, compare Orloff v. Allman, 819 F.2d 904 (9th Cir.1987), with Metge v. Baehler, 762 F.2d 621 (8th Cir.1985).

The principal question that has arisen in reconciling these sources of liability is whether establishing the "good faith" or "lack of knowledge" defense available under the statute also relieves the defendant of liability under traditional agency principles. Some courts have held that establishment of the statutory defense does not bar recovery on agency grounds, since Congress's purpose in the "controlling person" provisions was to extend liability to new classes of persons and not to restrict the application of existing bases of recovery. Others have held, however, that the "controlling person" provisions are the only basis for holding a principal liable for his or her agent's violations of the securities laws. For a thorough review of the law, see Marbury v. Kohn, 629 F.2d 705 (2d Cir.1980).

There is also a question whether the Supreme Court, in light of its 1994 decision in the *Central Bank* case (see § 39(b) below) eliminating liability for aiding and abetting violations of 1934 Act § 10(b), would recognize liability based on *respondeat superior*. The dissenters in that case expressed the view that decisions "impos[ing] liability in § 10(b) actions based upon *respondeat superior* and other common-law agency principles * * * appear unlikely to survive the Court's decision." Lower court decisions after *Central Bank* have split on the issue. Compare Seolas v. Bilzerian, 951 F.Supp. 978 (D.Utah 1997) (holding *respondeat superior* liability not affected by *Central Bank*) with Converse v. Norwood, 1997 WL 742534 (S.D.N.Y.) (asserting "in *Central Bank*, the Court implied that all forms of secondary liability are no longer viable").

(B) AIDING AND ABETTING

The idea that an "aider and abettor" is jointly liable with the actual perpetrator of an offense has its roots both in the criminal law and in § 876 of the Restatement of Torts, which imposes liability on a person who knowingly "gives substantial assistance and encouragement" to another person's breach of duty.

"Three elements are thus required for liability: (1) that an independent wrong exist; (2) that the aider or abettor knew of that wrong's existence; and (3) that substantial assistance be given in effecting that wrong." Landy v. FDIC, 486 F.2d 139, 162 (3d Cir.1973). Prior to 1994, the courts imposed liability for aiding and abetting in many cases involving violations of 1934 Act § 10(b) and other general antifraud provisions of the securities laws. However, in that year, the Supreme Court held, in a 5–4 decision, that there was no evidence that Congress intended to create any such liability, and that consequently a private plaintiff may not sue anyone as an aider and abettor of a 1934 Act § 10(b) violation. Central Bank v. First Interstate Bank, 511 U.S. 164 (1994).

The Court in *Central Bank* did not address the question of whether the SEC can still go after aiders and abettors in its injunctive actions. Congress answered that question in 1995 by adding 1934 Act § 20(e), which provides that in any action brought by the commission under 1934 Act § 21(d) "any person that knowingly or recklessly provides substantial assistance to another person in violation of" any provision of the Act "shall be deemed to be in violation of such provision to the same extent as the person to whom such assistance is provided."

Aiding and abetting remains an important issue in criminal and SEC enforcement actions. In 2010, Congress expanded the SEC's authority to pursue aiders and abettors by clarifying that reckless conduct is sufficient. In the private litigation arena, there is an increasing tendency of plaintiffs to try to characterize participants in a securities fraud as primary violators.

Primary Compared to Secondary Liability. Following the *Central Bank* decision, a key question in private litigation is whether the defendant was a primary violator rather than merely an aider and abettor. The line between primary and secondary is not always easily drawn. Some courts have held that in order to be a primary violator, the defendant must have drafted or uttered the statements forming the basis of the fraud suit. Other courts held that primary liability could be found if the defendant knowingly participated in the fraudulent scheme, even though he or she was not responsible for the statements at issue. The Supreme Court's decision in Stoneridge Investment Partners, LLC v. Scientific-Atlanta, Inc., 552 U.S. 148 (2008), likely put an end to this so-called scheme liability, at least in private suits. Among other things, the Court held that the defendant's involvement in the misstatements in questions must have been apparent to the plaintiff so as to satisfy the reliance requirement.

Rule 10b–5(b) prohibits any person from making untrue statements. While subsection (b) addresses anyone who *makes* a material misstatement, does that include someone who merely acts as the messenger and disseminates the information? The Fifth Circuit held that it does not and that Rule 10b–5 primary liability applies only to someone who disseminates the materially misleading statement. SEC v. Tambone, 597 F.3d 436 (1st Cir. 2010). As noted above, the SEC could pursue such a secondary violator under an abetting and abetting theory that would not be available in a private suit. Relying on the express language of Rule 10b–5(b), the Supreme Court in a sharply divided 5–4 decision ruled that primary liability exists, and hence a private right of action may only be brought, against someone who *makes* the materially misleading statement in question. Janus Capital Group, Inc. v. First Derivative Traders, 131 S. Ct. 2296, 180 L. Ed. 2d 166 (2011). In so ruling, the Court rejected the contention that "make" should be defined as "create," which would have allowed private plaintiffs to sue a person who provides the false or misleading information that another person puts into a statement. Id. The Court ruled that notwithstanding the close relationship of a mutual fund and its investment adviser, the adviser will not be held liable as a primary violator for statements made by the fund even where the adviser had a role in drafting the false statements. Id. This is an unfortunately narrow interpretation of Rule 10b–5 and, as the dissent pointed out, may act as an invitation for false information by dividing disclosures and drafting into two separate entities. The majority limited primary liability to makers as opposed to creators of misstatements.

The *Janus* ruling leaves a number of unanswered questions that are likely to lead to conflicts in the lower courts. For example, does the ruling have the same impact for entities and for individuals? In one case, the district court held that *Janus* did not require a corporate officer to be the actual *maker* of the statement so long as he or she had "ultimate authority" over the statement. In re Merck & Co., Inc. Securities, Derivative & "ERISA" Litigation, 2011 WL 3444199 (D.N.J. 2011). In contrast, another district court held that there is no distinction between entities and individuals and thus Rule 10b–5(b)'s requirement that the defendant have been the maker of the statement applies to any defendant. Hawaii Ironworkers Annuity Trust Fund v. Cole, 2011 WL 3862206 (N.D. Ohio 2011) (dismissing Rule 10b–5(b) claims but allowing claims under 10b–5(a) and (c) for deceptive conduct). These cases highlight the inconsistencies that have stemmed from the Court's unnecessarily narrow view of Rule 10b–5 in *Janus*.

In addition, the decision did not address the continued availability of scheme liability in SEC enforcement actions. Other decisions have held that scheme liability is sufficient to establish a primary Rule 10b–5 violation in an SEC enforcement action. In any event, someone who does not make the statement but still has substantial culpable participation may be pursued by the SEC as an aider and abettor of the maker of the statement. The Fourth Circuit held that the *Janus* ruling is limited to implied private suits and thus does not apply to governmental suits including criminal prosecutions. Prousalis v. Moore, 2014 WL 1799803 (4th Cir. 2014).

The Court in *Janus* focused on subsection (b) of Rule 10b–5 that expressly refers to someone who *makes* a statement. It is conceivable that someone other than the maker of the statement as the Court narrowly construes the term in *Janus* could be held liable as a primary violator for someone who engages in conduct that operates as a fraud in violation of Rule 10b–5(c), which makes it unlawful "[t]o engage in any act, practice, or course of business which operates or would operate as a fraud or deceit upon any person." Any such liability in a private suit would have to be in a context where the plaintiff had a basis for relying on defendant's participation in the fraud. See Stoneridge Investment Partners, LLC v. Scientific-Atlanta, Inc., 552 U.S. 148, 128 S.Ct. 761, 169 L.Ed.2d 627 (2008) The SEC can rely on either subsection (a) or (c) of Rule 10b–5 to find a violation by someone who has not made a statement but has employed "any device, scheme, or artifice to defraud" or anyone who engages "in any act or practice, or course of business which operates or would operate as a fraud or deceit." The SEC ruled that *Janus* is limited to Rule 10b–5(b) and thus does not apply to manipulative or deceptive conduct that violates Rule 10b–5(a) or 10b–5(c). And as discussed directly below, *Janus*'s requirement that the defendant must have actually made the statement, rather than merely participating in its preparation, does not apply to section 17(a) of the 1933 Act.

The impact of the *Janus* decision could be avoided should the SEC decide to reword the language of Rule 10b–5(b) to include someone playing a sufficiently active role in creating the offending statement. In addition, § 17(a) of the 1933 Act and § 34(b) of the Investment Company Act are not limited to someone who *makes* the statement in question. The Eleventh Circuit agreed and held that *Janus*'s requirement that the defendant have actually made the statement does not apply outside of Rule 10b–5(b) and section 17(a)(2). SEC v. Monterosso, 756 F.3d 1326 (11th Cir. 2014) ("Janus only discussed what it means to 'make' a statement for purposes of Rule 10b–5(b), and did not concern section 17(a)(1) or (3) or Rule 10b–5(a) or (c).").

Accountants and Lawyers. Among the categories of people most concerned about secondary liability for securities law violations are accountants and lawyers, who may in the course of their activities learn of such violations by their clients or others. Prior to 1994, liability might be asserted against them either on the ground that they aided and abetted (or participated in) the violation, or that they had an independent duty to disclose their knowledge to the victims or intended victims of the violations. While they can clearly no longer be held liable as aiders and abettors, the Supreme Court, in its *Central Bank* decision, stated specifically that "any person or entity, including a lawyer, accountant, or bank, who employs a manipulative device or makes a material misstatement (or omission) on which a purchaser or seller of securities relies may be liable as a primary violator under 10b–5, assuming *all* of the requirements for primary liability under Rule 10b–5 are met."

In Wessel v. Buhler, 437 F.2d 279 (9th Cir.1971), the court held that an accounting firm could not be held liable under Rule 10b–5 for failure to disclose to prospective investors its knowledge of irregularities and deficiencies in its client's financial statements. A similar approach was followed in Fischer v. Kletz, 266 F.Supp. 180 (S.D.N.Y.1967), at least as to unaudited interim financial statements. However, the court in *Fischer* indicated that accountants could be held liable for common law deceit, and perhaps also under Rule 10b–5, for failing to disclose information showing that financial statements, which they had previously certified, were inaccurate and misleading.

With respect to lawyers, the SEC took the position in one case that an attorney who learns that his or her client is engaged in a transaction which violates the securities laws has an obligation to refuse to give an opinion as to the validity of the transaction, to insist that the client comply with the securities laws, and, if the client refuses, to inform the SEC of the violation. The court did not pass on all of these questions, but did hold that a lawyer who knows that proxies necessary to effect a merger were procured by means of a misleading proxy statement, and takes no steps to prevent his or her client from consummating the merger, can be held to have aided and abetted a violation of the securities laws. SEC v. National Student Marketing, 457 F.Supp. 682 (D.D.C.1978).

In a subsequent disciplinary proceeding against lawyers for failing to prevent their client from filing false statements with the SEC, the Commission, while finding that the lawyers involved had not violated any standards in effect at the time, announced the following standard to be applied in

future cases: "When a lawyer with significant
responsibilities in the effectuation of a company's
compliance with the disclosure requirements of the
federal securities laws becomes aware that his client
is engaged in a substantial and continuing failure to
satisfy those disclosure requirements, his continued
participation violates professional standards unless
he takes prompt steps to end the client's non-
compliance." In re Carter, Sec. Exch. Act Rel. 34–
17597 (1981).

The obligations of securities lawyers have been
significantly heightened by § 307 of SOX. The Act
thus requires the SEC to impose the obligations to
report the wrongdoing within the corporation. The
Act does not require the attorney to blow the whistle
outside of the corporate entity (sometimes referred to
as a "reporting out" obligation). However, when the
SEC adopted its rules implementing the SOX "up the
ladder" reporting obligation on lawyers, it proposed—
but has not yet adopted—a more controversial
provision that if the up-the-ladder reporting does not
to a satisfactory solution the lawyer would have an
obligation to make a "noisy withdrawal" from
representation thus signaling the problem. Rule
205.3. See Sec. Exch. Act Rel. No. 34–48282 (2003).
The rules as adopted permit but do not require such
a "reporting out" of the problem. It remains possible
that the SEC will eventually adopt a mandatory
reporting out obligation. The SEC rules take a broad
view of what constitutes SEC practice so as to expose
the lawyer to the up-the-ladder obligations. The rules
apply to a wide variety of lawyers who might not
consider themselves as practicing securities law.

This would include, for example, if an attorney provides advice on the securities laws regarding any document that the attorney has notice will be filed with the SEC or is to be incorporated into a document filed with SEC. Rule 205.2(a)(1)(iv). The ABA's Model Rules of Professional Conduct were amended to comport with the SEC rules. Thus, Model Rule 1.13(b) was amended to provide that if a lawyer "knows" that a corporate employee has violated the law in a way that is likely to result in "substantial injury" to the corporation or other organization, "then the lawyer shall proceed as is reasonably necessary in the best interest of the organization." The Model Rules also impose a climbing the ladder requirement by explaining that "[u]nless the lawyer reasonably believes that it is *not* necessary in the best interest of the organization to do so, the lawyer shall refer the matter to higher authority in the organization, including, if warranted by the circumstances, to the highest authority that can act on behalf of the organization as determined by applicable law." ABA Model Rule 1.13(b).

In private damage actions against lawyers for allegedly aiding and abetting violations, the courts have refused to hold that a lawyer has an obligation to "blow the whistle" on his or her client's misdeeds. Barker v. Henderson, 797 F.2d 490 (7th Cir.1986). In Breard v. Sachnoff, 941 F.2d 142 (2d Cir.1991), the court held that a lawyer's failure to include information in an offering memorandum about his client's conviction for mail fraud could give rise to an inference of recklessness and might even "be considered reckless as a matter of law." And in

Molecular Technology v. Valentine, 925 F.2d 910 (6th Cir.1991), the court held that a lawyer could be held liable for misstatements of which he or she was aware. However, in Schatz v. Rosenberg, 943 F.2d 485 (4th Cir.1991), the court held that a lawyer could not be held liable for failing to disclose a client's misstatements of which the lawyer was aware to the other party in a transaction.

(C) JOINT AND SEVERAL LIABILITY

One of the principal concerns that led to passage of the PSLRA (see § 38(a) above) was the fact that "peripheral" defendants could be held liable for the full amount of the damages caused by the principal wrongdoer. The Act accordingly provides that a defendant in a private fraud action is jointly and severally liable for the full amount of the damages only if the trier of fact specifically determines that the defendant knowingly committed a violation of the securities laws. In all other cases, a defendant can be held liable "solely for the portion of the judgment that corresponds to [his] percentage of responsibility," as determined by the trier of fact. For this purpose, the jury must be specifically asked to determine, for each defendant, (a) whether he or she knowingly committed a violation, and (b) the defendant's percentage of "the total fault of all persons who caused or contributed to the loss." See 1934 Act § 21D(g); 1933 Act § 11(f)(2).

There are, however, a couple of strange exceptions to this limitation on joint and several liability. First, all defendants are jointly and severally liable to any individual plaintiff who has a net worth of less than $200,000 and is entitled to damages exceeding 10% of the defendant's net worth. Second, if any defendants cannot pay their share of the damages due to insolvency, each of the other defendants must make an additional payment—up to 50% of their own liability—to make up the shortfall.

(D) INDEMNIFICATION AND CONTRIBUTION

After recovery of a judgment against one or more defendants in a private damage action, a particular defendant may claim (a) indemnification by another party against his or her entire liability, or (b) contribution by other parties toward satisfaction of the judgment.

There is no specific provision governing indemnification in the federal securities laws; the SEC's position with respect to indemnification of directors, officers, and underwriters in public offerings registered under the 1933 Act is discussed in § 8 above. In an action under 1934 Act Rule 10b–5, a defendant who was found guilty of fraud was held not to be entitled to indemnification from another wrongdoer, but a company which was only vicariously liable for the wrongdoing of its agent was held to be entitled to indemnification. DeHaas v. Empire, 286 F.Supp. 809 (D.Colo.1968), aff'd in part, 435 F.2d 1223 (10th Cir.1970).

On the other hand, in an action under 1934 Act § 14(a), corporate directors who were held liable for negligence in connection with a misleading proxy statement were denied indemnification on policy grounds similar to those enunciated by the SEC with respect to 1933 Act registration statements. Gould v. American-Hawaiian, 387 F.Supp. 163 (D.Del.1974), aff'd, 535 F.2d 761 (3d Cir.1976).

In contrast to the situation regarding indemnification, several of the civil liability provisions of the securities laws contain specific language permitting any person held liable under those provisions to obtain contribution, "as in cases of contract," from any other person who, if joined as a defendant, would have been required to make the same payment. 1933 Act § 11(f); 1934 Act §§ 9(e), 18(b). See Globus v. Law Research Service, 318 F.Supp. 955 (S.D.N.Y.1970), aff'd, 442 F.2d 1346 (2d Cir.1971). On the basis of these provisions, an implied right to contribution has also been recognized in actions under 1934 Act Rule 10b–5. DeHaas v. Empire, above. Since contribution is to be "as in cases of contract," early decisions tended to allocate damages pro rata rather than in accordance with degree of fault. See Globus v. Law Research Service, above. However, 1933 Act § 11(f) bars recovery of contribution by any person guilty of fraudulent misrepresentation from a person not guilty thereof, and decisions under Rule 10b–5 have held that contribution should be awarded on the basis of "relative culpability." Smith v. Mulvaney, 827 F.2d 558 (9th Cir.1987).

The question of whether defendants held liable under 1934 Act § 10(b) and other antifraud provisions have a right to contribution from other defendants was not definitively resolved until 1993.

In that year, the Supreme Court held, in a 6–3 decision, that contribution is available, relying principally on the fact that Congress had specifically provided for contribution under 1934 Act §§ 9(e) and 18, which the Court viewed as addressing similar types of misconduct. Musick v. Employers Insurance, 508 U.S. 286 (1993). In 1995, Congress created an express right to contribution under the antifraud provisions of the 1934 Act and required that actions for contribution be brought within six months of the entry of judgment in the underlying action. See 1934 Act § 21D(g)(8), (9).

§ 41. DAMAGES

The remedy most commonly sought in a private action under the federal securities laws is damages for the financial loss allegedly caused by defendant's wrongdoing. Because of the great variety of situations giving rise to liability, it is difficult to generalize about the computation of damages. There are, however, certain types of transactions which lend themselves to particular theories of liability, and certain common questions which can arise in any type of securities case because of the distinctive attributes of securities and the entities which issue them.

Direct Damages. The simplest situation is where the plaintiff is suing the other party to a transaction in which the plaintiff bought or sold securities. If plaintiff is a buyer, alleging that he or she bought securities sold under a misleading registration statement, the measure of recovery under 1933 Act

§ 11(e) is the difference between the price the plaintiff paid for the security and either its value at the time the plaintiff brought suit or the price at which the plaintiff disposed of it. However, the seller may reduce or defeat the recovery to the extent that the defendant can show that the decline in value resulted from something other than the misstatements in the registration statement. (See § 11(a) above.) If the suit is for sale of unregistered securities or for misrepresentation under 1933 Act § 12, the buyer may sue either for a full refund of the purchase price, less any income received thereon, on tender of the security; if the purchaser no longer owns it, he or she may sue for "damages," which is normally the difference between the purchase price and the price at which he or she disposed of it. In Randall v. Loftsgaarden, 478 U.S. 647 (1986), the Supreme Court held that an income tax saving attributable to an investment was not "income received thereon" within the meaning of 1933 Act § 12, and that the purchaser was entitled to recover the full amount of his purchase price.

If the plaintiff is a seller, alleging that the buyer misrepresented or withheld material facts, his or her suit will generally be to enforce the implied civil liability under 1934 Act § 10(b) and Rule 10b–5. In this situation, the courts have generally held that the measure of damages is the difference between the price he received and "the fair value of what he would have received had there been no fraudulent conduct." Affiliated Ute Citizens v. United States, 406 U.S. 128, 155 (1972). However, if the security has increased in value since the transaction, the court

will often award the plaintiff the difference between
the sale price and the current value (or the price
realized by the defendant on resale), on the ground
that the "windfall" should more properly go to the
wronged party than the wrongdoer. See Janigan v.
Taylor, 344 F.2d 781 (1st Cir.1965). A second
rationale supporting this result is that if the
defendant had not induced the transaction by the
defendant's misrepresentations, the plaintiff would
have realized the profit himself or herself. Zeller v.
Bogue, 476 F.2d 795, 802 n.10 (2d Cir.1973). The
courts have not extended this approach to the
situation where a merger is approved on the basis of
a misleading proxy statement and the properties of
the acquired company increase in value following the
merger. Gerstle v. Gamble-Skogmo, 478 F.2d 1281
(2d Cir.1973). It has, however, been extended to a
tender   offer-merger   situation   where   the
misrepresentations relate to the value of the
consideration to be received. Osofsky v. Zipf, 645 F.2d
107 (2d Cir.1981).

Indirect Damages. Where the plaintiff is suing
someone other than the opposite party in a
transaction, damages are harder to compute.
Plaintiffs in these cases, which are normally class or
derivative actions, may have bought or sold securities
in stock exchange transactions; they are usually
suing either the issuer for having affected the market
price by misleading statements or people who were
trading on "inside" information at about the same
time. The problem is that any "loss" suffered by the
plaintiffs is matched by a "profit" realized not by the
defendant but by other innocent parties, and the

aggregate of all plaintiffs' "losses" may far exceed any "profit" realized by the wrongdoing defendants. In the misleading statement cases, the courts have tended to look to the out-of-pocket losses suffered by plaintiffs who bought or sold on the basis of the misleading statements. See Green v. Occidental (see § 20(b) above). In the insider trading cases, the current approach is to measure damages by the defendants' profit, rather than the plaintiffs' losses. Elkind v. Liggett & Myers, 635 F.2d 156 (2d Cir.1980); 1934 Act § 20A. (See § 19(b) above).

Common Problems. In cases where damages are to be determined on the basis of the difference between the "price" paid or received in a transaction and the "value" of the security at a particular time, a number of problems may arise.

Price. Where the transaction is for cash, the price must be adjusted to reflect other payments in connection with the transaction. When it is an exchange of one security for another, the "price" paid or received for one is the "value" of the other, and the valuation of the consideration can produce very large changes in the measure of damages. See Allis-Chalmers v. Gulf & Western, 372 F.Supp. 570 (N.D.Ill.1974), rev'd on other grounds, 527 F.2d 335 (7th Cir.1975).

Value. Determination of the "value" that a security would have had at a particular time if all relevant facts had been known is not an easy matter. In some cases, the court looks to the price which the security reached after the facts became known and the market had had a reasonable period to absorb the new information. See, e.g., Mitchell v. Texas Gulf Sulphur, 446 F.2d 90 (10th Cir.1971). However, the market price may have been affected in the meantime by factors other than disclosure of those particular facts. See Green v. Occidental, 541 F.2d 1335 (9th Cir.1976) (Sneed, J., concurring).

Large Blocks. The per share "value" of a large block of stock is not necessarily the same as the current market price of that stock in small transactions. When the block represents a controlling interest in the company, it may be valued at a premium over the current market price. Newmark v. RKO, 425 F.2d 348 (2d Cir.1970). But when it represents a minority interest in a company of which someone else has control, it may be valued at a substantial discount from the current market. Chris-Craft v. Piper, 516 F.2d 172 (2d Cir.1975), rev'd on other grounds, 430 U.S. 1 (1977).

Consequential Damages. When the violation consists of an improper course of conduct by a broker-dealer or other professional, such as churning or unsuitable recommendations, there will often be a question of how much of the customer's trading losses can be charged to the defendants. One court has followed the approach of taking the initial value of the portfolio, adjusting it by the percentage change in an appropriate index over the period of the violations, and subtracting the value of the portfolio at the end of the period. Rolf v. Blyth, 637 F.2d 77 (2d Cir.1980). Some courts have permitted the plaintiff in churning cases to recover the excessive commissions paid as well as the loss in value of the account. Miley v.

Oppenheimer, 637 F.2d 318 (5th Cir.1981); Mihara v. Dean Witter, 619 F.2d 814 (9th Cir.1980).

Punitive Damages. One of the principal reasons for allowing private rights of action, particularly where there is no plaintiff who suffers any ascertainable "damage" (e.g., insider trading in a public market) is to discourage violations by depriving the violator of his illegal profits. It would therefore seem logical, at least in that type of case, to permit recovery of punitive damages as an additional deterrent. However, the courts have held that punitive damages are barred by 1934 Act § 28(a), which provides that "[n]o person * * * shall recover * * * a total amount in excess of the actual damages to that person" in a suit under that Act, even though the language of that section is clearly aimed at preventing a double recovery under state and federal law, rather than at punitive damages. Green v. Wolf, 406 F.2d 291 (2d Cir.1968); Cyrak v. Lemon, 919 F.2d 320 (5th Cir.1990). Punitive damages have also been held to be unavailable in an action under the antifraud provisions of 1933 Act § 17(a), on the ground that the additional deterrent effect they might provide is outweighed by other policy considerations. Globus v. Law Research Service, 418 F.2d 1276 (2d Cir.1969). However, if the plaintiff combines his or her federal securities law claims with a common law fraud claim, he or she may be able to recover punitive damages on the latter claim in the same action. Coffee v. Permian Corp., 474 F.2d 1040 (5th Cir.1973).

§ 42.   EQUITABLE RELIEF

The federal securities laws contemplate "suits in equity" as well as "actions at law" by aggrieved persons. 1933 Act § 22(a); 1934 Act § 27. As an alternative to damages, private plaintiffs may seek rescission of a transaction, an injunction against threatened or further violations, or other forms of equitable relief.

Rescission. The Securities Act specifically contemplates rescission as the appropriate remedy where the defendant has sold securities without registration, or by means of misleading statements, and plaintiff still retains the securities. 1933 Act § 12. In actions under the Securities Exchange Act, plaintiffs may seek rescission pursuant to 1934 Act § 29(b), which provides that all contracts made in violation of the Act shall be void as against the violators. In Transamerica Mortg. Advisors v. Lewis, 444 U.S. 11 (1979), the Supreme Court specifically upheld the right of a plaintiff to obtain rescission of a contract, or an injunction against its continued operation, under a similar provision in IAA § 215. However, rescission is often an impracticable or inappropriate remedy.

For example, where the plaintiff is an aggrieved seller who claims the defendant purchased securities from the plaintiff without disclosing material facts, rescission may be unavailable because of an intervening restructuring of the issuing company or the resale of the securities to a third party. And where a merger has been approved and consummated on the basis of a misleading proxy solicitation in violation of 1934 Act § 14, the courts have held that 1934 Act § 29(b) does not require that the merger be set aside, and that plaintiff will normally be limited to money damages because of the practical difficulties and hardship to public shareholders that equitable relief would entail. Mills v. Electric Auto-Lite, 396 U.S. 375 (1970). On the other hand, courts have ordered a new election of directors when the original election was tainted by a misleading proxy statement. Gladwin v. Medfield, 540 F.2d 1266 (5th Cir.1976); Kennecott v. Curtiss-Wright, 584 F.2d 1195 (2d Cir.1978).

Injunctions. The situations most appropriate for injunctive relief under the securities laws are mergers and tender offers, which are both subject to disclosure requirements under 1934 Act § 14. Persons who believe that the disclosures are inadequate can seek a preliminary injunction against the holding of a shareholder's meeting or the acceptance of tendered shares until adequate disclosures have been made. See Studebaker v. Gittlin, 360 F.2d 692 (2d Cir.1966); General Host v. Triumph American, 359 F.Supp. 749 (S.D.N.Y.1973). The courts have taken the view that they should be generous in granting preliminary temporary relief prior to consummation of the transaction because "the opportunity for doing equity * * * is considerably better than it will be later on." Electronic v. International, 409 F.2d 937 (2d Cir.1969); Humana v. American Medicorp, 445 F.Supp. 613 (S.D.N.Y.1977).

Private plaintiffs have sometimes taken a position, similar to that of the SEC, that they should be entitled to an injunction against further violations by any person who is shown to have committed a securities law violation. However, in Rondeau v. Mosinee, 422 U.S. 49 (1975), the Supreme Court rejected this position and held that applications for injunctions by private plaintiffs under the federal securities laws should be judged by traditional equitable standards, which require the plaintiff to show danger of irreparable harm and other usual prerequisites for injunctive relief.

Other Forms of Relief. In private actions, as in SEC actions, involving looting or a pervasive pattern of violations, the court may order appointment of a receiver or other structural changes to prevent a repetition of the illegal activity. For example, in one action by shareholders against the directors of a major oil company for violating SEC proxy rules by failing to disclose illegal payments and political contributions, the court approved a settlement providing for a majority of "independent outside directors" on the board, the appointment of an audit committee, the nomination of six named persons as directors, and other relief. Gilbar v. Keeler, Civ. No. 75–611–EAC (C.D.Cal.1976).

CHAPTER IX

EXTRATERRITORIAL APPLICATION

The increasing "internationalization" and globalization of securities markets in recent years has raised difficult questions as to when, and to what extent, U.S. securities laws will apply to transactions which have connections with the U.S. and with one or more other countries. The transactions fall into three categories: (1) U.S. transactions in foreign securities; (2) foreign transactions in U.S. securities; and (3) foreign transactions in foreign securities which have some impact on U.S. investors or markets. Within each of these categories, several different questions can arise: (1) whether a U.S. court or the SEC has subject matter jurisdiction over the transaction involved; (2) whether the court can obtain personal jurisdiction over foreign defendants; (3) whether it is appropriate for U.S. courts to exercise jurisdiction under applicable principles of international law; and (4) whether a U.S. court or the SEC can fashion and enforce effective relief.

Many of the substantive provisions of the securities laws speak in terms of "the use of facilities of interstate commerce or of the mails" to effect a specified transaction. The term "interstate commerce" is defined in 1933 Act § 2(a)(7) and 1934 Act § 3(a)(17) to include commerce between any foreign country and the U.S., so that international transactions of that type are clearly covered. Under 1934 Act § 30(b), that Act does "not apply to any person insofar as he transacts a business in securities without the jurisdiction of the United States," but the meaning of "jurisdiction" in that context is unclear.

In an action under either the 1933 Act or the 1934 Act, process may be served on any defendant, "wherever the defendant may be found." 1933 Act § 22(a); 1934 Act § 27. The courts have held, however, that to satisfy due process requirements, "[t]he person sought to be charged must know, or have good reason to know, that his conduct will have effects in the state seeking to assert jurisdiction over him." Leasco v. Maxwell, 468 F.2d 1326 (2d Cir.1972). See SEC v. Unifund, 910 F.2d 1028 (2d Cir.1990).

§ 43.   U.S. TRANSACTIONS IN FOREIGN SECURITIES

Public Offerings to U.S. Investors. Public offerings to U.S. investors by foreign issuers are of course subject to the registration requirements of the 1933 Act to the same extent as offerings by domestic issuers. Indeed, Schedule B to the Act sets forth special disclosure requirements for the registration of securities issued by foreign governments, which do not share in the exemption for U.S. federal, state and local government securities. The SEC has adopted special registration and disclosure forms under both the 1933 and 1934 Acts for use by foreign issuers.

In 1991, in a major step toward internationalization of securities regulation, the SEC adopted a "multijurisdictional disclosure system" under which Canadian issuers that meet certain tests can register their securities for sale in the U.S. using disclosure documents prepared according to the requirements of Canadian regulatory authorities. See Sec. Act Rel. 33–6902 (1991); 1933 Act Forms F–7 through F–10. Simultaneously, the securities commissions of three Canadian provinces adopted comparable rules permitting U.S. issuers to register securities for sale in Canada using disclosure documents complying with SEC requirements.

Foreign issuers are also entitled to the same exemptions as domestic issuers (except for Regulation A, which under 1933 Act Rule 252(a)(1) is available only to U.S. and Canadian issuers). However, the entire offering must meet the terms of the exemption; a foreign issuer cannot claim the "private offering" exemption under 1933 Act § 4(a)(2) for a single sale to a U.S. purchaser in conjunction with a general public offering in another country. 1933 Act Rule 144A (see § 10(i) above), which permits unlimited resales of unregistered securities by and to qualified institutional buyers, was adopted in large part to facilitate offerings by foreign issuers to institutions in the U.S.

U.S. Trading in Foreign Securities. More difficult problems arise with respect to securities of foreign issuers that are purchased by U.S. investors in secondary transactions and come to be traded on U.S. exchanges or in the over-the-counter markets. Under 1934 Act §§ 12, 13, 14, and 16, issuers of all exchange-listed and certain OTC securities must register with the SEC and file annual and current reports. They are also subject to rules governing proxy solicitations and insider trading (see § 12 above). Since the foreign issuers in most of these situations have made no securities offerings in the U.S. and are not subject to U.S. jurisdiction in any way, there is no way for the SEC to enforce these requirements, other than to suspend U.S. trading in the securities, which would do much more harm to the U.S. investors than to the foreign issuers.

When the Securities Exchange Act was amended in 1964 to extend its coverage to OTC securities, these practical considerations led to suggestions that foreign issuers be exempted from the Act's requirements. Congress, however, was unwilling to appear to treat foreign issuers more leniently than domestic issuers, and instead gave the SEC authority to exempt foreign issuers if it found such exemptions to be "in the public interest and consistent with the protection of investors." 1934 Act § 12(g)(3). After much deliberation and delicate international negotiations, the SEC adopted 1934 Act Rule 12g3–2, under which the securities of a foreign issuer are exempt from 1934 Act § 12(g) if the issuer, or the government of its home country, furnishes the SEC each year with copies of all information material to investors that it has made public in its home country during the preceding year. A list identifying the items of information must also be furnished to the SEC, but there is no requirement that either the list or the information be translated into English.

§ 44. FOREIGN TRANSACTIONS IN U.S. SECURITIES

Foreign Public Offerings by U.S. Issuers. A foreign investor who purchases securities in an offering registered under the 1933 Act has the same right of action as a U.S. purchaser in the event there is a material misstatement or omission in the registration statement. However, the SEC has taken the position that, since the principal purpose of the 1933 Act is to protect U.S. investors, it will not make any objection to a U.S. corporation making a public offering of its securities abroad, solely to foreign investors, without registration under the Act, provided that the offering is made under circumstances reasonably designed to preclude redistribution of the securities within the U.S. or to U.S. investors. Sec. Act Rel. 33–4708 (1964). In 1990, the Commission codified this position when it adopted Regulation S, consisting of 1933 Act Rules 901–904. See Sec. Act Rel. 33–6863 (1990). Under these rules, an offering is exempt from the 1933 Act if no offers are made to persons in the U.S., no "directed selling efforts" are made in the U.S., and either (i) the buyer is offshore at the time of the origination of the buy order, (ii) the sale is made on an established foreign securities exchange, or (iii) the sale is made in a designated offshore securities market, and the transaction is not prearranged with a buyer in the U.S.

In 1995, the SEC expressed its concern about abuses of Regulation S, in which securities supposedly offered abroad quickly found their way back into the U.S. market. Accordingly, in 1997, the Commission proposed amendments pursuant to which securities sold under Regulation S would be deemed to be "restricted securities," which could be resold in the U.S. only in accordance with the provisions of 1933 Act Rule 144 (see § 10(i) above). Sec. Act Rel. 33–7392 (1997). In 1998, the Commission adopted this proposal. Accordingly, securities sold pursuant to Regulation S are subject to resale restrictions for one year. See 1933 Act Rule 903(b)(3). Regulation S securities are now classified as "restricted securities." See 1933 Act Rule 905. Additionally, as a result of the 1998 amendments, purchasers of Regulation S securities must certify that they are neither U.S. residents nor purchasing on behalf of U.S. residents.

Even if a foreign offering by a U.S. issuer is exempt from the 1933 Act registration requirements, a foreign purchaser may still be able to state a claim under the antifraud provision of the federal securities laws if misrepresentations were made in connection with the transaction. See Wandschneider v. Industrial Incomes, 1972 WL 312 (S.D.N.Y.).

In contrast to its position on foreign offerings by U.S. industrial companies, the SEC has held that a U.S. mutual fund offering its shares in other countries must comply with the disclosure requirements of the 1933 Act, including the furnishing of a statutory prospectus, translated where necessary into the language of the persons to whom the offer is made. The SEC's rationale for the distinction is that mutual fund shares, unlike other securities, "are vigorously merchandised abroad to large numbers of small investors" and that "disclosure at the point of sale helps protect the U.S. securities market as a whole by insuring that foreign investors will not seek redemptions because of later realization that they had been inadequately informed about their investment." Sec. Act Rel. 33–5068 (1970). However, the SEC permits mutual funds to sell shares abroad at a sales load different from that applicable to U.S. sales where the fund can show that it is not economically feasible to sell abroad at the U.S. sales load and where the proposed sales load is not inconsistent with the laws of the country involved. Id.

Foreign Trading in U.S. Securities. Foreign persons who engage in transactions in securities of U.S. issuers may be subjected to liability under U.S. securities laws, provided the requisite use of the mails or facilities of interstate commerce is shown. A foreign mutual fund which owned more than 10% of the stock of a U.S. corporation has been held liable under 1934 Act § 16(b) for profits realized from purchases and sales of its stock. Roth v. Fund of Funds, 405 F.2d 421 (2d Cir. 1968). The transactions in that case took place on a U.S. exchange, but the same result should be reached even if the transactions were effected abroad, since jurisdiction under 1934 Act § 16 results from the stock being registered under 1934 Act § 12, rather than from use of interstate commerce facilities.

With respect to liability under 1934 Act Rule 10b–5 for trading on inside information, one of the defendants in the landmark *Texas Gulf Sulphur* case was an engineer who lived in Canada and placed his order through a Toronto broker (he had, however, placed the order by telephone from New York and it was executed on a U.S. stock exchange). The court had no difficulty in finding the transaction subject to U.S. jurisdiction, nor in holding that the defendant could be validly served with process at his home in Canada. SEC v. Texas Gulf Sulphur, 258 F.Supp. 262, 287 (S.D.N.Y.1966), aff'd in part, rev'd in part, 401 F.2d 833 (2d Cir.1968). And a U.S. court has ordered a Swiss bank to disclose the names of its customers who traded in the stock of a U.S. company, in connection with an SEC investigation into insider trading. SEC v. Banca Della Svizzera, 92 F.R.D. 111 (S.D.N.Y.1981).

Under 1934 Act § 7, the Federal Reserve Board has issued "margin regulations" limiting the amount of credit that can be extended for the purchase of U.S. securities (see § 24(a) above). It is unclear whether these rules can be applied to foreign lenders who extend credit to U.S. purchasers of U.S. securities. See Metro-Goldwyn-Mayer v. Transamerica, 303 F.Supp. 1354 (S.D.N.Y.1969). However, in 1970, Congress amended 1934 Act § 7 to prohibit any "United States person" from obtaining credit from a foreign lender in a transaction which would have been prohibited if it had taken place in the U.S. Since that time, foreign banks have been held subject to the margin regulations if they engage in transactions that can be found to constitute doing business as a broker or dealer in the U.S. United States v. Weisscredit, 325 F.Supp. 1384 (S.D.N.Y.1971); UFITEC v. Carter, CCH ¶ 94,841 (Cal.Super.1974), affirmed 20 Cal.3d 238, 142 Cal.Rptr. 279, 571 P.2d 990 (1977).

1934 Act § 13(d), which requires certain disclosures by any person or group which acquires more than 5% of the stock of any company registered under 1934 Act § 12, has been held applicable to foreign investors, and the SEC has obtained injunctions against foreign investors and foreign banks, requiring their compliance with the disclosure requirements. See SEC v. General Refractories, 400 F.Supp. 1248 (D.D.C.1975).

§ 45. FOREIGN TRANSACTIONS IN FOREIGN SECURITIES

There are a number of cases in which the courts have applied the antifraud provisions of the federal securities laws to transactions in foreign securities taking place outside the U.S. In some cases, the basis of jurisdiction has been the harm to U.S. shareholders of the corporation which was the alleged victim of the fraud. Schoenbaum v. Firstbrook, 405 F.2d 200 (2d Cir.1968). In other cases, it has been based on the fact that some of the actions alleged to constitute the violation occurred within the U.S. Leasco v. Maxwell, 468 F.2d 1326 (2d Cir.1972); Travis v. Anthes Imperial, 473 F.2d 515 (8th Cir.1973).

In Bersch v. Drexel Firestone, 519 F.2d 974 (2d Cir.1975), the court held that the antifraud provisions should be applied to:

(1) Sales to Americans residing in the U.S. whether or not any important acts occurred in the U.S.;

(2) Sale to Americans residing abroad if acts in the U.S. contributed significantly to their losses; and

(3) Sales to foreigners outside the U.S. only if acts in the U.S. caused their losses.

With respect to sales to foreigners, however, one court went beyond this formulation, holding that "the federal securities laws * * * grant jurisdiction in transnational security cases where at least some activity designed to further a fraudulent scheme occurs within this country. * * * We are reluctant to conclude that Congress intended to allow the United States to become a 'Barbary Coast,' as it were, harboring international securities 'pirates.' " SEC v. Kasser, 548 F.2d 109 (3d Cir.1977); see also Zoelsch v. Arthur Andersen, 824 F.2d 27 (D.C.Cir.1987).

Formerly, the courts found a basis for jurisdiction in private and SEC actions if the conduct in question takes place in the United States, regardless of where the ultimate transaction occurs—this became known as the "conduct" test. However, in Morrison v. National Australian Bank Ltd., the Supreme Court ruled that it is not sufficient that the conduct take place in the United States. Morrison v. National Australia Bank Ltd., 561 U.S. 247, 274, 130 S.Ct. 2869, 2888, 177 L.Ed.2d 535 (2010). Section 10(b) and Rule 10b–5 apply only if the transaction takes place in the United States or if the securities are listed on a U.S. securities exchange. Thus, as a result of the ruling in *Morrison*, the conduct and effects tests have were replaced by a transaction test for private actions. While the transaction test adopted in

Morrison remains the rule in private suits, in 2010 Congress included a provision in the Dodd-Frank Act to give the SEC the authority to pursue fraud under either the conduct test or the effects test.[4] The success of this legislative fix is somewhat in doubt since Congress amended the jurisdictional provisions but left the language of § 10(b) intact. On the other hand, the Court's ruling in *Morrison* looked to the language of § 10(b). It is thus arguable that even with the expanded jurisdiction given by the 2010 amendment, the language of § 10(b) still warrants the *Morrison* test in government enforcement actions. While the legislative intent was clearly to the contrary, an overly literal court conceivably could limit the expanded jurisdiction as not applying to § 10(b).

The validity of service of process outside the U.S. on a defendant in this type of action will depend on the extent of the defendant's activities in the U.S. Compare Alco Standard v. Benalal, 345 F.Supp. 14 (E.D.Pa.1972), and Rosen v. Dick, 1974 WL 443, CCH 94,590 (S.D.N.Y.1974), with Bersch v. Drexel Firestone, 519 F.2d 974, 999 (2d Cir.1975). A foreign

---

[4] As amended, the jurisdictional provisions of the securities laws now provide that the SEC can pursue securities fraud for "conduct within the United States that constitute significant steps in furtherance of the violation, even if the securities transaction occurs outside the United States and involves only foreign investors" as well as "conduct occurring outside the United States that has a foreseeable substantial effect within the U.S." Dodd-Frank Wall Street Reform and Consumer Protection Act § 929P(b), Pub. Law 111–203, H.R. 4173 (111th Cong. 2d sess. 2010), adding 15 U.S.C. §§ 77v(c), 78aa(b), 80b–14(b). Richard W. Painter, The Dodd-Frank Extraterritorial Jurisdiction Provision: Was it Effective, Needed or Sufficient?, 1 Harv. Bus. L. Rev. 195 (2011).

entity alleged to have traded in U.S. stocks on U.S. markets on the basis of inside information was held to have acted in such a way as to "cause consequences" in the U.S. sufficient to support personal jurisdiction. SEC v. Unifund, 910 F.2d 1028 (2d Cir.1990).

An agreement by a U.S. party to a foreign transaction that any disputes will be resolved in a foreign forum under foreign law will be upheld if the choice of forum is not unreasonable under the circumstances and if the foreign law will not subvert the U.S. policy of insuring full and fair disclosure and deterring exploitation of U.S. investors. Bonny v. Lloyd's, 3 F.3d 156 (7th Cir.1993); Roby v. Lloyd's, 996 F.2d 1353 (2d Cir.1993).

CHAPTER X
STATE REGULATION

Prior to 1996, the various federal securities laws specifically preserved the power of the states to regulate securities activities. However, in that year, Congress passed the National Securities Markets Improvement Act, preempting significant areas of state regulation, as more specifically noted below.

Every state has some law specifically regulating transactions in securities. These laws are known as "blue sky" laws, after an early judicial opinion describing their purpose as the prevention of "speculative schemes which have no more basis than so many feet of blue sky." Hall v. Geiger-Jones, 242 U.S. 539 (1917).

While these "blue sky" laws vary greatly from state to state, they generally contain the following three types of provisions (although not all contain all three types): (a) prohibitions against fraud in the sale of securities; (b) requirements for registration of brokers and dealers; and (c) requirements for registration of securities to be sold in the state.

In 1956, the Commissioners on Uniform State Laws promulgated a Uniform Securities Act (USA) for adoption by the states. Reflecting the pre-existing pattern of state laws and the differences in regulatory philosophy among the states, the act is divided into four parts: (1) antifraud provisions, (2) broker-dealer registration provisions, (3) security registration provisions, and (4) definitions, exemptions, and administrative and liability provisions. States are thus free to adopt the provisions they find appropriate for their state.

While more than 30 states have adopted most or some of the provisions of the Uniform Securities Act, the movement toward uniformity has been hampered by several factors. First, some of the most important commercial states, including New York, California, Illinois and Texas, have not adopted any part of the Act. Second, almost all the states that have adopted it have made substantial changes from the approved text. Lastly, state administrators and courts interpret the same language differently, producing a difference in operation that is not apparent from a reading of the laws themselves.

Nevertheless, the promulgation and adoption of the Uniform Securities Act has produced a much more rational and consistent pattern of regulation than previously existed. This development has also been assisted by the North American Securities Administrators Association (NASAA), an association of state and provincial securities administrators, which from time to time issues "statements of policy" on various substantive and procedural questions and indicates to what extent those policies are followed by each of its members.

In 1985, the Commissioners promulgated a revised Uniform Securities Act, modified for the stated purposes of (1) updating licensing and registration procedures to reflect federal and state developments, (2) expediting the registration process for seasoned issuers, and (3) strengthening the powers of state securities administrators. Section references herein are to the 1985 version of the Uniform Act. There have been subsequent amendments to the USA over time.

§ 46.   REGISTRATION OF SECURITIES

With the exception of the New England and Middle Atlantic states, most of which have only rudimentary provisions for the registration of securities, almost every state requires that some affirmative action be taken to register securities before they can be sold in the state. This means that, in addition to complying with the federal Securities Act of 1933, an underwriting syndicate making a national distribution of a new issue must take steps to "blue sky" the issue in more than 40 states.

(A)   PROCEDURES

Most states which require registration of securities issues provide two alternative methods of registration: "notification" and "qualification." Some states provide a third method: registration by "coordination" for issues simultaneously being registered with the SEC.

Securities may generally be registered by "notification" only if they meet certain tests for stability and earnings coverage. Registration is accomplished by filing a statement showing compliance with the statutory test and describing of the securities being registered and the terms of the offering. The registration automatically becomes effective within a prescribed period, unless the state administrator takes action to prevent it.

The 1985 Uniform Act replaces "registration by notification" with a similar procedure called "registration by filing." To qualify for this procedure, a company must have been in business for at least 36 months, have a class of securities registered under 1934 Act § 12, and meet certain tests for net worth and volume of securities publicly traded. USA § 302. Unlike registration by "notification," an application for registration by "filing" cannot be denied by the state administrator on the basis of the "merit" standards discussed in subsection (b) below. USA § 306(b)(2).

Registration by "coordination" is substantially similar to registration by "notification" or "filing" except that the only information normally required to be filed is a copy of the prospectus filed with the SEC under the 1933 Act. See USA § 303.

Registration by "qualification" is the method generally prescribed for those issues which do not meet the tests prescribed for registration by other methods. The issuer must file a statement containing information roughly comparable to that required in a 1933 Act registration statement, and registration does not become effective until the administrator takes action to approve it. See USA § 304.

(B) STANDARDS

In contrast to the 1933 Act, under which the SEC has no power to approve or disapprove the sale of securities, most state laws authorize the administrator to deny an application for registration, even though the facts regarding the security and the issuer are fully disclosed. The standards for granting or denying an application range from those which authorize denial only on grounds of "fraud" to those which authorize the administrator to bar any issue unless the administrator finds its terms to be "fair, just and equitable." Interpretations of these vague standards also vary greatly from state to state. The 1985 Uniform Act offers alternative wordings for adoption by the states, authorizing denial of registration if the administrator finds either that the offering would "tend to work a fraud upon purchasers" or that it is "unfair, unjust or inequitable," as well as in situations where it "would be made with unreasonable amounts of" underwriting compensation, promoters' profits, or options. USA § 306(a)(5), (6). The associations of North American Securities Administrators and Midwest Securities Administrators have also issued a number of "Statements of Policy," indicating what levels of compensation or other arrangements with insiders would be considered unfair in determining whether registration of a particular issue should be granted.

(C) EXEMPTIONS

Most states exempt from their registration requirements the principal types of securities exempted from the 1933 Act—government securities, instruments issued by various types of institutions, and securities issued by companies subject to special regulatory statutes (such as banks and common carriers). In addition, most states exempt one important class of securities which are not exempt from the 1933 Act—namely, those listed on major stock exchanges or on NASDAQ. See USA §§ 401(a)(7), (8).

(D) FEDERAL PREEMPTION

In 1996, Congress prohibited state regulation of offerings of several important categories of securities:

(1) Securities listed or to be listed on the New York or American Stock Exchange or the NASDAQ National Market System (most states already exempted these securities);

(2) Securities issued by investment companies (mutual funds);

(3) Securities exempted from 1933 Act registration requirements by:

(a) 1933 Act § 3(a), except § 3(a)(2) (municipal securities), § 3(a)(4) (nonprofit organizations), or § 3(a)(11) (intrastate offerings);

(b) 1933 Act § 4(a)(1) or 4(a)(3), with respect to securities of issuers filing reports under the 1934 Act; or

(c) Any SEC rule adopted under 1933 Act § 4(2) (i.e., Rule 506);

(4) Securities offered only to "qualified purchasers" (a term to be defined by the SEC).

While the states are barred from regulating or
imposing disclosure requirements on these types of
offerings, they remain free to charge fees or to bring
antifraud proceedings. See 1933 Act § 18.

Private Placements. Traditionally, most state
statutes did not contain exemptions comparable to
the 1933 Act exemption for "transactions by an issuer
not involving any public offering," although many
had exemptions for "isolated transactions" or "preorganization subscriptions." The 1985 Uniform Act
exempts offerings that involve no general solicitation
and result in sales to no more than 25 purchasers in
the state who are purchasing for investment and not
for resale. USA § 402(11). The "accredited investor"
concept in Regulation D (see § 10(c) above), finds a
counterpart in state provisions, which commonly
exempt sales to broker-dealers or other financial or
institutional investors. See USA § 402(10). The
North American Securities Administrators
Association in 1983 promulgated a "Uniform Limited
Offering Exemption," which has been adopted by
more than 20 states, under which any offering which
meets the tests of the SEC's Regulation D is also
exempt from the state's registration requirements.

Secondary Transactions. State securities laws do
not embrace the "underwriter" concept of 1933 Act
§ 2(a)(11), which has given rise to so much difficulty
in determining when a person other than the issuer
must register securities for sale under federal law
(see § 10(e) above). Most state laws have an
exemption for "isolated non-issuer transactions" and
for other non-issuer sales of securities registered

under 1934 Act § 12 or listed in "standard manuals" (such as Moody's and Standard & Poor's). See USA § 402(2), (3). Under the Uniform Act, a registration of securities remains in effect for one year (unless suspended or revoked), and "all outstanding securities of the same class * * * are considered to be registered for the purpose of any non-issuer transaction" during that period. USA § 305(i).

§ 47.   BROKER-DEALER REGISTRATION

Almost every state requires securities broker-dealers and their agents to register with a state agency. Most of the statutes also contain provisions for denial or revocation of registration or imposition of other sanctions. See USA §§ 212, 213. The coverage of these provisions varies; some states define the term "broker-dealer" to include an issuer selling its own securities, but most do not. See USA § 101(2). In 1996, Congress prohibited the states from regulating broker-dealers with respect to their capital, custody, margin, financial responsibility, record-keeping, and financial or operational reporting requirements. 1934 Act § 15(h).

With respect to investment advisers, the 1996 legislation preempted state regulation of investment advisers with more than $25 million of assets under management, and exempted from the Investment Advisers Act advisers with less than $25 million under management that are regulated by their home states. IAA § 203A.

§ 48. ANTIFRAUD PROVISIONS

In almost every state, the securities law contains some sort of general prohibition against fraud and authorizes the appropriate government official to obtain injunctive relief or bring a criminal prosecution. The definition of fraud is usually worded in very general terms; the Uniform Act uses the language of 1934 Act Rule 10b–5 (see § 18 above) and makes it applicable to any "offer to sell, sale, offer to purchase, or purchase, of a security." USA § 501.

§ 49. SANCTIONS FOR VIOLATIONS

Most state laws provide for a range of sanctions against persons who violate the registration or antifraud provisions. The Uniform Act authorizes the administrator to conduct investigations, issue subpoenas, and bring injunction actions, in addition to imposing criminal penalties for violations. USA §§ 601–604. The 1985 Uniform Act augments the administrator's authority by giving the administrator the power to issue cease and desist orders. USA § 602. The weak point of these provisions is that most states have a very small staff engaged in administration and enforcement of their securities laws, so as a practical matter, the only significant sanction against violators is the threat of civil liability.

§ 50. CIVIL LIABILITIES

The traditional state securities law generally provides that any sale "made in violation of any provision" of the law is "voidable" and that the purchaser is entitled to rescind the transaction and recover the purchase price. The types of violations which give rise to this right of rescission may include a technical violation, failure to register, or a violation of the antifraud provisions. Thus, an issuer or broker-dealer making a public distribution runs the risk that a technical failure to comply with any provision of the securities law of a particular state will give all purchasers in that state an absolute right to the refund of their investment if the security declines in value. Enforceability is facilitated in many states by a requirement that issuers or broker-dealers post a surety bond for satisfaction of their liabilities.

The Uniform Act departs from the "voidability" concept to follow the approach of 1933 Act § 12. Any person who offers or sells a security (1) in violation of the registration requirements or certain other important provisions or (2) by means of a misstatement or omission of a material fact, is made liable to refund the purchase price upon tender of the security, or to pay damages to the purchaser if the purchaser no longer owns the security. USA § 605.

Persons Liable. Many state laws impose civil liability not only on the "seller" but also on any persons, or specified classes of persons, who "participate" or "aid" in the sale. The Uniform Act imposes liability on partners, officers, and directors of the seller, whether or not they aid in the sale, and on other employees, broker-dealers, and agents who "materially aid in the sale," subject in each case to a defense of "due diligence." USA § 605(d).

Implied Liability. In situations where the state law provides no express right of action to the purchaser in a transaction which violates the law, many courts have implied a right to rescind the transaction. The Uniform Act, however, contains a specific provision that it "does not create any cause of action not specified in" the Act. USA § 609(b). Since the Act creates no right of action for a violation of its general prohibition against fraud, this provision forecloses the development of implied rights of action for fraud which the federal courts have recognized under 1934 Act Rule 10b–5 (see § 18 above). This means that defrauded *sellers* of securities have no right of action under the Uniform Act.

Preemption of Class Actions. The Securities Litigation Uniform Standards Act of 1998 (SLUSA) mandates that most class actions involving publicly traded securities be brought in federal court. This in essence preempts a good deal of private litigation under state securities laws. SLUSA preemption also applies to fraud related claims but does not preclude state law claims on other theories such as conversion, breach of contract, or breach of fiduciary duty.

§ 51. JURISDICTIONAL QUESTIONS

Most state securities laws apply to any offer or sale of securities in the state, but contain no explicit provisions defining when an offer or sale is made "in the state." Since many securities transactions involve a buyer in one state and a seller in another, difficult problems arise in determining (a) to which transactions the law of a particular state applies, and

(b) which state law governs the validity of a transaction which has contacts with more than one state. For example, is an advertisement in a newspaper published in State A but also circulated in State B an "offer" in State B? If a broker in State A makes an offer by telephone to a customer in State B, who accepts the offer by mailing a check to the broker in State A, is the transaction voidable if the broker and the security were registered in State A but not in State B?

Applicable Law. Since most civil actions under the blue sky laws are actions for rescission, courts traditionally tended to look to the conflict of laws principles applicable to contract claims. These courts held that the contract was not voidable if it was valid under the law of the state where the contract was made or to be performed. See, e.g., Robbins v. Pacific Eastern, 8 Cal.2d 241, 65 P.2d 42 (1937). Under this approach, an issuer or broker-dealer could offer and sell securities to residents of a state with a "strict" blue sky law—without complying with the terms of that law—simply by making sure that the contract was technically made and performed in its own state. A more recent approach is to hold that, when a customer is solicited in his or her home state, the securities law of that state must be complied with, no matter where the transaction is technically consummated. See Green v. Weis, 479 F.2d 462 (7th Cir.1973). Where that approach is followed, the courts are also likely to hold that the law of the offeree's state cannot be avoided by providing in the contract that it shall be construed in accordance with the law of another state. Boehnen v. Walston, 358 F.Supp. 537 (D.S.D.1973).

The Uniform Act adopts the latter approach by making the registration requirements applicable either when (1) an offer to sell is made in the state, or (2) an offer to buy is made and accepted in the state (since many offers take the form of the seller's solicitation of the purchaser's offer to buy). An offer to sell is deemed to be made in the state if it originates from the state or is directed to and received in the state. An exception to this is that advertisements in out-of-state newspapers or radio stations are not deemed to be made in the state. An offer to buy is deemed to be accepted in the state when it is first communicated to the offeror in the state. USA § 801. Even this detailed specification can raise interpretive problems, however, particularly if the adopting state modifies the language of the Uniform Act. See Kreis v. Mates, 473 F.2d 1308 (8th Cir.1973).

Constitutional Questions. In Merrick v. N.W. Halsey, 242 U.S. 568 (1917), the Supreme Court held, without discussion, that application of a state's blue sky laws to offers directed into the state by an out-of-state broker-dealer was not an unconstitutional interference with interstate commerce. And in Travelers Health Ass'n v. Virginia, 339 U.S. 643 (1950), the Court held (5–4) that the Due Process Clause did not bar Virginia from issuing a cease and desist order under its blue sky law against a Nebraska association which solicited Virginia residents by mail and encouraged Virginia members to submit the names of their friends to the association's home office. With respect to the constitutionality of the state laws regulating takeovers, which were widely adopted during the 1970s, see § 15(b) above.

Personal Jurisdiction. Under what circumstances can an issuer or broker-dealer that offers and sells securities to residents of a state be subject to suits in the courts of that state if it does not maintain any place of business there? Many state blue sky laws require an out-of-state applicant for registration to file a formal consent to service of process. See USA § 414(g). With respect to sales made without registration, in violation of state law, a number of states provide for "substituted" service of process. Under these provisions, an out-of-state person who sells securities in the state in violation of its laws is deemed to have irrevocably appointed a named state official as his or her agent for service of process in any legal action or proceeding growing out of that conduct. See USA § 414(h); Paulos v. Best Securities, 260 Minn. 283, 109 N.W.2d 576 (1961). The constitutionality of these provisions, like other "long-arm" statutes, has been consistently upheld under the principles laid down by the Supreme Court in McGee v. International, 355 U.S. 220 (1957).

INDEX

References are to Sections
